Malawian Oral Literature

The Aesthetics of Indigenous Arts

First edition published 1988
© 1988 Centre for Social Research
Sponsored by the Harold Macmillan Trust, London

© 2020 Moira Chimombo

Published by
Luviri Press
P/Bag 201 Luwinga
Mzuzu 2
Malawi

ISBN   978-99960-66-52-8
eISBN 978-99960-60-53-5

Luviri Press is represented outside Malawi by:
African Books Collective Oxford (order@africanbookscollective.com)

www.luviripress.blogspot.com
www.africanbookscollective.com

Malawian Oral Literature

The Aesthetics of Indigenous Arts

Steve Chimombo

Luviri Press
Mzuzu
2020

To Moira, Tina, Zangaphee, and Napolo who, as usual, are an unending source of inspiration. *Tili tonse*.

PREFACE

This book is about *Ulimbaso*, the aesthetics of the Chewa people (Nyanja and Mang'anja included) and by extension the Bantu speaking peoples of Southern Africa; how these people talk about their verbal and visual art objects and how they perceive these art objects in relation to one another.[1] *Ulimbaso*, as conceived here, underlies all artistic creation and perception: *-ul-* refers to inspiration, *-mb-* to form and *-so-* to artistry. *-Ul-* operates on the artist from the onset of inspiration to the production of the art object; *-ul-* is taken from *ula* or *laula*, oracle, and its divine connotations as the source of wisdom, creativity and human action. *-Mb-* is at the centre of the verbal arts (*mwambi/mwambo, nyimbo/chamba,*) and the visual arts (*choumba/cholemba*). *-So-* concerns *luso*, artistic creation and *kaso*, the appreciation of the finished product.

A common-sense view of aesthetics – the ability to perceive art as pleasing or beautiful, and the opposite – derives from many sources. The sources include childhood experiences, what friends, relatives, and even enemies say about their own perceptions. Other sources are formal instruction or what has been read on the subject. Formal teaching or readings on aesthetics, however, have for long inhibited the articulation of indigenous African aesthetics since they have always been based on western art and formulations. In post-independence Africa there is no excuse for continued suppression of indigenous aesthetics or actual research in the field. *Ulimbaso* is a dynamic theory of art creation and appreciation based on how the Chewa man articulates his own artistic vision. The examples are taken from the Nyanja of the southern region and the Chewa of the central region of Malawi. These languages and their dialects demonstrate how a linguistic model of aesthetics can be constructed from within the culture itself.

---

[1]   Chichewa is the official language of Malawi, Central Africa. It includes Chinyanja, Chimang'anja, and some other dialects spoken in the central and southern regions of the country. It is also spoken in parts of Zambia and Mozambique. Hereafter, it will be used to include the languages mentioned.

For the contours of *Ulimbaso* to be seen, it was necessary to completely ignore (even to abandon) previous non-Malawian pronouncements on aesthetics. The retreat into or communion with his own language made it possible for the author to listen to the artistic heartbeat of his own people and record what he saw and heard there. This book, then, is a record of that sojourn or hibernation and the return with *Ulimbaso* as a truly original and indigenous aesthetic.

To arrive at *Ulimbaso*, detours had to be made into the debris, flotsam, or fuzz inhibiting clear vision, accessibility and apprehension of the people's aesthetics. Before presenting the *Ulimbaso* theory itself, Part One: Theory: Studying Malawian Arts, discusses the problems of collecting, confusions of terminology, and illusiveness of the material. The rest of the book, for both thematic consistency and the demonstration of the applicability of *Ulimbaso*, is based on the manifestations of the trickster and dupe series encountered in narrative, song, dance, rock art, and graphics (cartooning). Part Two applies the theory to narrative texts using "The Hare and the Well" variants. Part Three applies the theory to song, ritual, and dance. Part Four demonstrates *Ulimbaso* in practice on rock art and canvas, and in graphics with particular reference to current cartooning.

Thus, the book covers the theory and practice of *Ulimbaso* applied to very specific major art forms of Malawi. Does *Ulimbaso* work? Does it live up to its claims? Is it generalisable to other non-Malawian art forms? These are the questions the book provides answers to with reference to Malawi and, it is hoped, will initiate discussion with reference to other African cultures.

ACKNOWLEDGEMENTS, FIRST EDITION

Some of the chapters in this book were published before, as articles in periodicals: "Terminological Problems" appeared in *Outlook;* "*Ulimbaso,* an Integrated Theory of Art" as "The Aesthetics of Indigenous Arts" in *Review of Ethnology*; "A Taxonomy of Aesthetic Terms" and "The Trickster and the Media" in *Baraza*; "A Model of Narrative Performance," "Sample Oral Text" and "Analysis" appear as "Folk Story Analysis: Basic Approaches" in *Kalulu*; "Folk, Flora and Fauna" in *Nyala*; "The Dupe in a Modern Context" in *Saiwa*. I wish to thank the editors for permission to include the material in the present volume.

I am grateful to a large number of people, colleagues in various departments of the University of Malawi: Fine and Performing Arts, French, Chichewa and Linguistics and English who made useful comments on earlier drafts of different parts of the book. Above all the book owes most of its existence to several generations of students who have taken my introductory and advanced courses in oral literature at Chancellor College since 1972.

At various stages, I was the beneficiary of grants from the Research and Publications Committee which enabled me to do field work and transcribe and publish portions of the book. Separate monographs like *The Folklore of Makoka Village, Malawian Arts: A Bilingual Guide*, and *A Bibliography of Oral Literature Research* are the products of the grants.

Various individuals must also be mentioned: Researchers like Dr. M. Schoffeleers; the story teller, Mr. Simika; the interviewees, Dr. J. Kuthemba Mwale, Mrs. Rhoda Botha, and Mrs. Chitekesa; the indefatigable secretary, Miss Lysca Chisale.

The Harold Macmillan Trust deserves special mention for funding the publication of the book.

Steve Chimombo, 1988

ACKNOWLEDGEMENTS, SECOND EDITION

I always enjoyed helping my late husband with editing his work. I never ceased to be amazed by the extent and thoroughness of his research and the breadth of his interests. *Malawian Oral Literature: The Aesthetics of Indigenous Arts* demonstrates admirably the originality of his scholarship. It continues to be recommended as a course text for the study of Oral Literature, but has been out of print for some years. With the establishment of new universities in Malawi and the continuing demand for copies both locally and internationally, I realized the necessity to bring out a second edition. However, it was a daunting task, since the original text was produced on an electronic typewriter, so it would have had to be completely retyped if it hadn't been for the possibility of scanning it. The production of this edition would therefore have been impossible without the offer to scan and the untiring help of Prof. Klaus Fiedler to get it ready for printing and distribution. *Mulungu awadalitse*.

Moira Chimombo, February 2020

TABLE OF CONTENTS

LIST OF FIGURES

LIST OF TABLES

INTRODUCTION

Designing Indigenous Aesthetics

Most of the critical debates on African literature, whether of form or content or even the language of expression, raise fundamental questions of aesthetics: What is *African* literature and what is the appropriate response to it? And most arguments for "decolonising" African literature are really searches for *authentic* African aesthetics. The search has been on since the early 1970s: *Black Aesthetics: Papers from a Colloquium held at the University of Nairobi.*[1] And it is still on with the most recent publication: *Towards Defining the African Aesthetic.*[2] All publications to date reveal that the elusive African aesthetics has yet to be found or formulated.[3]

The obvious reason for failing to come up with an African aesthetic is the lack of clear and simple guiding principles. Before discussing *Ulimbaso* as a solid indigenous aesthetic, the author will summarise the guiding principles used in its formulation.

An indigenous aesthetic must be:

1. based within the culture and the language of the people it is supposed to serve.

2. based on the language of the people themselves.

---

[1] Andrew Gurr and Pio Zirimu, eds., *Black Aesthetics, Papers from a Colloquium held at the University of Nairobi, June, 1971* (Nairobi: East African Literature Bureau, 1973).

[2] Lemuel A. Johnson, *Toward Defining the African Aesthetic, Annual Selected Papers of the African Literature Association* (Washington, D.C.: Three Continents Press, 1982).

[3] See Chapter Three.

3. based on the reality of the art forms devised and recognised by the people themselves.

4. consistent in its uses, i.e. it must not depend on the whims of the artist or the critic.

5. stable and comprehensive enough to be used for all the art forms in the culture.

6. well-established and long-lasting, i.e. it must be based on antiquity or at least have its origins in the art forms it describes.

7. flexible enough to incorporate new art forms or the development in new directions of the indigenous art forms.

8. open enough to new terms to describe the new art forms or to refine existing ones to apply to the new.

9. able to move towards the universal, in other words, however locally based, it must have some general features which are shared with other cultures different from its own.

The majority of the nine guiding principles outlined above are self-evident, yet they seem to elude investigators, thereby confounding their own formulations of African or other indigenous aesthetics. Some of the confusions in setting out clearly the aesthetics of a people are related to the failure to be governed by the principles given above, and can be seen to emanate from external or internal problems. These problems are explored in the next section.

Problems in Art Appreciation

External Problems

The major problems in designing an appropriate aesthetic arise from the use of external approaches. These fall into five categories.

1. Non-indigenous classification systems

Once art forms are classified using foreign categories, the clear perception of form and content is automatically inhibited. For example, African verbal arts have been divided into two:

the spoken and the sung[4]

and into three:

the spoken, the sung and the acted.[5]

These double or triple modes of classification, with their insistence on the verbal, exclude other art forms (e.g. the visual) which are inextricably interrelated with all the rest. As will be seen later, in the Chichewa-speaking group there is no such linguistic discrimination, since all the arts are united under the -mb- principle. Furthermore, the isolation of the performing arts creates a "new" art form, drama, theatre or plays, which did not exist in such elaborate forms before in the society under review. Thus, by using non-indigenous taxonomies there is a fragmentation of what hitherto had been a unified view of the arts.

2. Non-indigenous terms

The use of foreign categories gives rise to the use of new terms either by creation or through translation. This sometimes results in distortions of the indigenous terms and forms. Finnegan's "dramatised" forms, for example, caused problems in Chichewa of what to call sustained non-ritual arts.[6] Hitherto *chamba* (or *gule*) served for both dance and ritual drama. Once these became sustained and developed into modern theatre or drama, there was no term for it. *Sewero* (plural *masewero*), which originally meant any non-ritual or non-religious dance or game or recreation, was borrowed instead. The term and the new meaning have since stuck.

Perhaps the use of *sewero* in the new sense was excusable. However, the translation and use of foreign words where local ones existed is not. One

---

4   W.H. Whiteley, ed., *A Selection of African Prose*, Vol. I (London: Oxford University Press, 1964).

5   Ruth Finnegan, *Oral Literature in Africa* (Nairobi: Oxford University Press, 1976).

6   Finnegan, *Oral Literature in Africa*.

scholar defines *mwambi* as *alegole* (from "allegory"), when *mwambi* or other terms, as we are going to see, are available.[7]

3. Non-indigenous forms

The penchant for forcing correspondences between African and non-African forms creates another distortion: equating foreign forms with indigenous ones. Although, by description, the expression *kuyimba nthano* (singing a story) exists in Chichewa, the society distinguishes between *nthano,* narratives with songs, and *nthanthi*, narratives without. The distortion is to equate the *nthano* narratives with songs with *cante-fable* and leave it at that.[8] The problem here is that there are several degrees of singing in *nthano*. Some have one song thematically and structurally related to the story and sung at strategic points in the narrative's development. Others have songs that are not related to the story but are introduced arbitrarily at any point to make a dull story and a bored audience more lively. Is this a cante-fable? Some *nthano* have two or more different songs sung by different characters. The songs are also related thematically and structurally to the narratives. Others have songs sung by different members of the audience (*kutengulira*) to harmonise with the narrator's song or relieve the story-teller or simply because the singer has been touched by the story and so bursts out into a favourite song. Is this a cante-fable?

4. Non-indigenous aesthetics

The wholesale importation of foreign aesthetics distorts old and especially emerging art forms. A serious local case is the injunction by an established writer that some Chichewa poetry rhymes.[9] Whole generations of not only young writers but also school children (since the advice was given in a textbook) have adopted this view when it is actually known that Bantu languages have got their own techniques for creating euphony and rhythm.

---

[7]   John Loga, *Muni wa Chichewa: Ulalo 3* (Blantyre, Malawi: Blantyre Print and Packaging, 1972), p. 176.

[8]   Enoch Timpunza Mvula, "Chewa Folk Narrative Performance," *Kalulu*, 3 (May 1982), p. 32.

[9]   J.W. Gwengwe, *Ndakatulo* (Nairobi: Oxford University Press, 1976), pp. v-vi.

5. Misunderstanding indigenous arts

Several other inhibitors to appreciating indigenous arts are misunderstanding, misinformation, and misinterpretation by critic and informant alike. When an art object is being appraised by western missionaries, traders and administrators, or western-educated locals, the emotional, psychological, attitudinal, and sometimes even physical distance, is likely to distort the way art forms are viewed. The case of *mwambi* as allegory has already been cited. To extend the example, the source gave S. Kumakanga's *Nzeru za Kale*, a collection of proverbs with the accompanying narratives to explain them.[10] Admittedly, proverbs are moralistic, but Kumakanga's stories do not come close to allegory in the western sense, unless we take all folk narratives as allegorical in the metaphoric sense.

To conclude, it will be seen that the problems discussed above are created by the art viewer. The problems do not lie in the art forms themselves. And, if the *ulimbaso* theory is taken as the key to all art appreciation, all the above external problems disappear. However, some of the problems are inherent in the indigenous formulations themselves, as the next section demonstrates.

Internal Problems

The four art forms isolated here: *zolankhula* (spoken) *zoyimba* (sung), *chamba* (dance), and *zopanga* (visual arts), face different degrees of terminological and even classificatory difficulty which can only be resolved at a very high level of abstraction.[11]

1. Zolankhula

Chichewa prose forms have at least ten vernacular terms: *mwambi, mwambo, nthano, nthanthi, chifanizo, nthabwala, mbiri, nkhani, ndawi,* or *chisimo*. All these have some shared features: e.g. *mwambi/mwambo*

---

[10]   S. Kumakanga, *Nzeru za Kale* (Lilongwe: Longman, 1931).

[11]   Apart from general usage, the author is following closely the basic dictionary definitions given in David Clement Scott and Alexander Hetherwick, *Dictionary of the Chichewa Language* (1929) (Blantyre: CLAIM, 1970).

spoken and narrative to a greater or lesser extent. Some of them belong to *zoona* (of the real world), others to *zopeka* (the fictive) in various degrees. As the diagram at the end of the chapter (Figure 1) shows, there are relationships and distinctions between the forms.

a. *Mwambi* as a genre is spoken, narrative and fictional. All the *zopeka* (fictive) forms are its subcategories:
   i. *Nthano*: narrative, fictional, with song.
   ii. *Nthanthi*: narrative, fictional, without song.
   iii. *Chifanizo*: narrative, fictional, parabolic.
   iv. *Nthabwala*: narrative, fictional, joke or prank.
   Maloto, (dreams, spoken and written) and *ndakatulo* (verse) would be included here.

b. *Mwambo* as a genre is spoken, narrative and factual. All the *zoona* (factual) forms are its subcategories:
   i. *Mbiri*: narrative, historical, factual.
   ii. *Nkhani/mkambo*: conversational speech, report, news.
   iii. *Ndawi/ndaji/ndagi/chilape*: custom, riddle.
   iv. *Chisimo*: custom, proverb.

c. *Miyambo* is the plural form of *mwambo*, but here are grouped all non-narrative short forms, customs, traditions, sayings, instructions, etc.:
   i. Formulaic: *temberero* (curse), *lumbiro* (oath), *tamando* (praise or panegyric), *tukwana* (swear).
   ii. Ritualistic: *pemphero* (prayer), *pembedzo* (worship), *ombedza* (divination), *lodza* (bewitchment), *logololo* (exorcism), *dalitso* (blessing), *nsembe* (sacrifice).
   iii. Idiomatic expressions: *mkuluwiko/chining'a/ku-phiphiritsa* (euphemism), *dzina/mfunda* (naming), *chifanifani* (simile), *idyofoni/mvekero* (ideophone).
   iv. Conversational: *bodza* (gossip), *langizo* (instruction), *lalika* (oratory or sermon), *nyoza* (insult), *tonza* (tease), *lonjera* (greeting), *tsazika* (parting).

2. *Zoyimba: nyimbo/chamba* (sung forms).

There are no problems of generic distinctions in the sung forms: the context, the occasion, the purpose all distinguish the form and content, as the axis below reveals:

Nyimbo ya	*Chamba cha*

   a. *Nyimbo*: song, for example:
      i. *nyimbo yapaukwati*: wedding song.
      ii. *nyimbo yapamaliro*: funeral song.
   b. *Chamba*: dance, for example:
      i. *chamba cha chioda*: *chioda* dance.
      ii. *chamba cha dzoma*: *dzoma* dance.
   c. *Ndakatulo*: poem, for example:
      i. *ndakatulo ya chikondi*: a love poem.

As can be seen, the *nyimbo/chamba* axis is more unified, since all the *nyimbo* (songs) have got their own *chamba* (dance) to go with them. The only problems, discussed and resolved above, arise when the songs and dances become more elaborate and sustained so that they move towards drama and theatre in the western sense.

3. *Zochita: chamba* (performing arts).

As in *zoyimba* above, *zochita* (the performing arts) are related to *nyimbo* and *chamba* when they depend on dramatic performance. All the dances come under this category as subcategories.

   a. *Chamba*: ritual drama.
   b. *Sewero*: play, game.

The problem raised by the new meaning attached to *sewero* has been discussed above.

4. *Zopanga*: the visual (plastic) arts.

Under this category come art forms dealing with *kuumba* or *kuomba* (ceramics or pottery), *kulemba* (etching, drawing, engraving) and *kujambula* (painting). The terms are very specific to the kinds of action performed.

   a. *Choumba*: ceramics, pottery, sculpture.

b. *Cholemba*: drawing, etching, engraving, ornamentation, decoration, design, carving, tattoo, calligraphy.
c. *Chojambula*: painting, photography.
d. *Kuluka*: weaving, basketry.
e. *Kusula*: smelting, all metalwork.
f. *Kusoka*: sewing.
g. *Kutiwa*: plaiting.

The problems in this category come in the use of *kulemba* and *kujambula*. *Kulemba* incorporates all patterns on objects with or without paint or dye, while *kujambula* is restricted to painting on canvas or a flat surface. The use of *kujambula* for photography and film is a recent innovation and is not a problem.

The larger problem, which could have been considered under external problems, is more conveniently discussed here. "Carving" is used to refer to "carving a canoe/drum," i.e. a purely functional or physical activity; it only becomes an art form when it has *kulemba* or *kujambula* or the other categories of decoration on it.[12] More of this under the *-mb-* theory of art.

---

[12] Carving is *sema*: to dig out, to adze. It moves towards fictional representation in expressions like *kusemera chinyau*, literally meaning "to carve a mask for somebody," but meaning "to invent a story for the purpose of putting someone in difficulty," or "to frame" in American parlance.

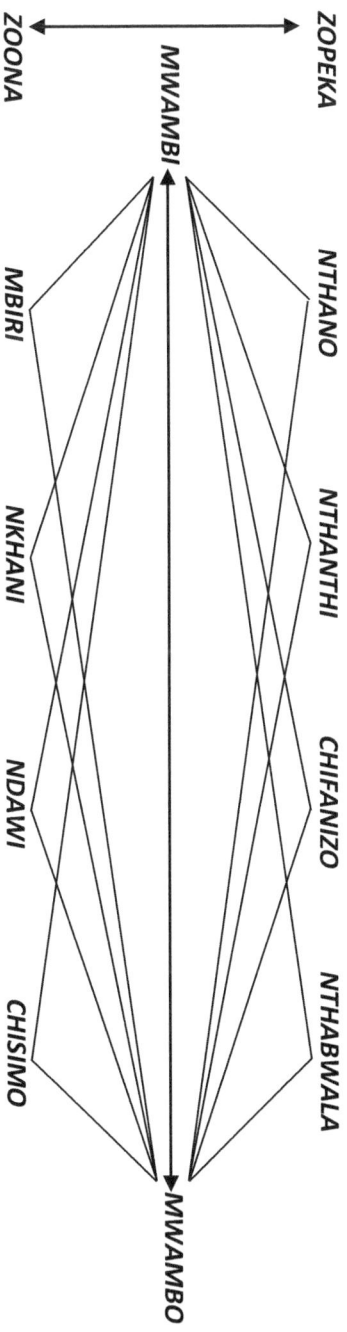

FIGURE 1: INTERRELATIONSHIPS OF PROSE FORMS
ZOPEKA/ZOONA: KUGWIRIZANA KWA MAINA ENA A LUSO LOLANKHULA

PART ONE

THEORY: STUDYING MALAWIAN ARTS

CHAPTER ONE:
TERMINOLOGICAL PROBLEMS IN
MALAWIAN VERBAL ARTS

After examining the oral literature of the Nyanja, Finnegan remarked:

> ... proverbs are not always distinguished by a special term from other categories of verbal art. The Nyanja *mwambi*, for instance, refers to story, riddle, or proverb ...[1]

This comment suggests that the problems are inherent in the vernacular terms or forms. However, some of the terminological problems are found also when western classificatory systems or terms are used to describe purely local phenomena. This chapter examines some of the definitional problems encountered when discussing the major Malawian folklore items. Although the discussion starts with an examination of the western (English) terms used for Yao, Tumbuka and Nyanja (Chewa), the major emphasis in the second part is on Chichewa terms, not for any ethnocentric reasons but because of the scarcity of vernacular publications in the other languages. The chapter concludes with a reclassification of the major and minor verbal arts.

English Terms: Vernacular Forms

Terminological or definitional problems of Malawian folklore, especially oral literature, have existed since the first publication on the subject in the 1880s.

The Yao Case

Macdonald isolated "at least four distinct forms" of traditional Yao literature: *ndawi* or conundrums, some of which he noted were in the form of a "little story"; *ndano*, tales; *nyimbo* or songs, and *chitagu* or

---

[1] Finnegan, *Oral Literature in Africa*, p. 390.

catchword composition. The comments under *ndano* are relevant to the problem.

> These are also called *ndawi*, because many of them resemble the conundrums in having a double meaning. Some of these, we might almost say most of these, when complete have songs in them, which are repeated every now and then at each crisis in the tale. They are often recited in this form on public occasions.[2]

The narrative forms, it seems, have interchangeable names *ndano* or *ndawi*, simply because of having double meanings. Note also that *ndano* proper sometimes have songs in them, although Macdonald does not give them any special name.

Another problem here is the isolation of a minor verbal form, *chitagu*, which among the Yao holds no special significance except the recreational aspect of playing upon words. Macdonald states that "long tales are carried on in this way"; however, my informants do not include narratives under *chitagu*. The term *kutagulira* is a conversational form belonging more to oratory than recitals or narratives.

Significant also is not so much the promotion of a minor form to a major one but the translation of *ndawi* as conundrum instead of riddle as a major term. Macdonald seems to put conundrums on the same footing as riddles, since in the same publication he uses the two terms interchangeably too.

Apart from the problems mentioned above, Macdonald's four-way classification excludes some major categories. Proverbs, for example, do not appear under the above, even as a subcategory; only the following appears:

> Natives have plenty of such traditional literature, which accompanied by their shrewd observations on men and manners, makes their society highly interesting.[3]

---

[2]   Duff Macdonald, *Africana or the Heart of Heathen Africa*, Vol. 1 (1882) (London: Dawsons, 1969), p. 48.

[3]   Macdonald, *Africana*, Vol. 1, p. 122.

This could refer to proverbs, which the Yao might not have a special label for. However, even if the "natives" did not have a special term for proverbs there are more significant forms than the *chitagu* isolated above.

The Tumbuka Case

T. Cullen Young, unlike Macdonald, recognises the existence of proverbs, although he does not give the vernacular terms. This in itself is a problem for other researchers, since for identification and even comparative purposes the vernacular terms are essential. The comments on proverbs deserve quoting in detail because they not only echo Macdonald but reveal similar problems of extending western terms to the local forms.

> The⁻ proverbial wisdom of this federation of early peoples, as well as the language in which many of these proverbs are couched, presents points of interest ... I shall let these African Aphorisms speak for themselves.[4]

It is not clear, in the absence of the vernacular terms, whether or not the locals would have used "proverbs" and "aphorisms' as interchangeably as Cullen Young does for the same forms.

Cullen Young's problems are augmented in another publication which gives a more general term, "sayings", for the same forms.

> The great bulk of the sayings recorded here—some witty, all wise—have already appeared ... these Aphorisms naturally use a "slang," rather than a "cultured," form wherever a choice of that sort offers.[5]

The distinction between "slang" and "cultured" in the local tongue is problematic apart from whether proverbs are distinctly "formulaic" and "cultured" whereas sayings are *colloquial," "idiomatic," or "cliché-like" expressions.

---

[4] T. Cullen Young, "Some Proverbs of the Tumbuka-Nkamanga Peoples of the Northern Province of Nyasaland," *Africa*, 10, 3 (July 1931), p. 344.

[5] T. Cullen Young, *Notes on the Customs and Folklore of the Tumbuka-Kamanga Peoples* (Livingstonia, Malawi: The Mission Press, 1931), p. 265.

The problem with Cullen Young's categories extends to the narrative forms where terms like "fable," "tale," and "story" are used interchangeably.

> The Fables that here follow have been chosen not because all or, indeed any of them are of unquestionable antiquity, but because all of them are being used in the country at this moment for the purpose of pointing some moral which, to the teller of the fable appears to be implicit in the tale itself.[6]

As in the comments on proverbs, liberties are taken on whether or not the locals use the terms "fables," "tales" and "stories" as interchangeably as Cullen Young does.

The Nyanja/Chewa Case

The terminological confusions above in the other languages were also apparent in the case of Chinyanja or Chichewa. Riddles, proverbs, stories, or rituals, seem to have been classified interchangeably as *mwambi* or *mwambo*. Worse still, some collectors did not even recognise the confusion as a terminological problem. It is only Ernest Gray in 1944 who confronted the problem in a brief introductory section of his collection of proverbs.[7]

Using *Mwambi* as proverb, Gray goes on to illustrate the confusion from the other dictionaries and grammars of the language:

> Scott's *Mang'anja Dictionary*: "A story, a custom, a guess, tradition, true narrative, instruction." After these definitions Scott gives a few riddles headed, "Some Riddles, *mwambi*." These are followed by a few proverbs headed, "Some Proverbs, *ntanu* or *mwambi*."[8]

The problem which Scott did not see here is the confusion of two basic terms: *mwambi* (plural *miyambi*) for narrative and *mwambo* (plural *miyambo*) for customs, traditional wisdom and instruction. The confusion extends to *ntanu* as proverbs. Scott did not realise that the short sayings

---

6   Cullen Young, *Notes on the Customs and Folklore of the Tumbuka-Kamanga Peoples*, p. 179.

7   Ernest Gray, "Some Proverbs of the Nyanja People," *African Studies*, 3 (Sept 1944), p. 102.

8   Gray, "Some Proverbs of the Nyanja People," pp. 102-103.

are truly proverbs but the *ntanu* (*nthano*) are the long narratives used to explain the sayings.

The Scott and Hetherwick Dictionary later committed the same offense. When Hetherwick includes the example *Mwambi ndi kungophiphiritsa*,[9] i.e. *mwambi* is just to confuse, he is himself confusing another form more related to parable, fable and allegory than he realised. In this case, other vernacular terms to be discussed later were needed.

The two grammar books quoted by Gray can also be accused of similar confusions. First, Hetherwick's *Manual of the Nyanja Language* has *mwambi* for custom when it should have been mwambo.[10] Secondly, Sanderson and Bithrey's *An Introduction to Chinyanja* has *mwambi* as "A story a riddle, a proverb."[11] The confusion can be sorted out as above and in the manner this chapter demonstrates.

After noting the confusions over terms and their definitions in the 1930s, Gray took pains to sort out some of them.[12] He isolated five terms synonymous with proverbs and four cognates. The five terms used interchangeably with proverbs were *mwambo* (*miyambo*), *mwambi* (*miyambi*), *nthanthi* or *ntanti* (singular and plural), *nthanu* (singular and plural) and *chisimo* (*zisimo*). The four cognates were *nkhani*, *luso*, *lunta* *(sic)* and *ndota*. This was the first and last serious attempt outside the dictionaries quoted earlier at trying to find a system underlying the Chichewa folklore terms. However, there are also some serious problems with Gray's classification requiring a complete reclassification system and even a redefinition.

Some of the problems with Gray's approach are simply attitudinal. The first problem is to suggest that the confusion might be due to "the admixture of tribes and languages."[13] As this discussion demonstrates the Chichewa cluster of languages (Chinyanja and Chimang'anja) has a unified

---

9   Scott and Hetherwick, *Dictionary of the Chichewa Language*, p. 353.

10   Quoted by Gray, "Some Proverbs of the Nyanja People," p. 103.

11   Quoted by Gray, "Some Proverbs of the Nyanja People," p. 103.

12   Gray, "Some Proverbs of the Nyanja People," pp. 102-103.

13   Gray, "Some Proverbs of the Nyanja People," p. 102.

and systematic classification system for all the arts. The second attitudinal problem is to assume "that the Nyanja are not of an analytical turn of mind."[14] That the assumption is erroneous is demonstrated by the fact that the people distinguish between not only different artistic *forms* but also various degrees of verbal *content*. Furthermore, the unified linguistic system presented here could not have been devised by a non-analytic people. The third serious methodological problem is that Gray, in spite of his attempts to get at the root of the system, was still using external non-Nyanja or Bantu modes of classifying folklore instead of working from within the ethnolinguistic framework set up by the data. Apart from using western conceptions of how folklore should be classified Gray placed the proverb as a genre at the centre of the system, when it is only a subcategory of other major genres, as we are going to see. Gray also misses very important subcategories in his five-by-four classification. All in all, there is a need to re-examine, reclassify and regroup the verbal arts in Chichewa in a more comprehensive and consistent manner. Below is a critique of Gray's definitions or explanations for each term.

1. *Mwambo (Miyambo)*

To quote Gray:

> This is, perhaps the most widely-used term. It is applied to all types of traditional wisdom. Customs, rites, proverbs, riddles, stories, and songs are all called *Miyambo*.[15]

There is confusion here between terminology and the context in which certain folklore material is found. All the above items can appear in the context of an initiation ceremony under *mwambo*. This can be illustrated by a sentence like: *iyi ndi miyambi yapamwambo* (these are the teachings given during ceremonies). No one, even during such ceremonies, would confuse a song with a story, although they can appear in the same rite or context.

---

[14] Gray, "Some Proverbs of the Nyanja People," p. 102.

[15] Gray, "Some Proverbs of the Nyanja People," p. 103.

Gray goes further on the same page:

> The term is also used for the instruction of wisdom, the narration of customs and traditions. *Kulanga mwambo* is to teach or instruct. *Amace ali kumuuza iye mwambo* means, "Her mother is teaching her duties (or responsibilities)." Solomon's Proverbs are called *miyambo*.

As above, the teachings and Solomon's proverbs are called *Miyambo* not because of their form but their context.

2. *Mwambi (Miyambi)*

> This term ... has a less wide connotation. It is commonly used when speaking of proverbs, but is also used when speaking of many types of folklore.[16]

In fact, however, *mwambi* is the major generic term for all narratives: it contains all the subcategories Gray later isolates as distinct forms, i.e. he makes major forms minor: *mwambi/mwambo* are the major verbal arts, while the rest are subcategories, as will be discussed in a reformulation of the arts later.

3. *Nthanthi* or *Ntanti* (singular and plural)

> This term is the one Sanderson and Bithrey give. It is the one most commonly used among the Nyanja I know. It is also used for a folk story of the type upon which many of the proverbs are based.
>
> Hetherwick says that whilst "*mwambi* is true and of long ago, *ntanti* is not necessarily true." The verb *kutanta* means to straighten out, to stretch across, and is used of anything without bends or turnings. The word *ntanti* might therefore be used to differentiate between this straight-forward type of story without interruptions, and *nthanu*.[17]

There are no problems with this definition.

---

16   Gray, "Some Proverbs of the Nyanja People," p. 103.
17   Gray, "Some Proverbs of the Nyanja People," p. 103.

4. *Nthanu* (singular and plural)

> This term is generally used to denote a story punctuated by sung choruses, but it is also used for narrated custom and for proverbs.[18]

Gray does not distinguish between *ntanti/nthanthi* as an unsung narrative and *ntanu/nthanu/nthano* as all narratives whether or not sung. Furthermore, it is rare for the term to refer to custom or proverb. It only refers to proverbs when they have narrative explanations to describe their origins.

5. *Chisimo* (*Zisimo*)

> I have never heard this term used with reference to folklore, but a Chewa informant uses it in the written introduction to a collection of proverbs ... Amongst other wider meanings Hetherwick gives "nature, manner, custom, proverb."[19]

The term could derive from *kusimba* (*chisimo*), i.e. to recount or to narrate. However, it moves more towards fable or parable than towards proverbs, as such. It can refer to proverbs as above only if there is a narrative explanation behind it.

Gray puts the other four categories under "Other cognate words":

6. "*Nkhani*: a narrative, a story or speech, news."[20]

As a later section demonstrates, this is a more general term for factual and fictional narratives or accounts. When discussing particular genres, however, the specific term is used.

7. "*Luso*: wisdom, cleverness, experience."[21]

8. "*Lunta*: wisdom, wit, sense, understanding."[22]

---

[18] Gray, "Some Proverbs of the Nyanja People," p. 103.

[19] Gray, "Some Proverbs of the Nyanja People," p. 103.

[20] Gray, "Some Proverbs of the Nyanja People," p. 103.

[21] Gray, "Some Proverbs of the Nyanja People," p. 103.

[22] Gray, "Some Proverbs of the Nyanja People," p. 103.

Both *luso* and *luntha* are well-defined; however, they would hardly be used for genres, only the manner of performance.

9. "*Ndota*: wisdom (of an oracular character), instinct, guessing, divination."[23]

As above, it is also well-defined, but mostly used for persons of old age and therefore full of worldly ancient wisdom, e.g. *nkhalamba za ndota* (old sages).

The dissatisfactions with Gray's categories consist not only in the definitions and confusions but in the failure to distinguish form, context and content. Some minor forms, e.g. *chisimo*, are given major status and some major forms, e.g. *nkhani*, minor status. Furthermore, some non-verbal skills are given verbal status, e.g. *ndota*, *luso* and *luntha*.

An Investigation into Current Vernacular Usage

An investigation into the current usage of some of the major Chichewa folklore terms was conducted. Thirty-one usages were examined from twenty-seven different published sources by nineteen different Chichewa or Chinyanja authors. The results are given below:

1. *Mwambi*

Three factual sources and two fictional sources used *mwambi* (*miyambi*) to refer to factual or fictional narrative speech, news or reports. Phiri and Ntara use *mwambi* to refer to a proverb.

> Pali mwambi uja ukuti: "Konza kapansi kuti ka m'mwamba katsike."[24]
> Fanizo (kapena mwambi) la akulu likuti, Dziko ndi anthu, thengo ndi mambala.[25]

---

[23]   Gray, "Some Proverbs of the Nyanja People," p. 103.

[24]   Paladio G. Phiri, *Nsembe ndi Miyambi ya Achewa* (Kachebere Major Seminary, n.d.), p. 3.

[25]   S.Y. Ntara, *Msyamboza* (Nkhoma: CCAP, 1965), p. iii.

These are straightforward cases. Note however, that Ntara introduces the term *fanizo* which will be discussed later.

Loga uses *mwambi* to refer to *alegole*, i.e. allegory or folk-narrative.

> *Ndi mkambo wa nthano omwe umakhala ndi ndanda wa zochitika omwe umagwirizana ndi m'ndandanda mau mu sentensi pokamba zochitika kuti umasulire kapena kuonetsa cholinga cha mauwo.*[26]

There are two other terms used synonymously above, *mkambo* and *nthano*. These terms will also be discussed later.

In a work of fiction, Mphonda uses *mwambi* to denote a folk narrative:

> *Poyamba kufotokoza mwambi uliwonse (kapena nthano) pamakhala liu lake loyamba kunena limene amati: 'kunangokhala', ndipo akumva amayankha: 'kalipenda', 'tili tonse' kapena 'adisi njoo' ndipo pomaliza wonena uja amati 'mbatata yangayo' omvera aja nabvomera nati 'yapsyerera'.*[27]

It will be noticed that Mphonda is describing the formal opening and closing formulas for a folk story here.

In another fictional work Ntaba uses *mwambi* to refer to a novel, a long short story or a fictional account.

> *Masiku amenewo ambirife tisadadziwe kuwerenga, timamva miyambi ya kalulu ndi nyama zinzake kwa akulu-akulu. Koma lero tikumva miyambi osati ya nyama zokha komanso ya anthu kuchokera. m'mabuku. Miyambi yonseyi ili ndi cholinga chawo ... Bukhu lino lalembedwa mosasiyananso ndi "Kale-kale padali Kalulu ndi Njobvu." ... ndi mwambi wanga wa makono kuyesa kusanthula zobvuta zake zosakhutitsidwa ndi zazing'ono zimene tili nazo. Ngakhale lalembedwa m'Chichewa ndipo ndatchula makwacha ndi atambala, nkhaniyi, mayina onse, si zam'dziko muno kapena dziko lirilonse. Si mbiri yakale, yatsopano, kapena yamtsogolo ya dziko*

---

[26] Loga, *Muni wa Chichewa*, p. 176.

[27] A.H. Mphonda, *Miyambi Yatsopano* (1965) (Limbe: Malawi Publications and Literature Bureau, 1975), p. vii.

lirilonse. Choncho zochitika muno sizikhudza aliyense. Bwinze, Gong'o, Sofiya, Bimbo, Agabu, ndi Thyola ali m'maloto.[28]

Ntaba uses other synonyms like *nkhani* and *mbiri. Maloto*, dreams, for a fictional construct has also been used above.

From the above usages it is clear that *mwambi* understood to be a fictional or factual narrative. It also includes the proverb.

2. Mwambo

The second term is *mwambo* (*miyambo*). Five sources were examined, with the usages discussed below.

Gwengwe uses *mwambo* to refer to customs, traditions, arts and crafts, civilisation, religion (and beliefs), *rites de passage*, language, in short, the culture of a people. His *Kukula ndi Mwambo* is on all aspects of Chewa culture.

> *[N]zeru zao [zamakolo], nchito zao, mkhalidwe wao, m'mene anali kusungira dziko lao, chipembedzo chao, zimene anali kuzikhulupirira kuti zinali ndi mphamvu, zosiyana-siyana, zimene anali kuchita pa ubwana wao, chilankhulidwe chao, ndi zina zotere.*[29]

Chakudza also describes all aspects of Chewa culture.[30]

Mwambo is also used to refer to specific rites or rituals. Makumbi's *Maliro ndi Miyambo ya Achewa* is on funeral rites of the Chewa. Makumbi says:

> *Colembera bukhuli, ndico kuti tilondole za miyambo ya Acewa kuti mbiriyi isungidwe kuti ana amtsogolo adzaidziwe ... ndifuna kulondola maliro ndi miyambo ya Acewa, mmene iwo anasamalitsa miyamboyi.*[31]

---

[28] Jolly Max Ntaba, *Mtima Sukhuta* (Limbe: Popular Publications, 1985), p. 5.

[29] John W. Gwengwe, *Kukula ndi Mwambo* (1965) (Limbe: Malawi Publications and Literature Bureau, 1970), p. iii.

[30] Z.P. Kamende, *Chakudza* (Limbe: Malawi Publications and Literature Bureau, 1967).

[31] Archibald Makumbi, *Maliro ndi Miyambo ya Achewa* (1955) (London: Longman Group Ltd., 1970), p. iv.

Makumbi uses *mbiri*, a term remarked on earlier and to be discussed later.

Gumbi in *Tili Tonse* uses *mwambo* in a similar way to the above but here it refers to the tradition or practice of story-telling.

> *Ndifunanso kuwakumbutsa amayi kuti asataye mwambo wa makolo womayimbira ana nthano asanapite kogona.*[32]

Mwambo refers to laws, codes, ordinances and regulations as in:

> *Dziwani kuti zolembedwazi ndizo Mwambo wa pa Mseu umene anaunena pa Malamulo a Magalimoto ndi njinga za moto.* (Motor Traffic Ordinance).
>
> 1 *Mwambo wa pa mseu ndiwo wotsogolera anthu oyendetsa magalimoto ndi njinga kuti apewe zoopsya. Mwambowu utikumbutsa kuti tiyenera kusamalira anthu ena osangoganiza za ife tokha.*[33]

It seems *mwambo* (*miyambo*) is straightforwardly used to refer to customs, rites, instructions, regulations, arts, crafts and culture. It is not confused with any of the fictional narratives in form and content, although other non-Chichewa users, to be discussed below, do confuse *mwambo* with *mwambi* above.

3. *Nthano*

Four sources were examined for the use of *nthano*. All referred to fictional narratives.

Ntaba's *Mwana wa Mnzako* is a novel prefaced by:

> *Nthano ya Liyoyo ndi chitsanzo chabe chofotokoza ndi kumasulira zimene tateyu akufotokozera mwana wake; nkhani ya Liyoyo ndi chitsanzo ngati chida cha mphunzitsi pophunzitsa.*[34]

Zingani's *Njala Bwana* is a long short story also prefaced by:

---

[32]   E.M.S. Gumbi, *Tili Tonse* (Limbe: Popular Publications, 1984), p. v.

[33]   Malawi Government, *Malamulo a Pamseu* (Zomba: The Government Printer, 1962), p. 1.

[34]   Jolly Max Ntaba, *Mwana wa Mnzako* (Limbe: Popular Publications, 1982), p. 4.

*Adandipatsa malingaliro amene ndagwiritsira ntchito m'nthanoyi
ndi ana anga ...* [35]

Gumbi's *Tili Tonse* is a collection of folk stories:

*Amayiwa adandiphunzitsa luntha lopeka nthano za matanthauzo
ndiponso kuyimba kumene.* [36]

Kalindawalo's novel *M'thengo Mdalaka Njoka* declares:

*Nkhaniyi ndi yopeka; zonse zimene zalembedwa m'bukhumu ndi
nthano chabe yochokera m'maganizo mwangamu.* [37]

Note Kalidawalo's use of the term *nkhani.*

In the above sources, *Nthano* refers to a folk story, a short story, or a novel. In other words, the term covers all fictional narratives.

4.   *Nkhani*

Nkhani has been used above to refer to both factual and fictional narratives or accounts, speeches, reports or news. It is also used as such in the five examples below.

Two factual accounts use *nkhani* in the following manner.

Ngawi says:

*Ndayesa kuti ndi chinthu chabwino kuti ndilembe kanthu pa nkbani
yokhudza za ntchito popeza kuti anyamata kaya asungwana
akamaliza maphunziro ao sadziwa zomwe ayenera kuchita.* [38]

In an earlier publication, Chafulumira prefaced his remarks with:

*M'buku muno mwalembedwa nkhani zimene zingathe kupatsa
anthu a banja nzeru zokometsa banja.* [39]

---

[35]   Willie Zingani, *Njala Bwana* (Limbe: Popular Publications, 1984), p. v.

[36]   Gumbi, *Tili Tonse*, p. iv.

[37]   A. Kalindawalo, *M'thengo Mdalaka Njoka* (Lilongwe: Longman [Malawi] Ltd., 1974), p. ii.

[38]   K.J. Mgawi, *Gwira. Pali Moyo* (Blantyre: CLAIM, 1985), p. iii.

[39]   E.W. Chafulumira, *Banja Lathu* (1942) (Lusaka: NECZAM, 1972), p. vii.

Three other sources use *nkhani* for fictional constructs.

Ntaba's novel *Ikakuwona Litsiro Sikata* opens with *"Tamverani tsono nkhani yangayi."*[40]

Kalindawalo's *M'thengo Mdalaka Njoka*, the novel referred to in the last section, states in the preface *"Nkhani imene yalembedwa m'bukhu lino ikukhudza mabvuto woterewa."*[41]

Zingani is not certain whether his long short story *Madzi Akatayika* is a factual or fictional construct:

> *Nkhani yonseyi ndi yopeka. Ngati zina zifanana ndi zomwe zinakuonekeranipo, ayi musandikwiyire, zangochitika mwangozi. Cholinga changa ndi kuyesa kulemba zimene zimachitika m'moyo mwathu, osati kulemba mwadala mbiri ya munthu wina ali yense.*[42]

Note also the use of *mbiri* to be discussed below.

It is interesting to find another source extending the coverage of the word. Paliani's *1930 Kunadza Mchape* uses *nkhani* to include a narrative dramatic (play) form: *"sewero'li ndi nkhani yopeka."*[43]

5. *Mbiri*

Mbiri seems also to be used in several senses: factual and fictional narrative, history and even biography in the six sources below.

Soka's *Mbiri ya Alomwe* is translated as a historical account of the Lomwe:

> *Kumene anali ndi kumene ali lero; momwe anali kukhalira ndi momwe ali kukhalira lero.*[44]

---

[40] Jolly Max Ntaba, *Ikakuona Litsiro Sikata* (Blantyre: Dzuka Publishing Co., 1986), p. 2.

[41] Kalindawalo, *M'thengo Mdalaka Njoka*, p. ii.

[42] Willie Zingani, *Madzi Akatayika* (Blantyre: Dzuka Publishing Co., 1984), p. vi.

[43] Sylvester Paliani, *1930 Kunadza Mchape* (Lilongwe: Likuni Press and Publishing House, 1971), p. 5.

[44] L.D. Soka, *Mbiri ya Alomwe* (1953) (Limbe: Malawi Publications and Literature Bureau, 1975), p. v.

Ntara's three publications are relevant also. In *Nthondo*, a fictional biography, *mbiri* is a fictitious story of a person with factual undertones:

> *Bukuli ndi mbiri yopeka, koma ngakhale iri mbiri yopeka, mwina njonena zoona, cifukwa zonse zimene ndinalembamo, inu ambiri munamva monga momwe ndinamvera ine. Polembera mbiri iyi ndinayesetsa kutola makhalidwe ndi malankhulidwe a anthu ndi kusanganiza kumbiriyi kuti ikhale bwino. Ndiponso ndinayesetsa kukumbukira zonse zimene ndinazimva kale.*[45]

In *Msyamboza*, which is an account of an actual historical figure, *mbiri* refers to biography:

> *Mbiri zolembedwa m'mabuku ziri ndi phindu lalikulu kwa anthu odziwa kuwerenga. ... Pano (kunena m'buku ili) panalembedwa mbiri ndiyo ya mfumu dzina lace Msyamboza ... Tikatsata bwino mbiri yace, tidzaona kulephera kwace kwa munthu ndi kupambana kwace.*[46]

Ntara's *Namon Katengeza* is about another historical figure; *mbiri* denotes a straight biography in this case:

> *Ndinasauka polemba mbiri imeneyi chifukwa kutsata moyo wa munthu ... nkobvuta ... polemba mwatsatanetsatane mbiri ya moyo wa mbusayo.*[47]

The story of Mchape, another historical figure, is also *mbiri* in the biographical sense in Paliani's *1930 Kunadza Mchape*:

> *Ngakhale ziri zoona kuti mbiri ya Sing'anga wochuka'yu wochedwa Mchape inayamba kugwedeza dziko lino m'chaka cha 1930 ... sewero'li ndi nkhani yopeka ...*[48]

---

[45]   S.Y. Ntara, *Nthondo* (1936) (Nkhoma: CCAP, 1966), p. 3.

[46]   Ntara, *Msyamboza*, p. v.

[47]   S.Y. Ntara, *Namon Katengeza* (Nkhoma: CCAP, 1964), p. iii.

[48]   Paliani, *1930 Kunadza Mchape*, p. 5.

Two fictional narratives suggest that *mbiri* is also an account of a fictional construct. Gwengwe's *Kathyali Psyipsyiti* says *"Mbiri imene iri mbukuyi ndiyo yopeka."*[49]

Zingani's *Madzi Akatayika*, however, suggests both fact and fiction:

> *Cholinga changa ndi kuyesa kulemba zimene zimachitika m'moyo mwathu; osati kulemba mwadala mbiri ya munthu wina aliyense.*[50]

The six sources, then, suggest that *mbiri* should cover factual and fictional accounts, narratives, histories and biographies (and, by extension, autobiographies).

6. Sewero

Sewero is another problematic term. In all dictionary definitions, *Sewero* is always defined as *chamba, gule, kubvina*, i.e. dance or play in the sense of game. One source out of the four in this section uses it in this original sense. Koma-koma in *Mganda Kapena Malipenga* opens with the statement:

> *Mganda sichinthu chonga nyama kapena munthu ai, koma ndi masewera amene amakonda kuchitika m'dziko lathu lino la Malawi ... Masewera amenewa amafanana kwambiri ndi asirikari pamene amaguba perete.*[51]

The definition starts out with the original meaning of *sewero* for dance, then moves towards mime or imitation, which is its modern use. *Sewero* has now come to mean any play, drama or theatre (although it still retains the other meanings of a dance and a game). The rest of the examples below use *sewero* in its modern sense.

Paliani's *Sewero la Mlandu wa Nkhanga* was prefaced as:

---

[49] John W. Gwengwe, *Kathyali Psyipsyiti* (Blantyre: Malawi Publications and Literature Bureau, 1968), p. iii.

[50] Zingani, *Madzi Akatayika*, p. vi.

[51] W.P. Koma-koma, *Mganda Kapena Malipenga* (Limbe: Malawi Publications and Literature Bureau, 1965), p. 7.

> *Seweroli mutha kuona kuti lingathe kuseweredwa panja kapena m'nyumba pali makatani kapena opanda makatani kapena kuti anthu atha kungoliwerenga chabe monga nkhani ina iliyonse yopatsa chidwi.*[52]

Even as early as 1952, when drama in the western sense was not common in the country, the term had already acquired its new meaning. Paliani's *1930 Kunadza Mchape* supports the earlier usage: *"sewero'li ndi nkhani yopeka."*[53]

Chipinga's *Atambwali Sametana* follows the modern meaning:

> *Polemba bukhuli ndayesetsa kuti sewero iri la Atambwali Sametana (Saguza ndi Paguza) limveke bwino ndipo lisangalatse maganizo anu ...*[54]

As with the other terms, then, *sewero* has extended its meaning from dance and game to a scripted and performed extended play.

7. Ndakatulo

There are four recent publications which have popularised the term *ndakatulo* to refer to written, spoken or sung poetry. Chadza, in *Nchito ya Pakamwa*, the earliest publication of this genre, defines the term as follows:

> *ziri ngati nyimbo zodzipekera yekha munthu zokhala ndi matan-thauzo ace. Ndakatulo zambiri mayimbidwe ace sadziwika koma pakuziwerenga, camumtima kaya momveka, zimakometsera cinenero.*[55]

Nankwenya, in *Zofunika Mgramara wa Chichewa*, follows the above definition almost verbatim.[56] Gwengwe, in *Ndakatulo*, a collection of his

---

52 Sylvester Paliani, *Sewero la Mlandu wa Nkhanga* (1952) (London: Macmillan, 1982), p. iii.

53 Paliani, *1930 Kunadza Mchape*, p. 5.

54 C.C.J. Chipinga, *Atambwali Sametana* (Blantyre: Malawi Book Service, 1972), p. ii.

55 E.J. Chadza, *Nchito ya Pakamwa* (1963) (Lusaka: The Zambia Publications Bureau, 1967), p. 5.

56 I.A.J. Nankwenya, *Zofunika Mgramara wa Chichewa* (Lilongwe: Longman (Malawi) Ltd., 1974), p. 147.

poetry, does not define the term.[57] He only gives the functions and the pedagogy of verse. *Akoma Akagonera*, a collection of poetry, has a longer description of this genre by Mvula, the editor:

> *Ndakatulo ndi chidule cha nkhani kapena mbiri yayitali. Mawu amene anenedwa polira kapena polankhula munthu akakondwa; kapenanso akamva chisoni, amachokera mumtima. Munthu sachita kukhala pansi kuti apeke ndakatulo ayi. Kawirikawiri munthu amangozindikira akuyimba ndakatulo … Mwina munthu amakhala ndi nkhani imene safuna kuti iyiwalike. Kuti nkhaniyo isungike, amatenga mitu ikuluikulu yokhayokha ya nkhaniyo napeka nyimbo kapena ndakatulo. M'nyimboyo amaika mawu oyenera, woti afike pamtima ndi cholinga chake; ndiponso wokuluwika … Izi amazifotokoza mwachidule ndiponso mophiphiritsa polakatula … Ndakatulo zili ngatinso tsenga, ndagi, kapena mikuluwiko ingapo yoti munthu aganizire mozama kupsyola m'mene aganizira masiku onse. M'ndakatulo timapeza chinenedwe cholemera, chakuya, cha paphata pamaganizo anzeru … Ndakatulo ndi maziko otiphunzitsa mkhalidwe wa anthu … [Alembi] ayesa kutendera zolembalemba zawo ndi mikuluwiko, ndi maidyofoni. Zonsezi ndi nsinjiro za ndakatulo za m'chinenedwe chathu.*[58]

8. Nyimbo

Apart from Christian hymns, vernacular publications on folksongs have not appeared. In any case, there is no confusion here.

9. Mkuluwiko

Mikuluwiko, kuphiphiritsa, kukunkhuniza, ntchintchi or *chining'a* are expressions referring to idiomatic metaphoric and euphemistic language with a veiled or hidden meaning. Ntara's *Mau Okuluwika M'cinyanja*, the first collection of its kind, explains the functions of this term.

---

[57] Gwengwe, *Ndakatulo*, pp. v-vi, 1-4.

[58] E.T. Mvula, *Akoma Akagonera* (Limbe: Popular Publications, 1981), pp. v-vii.

Tilankhula mokuluwika kuti anthu ena asatsate nkhani zonse zimene tilikukamba.[59]

Nankwenya, in *Zofunika Mgramara wa Chichewa*, is more straightforward: *"Mau okuluwika ndiwo mawu amene matanthauzo ake ali obisika."*[60] Loga in *Muni* defines *chining'a* in the following manner:

> *ndi mau a kalankhulidwe ka m'njira yadongosolo la mau mwandunji, pogwiritsa ntchito mafulezi mu m'ndandanda osiyana ndi kalankhulidwe (koma kodziwika) ka masiku onse achinenero. Kusiyana kwa mkambidweku, ndipo kagwiritsidwe ka ntchito ka mau kapena mafulezi kotereku kumakhala ndi tanthauzo lomwe m'ndondomeko wake wa mauwo kawiri-kawiri sugwirizana ndi malamulo akalembedwe koyenera.*[61]

Mikuluwiko thus form a category on their own.

10. Mvekero (Ideophones)

Three Chichewa writers treat ideophones and onomatopoeic words as a separate verbal art. Nankwenya, in *Zofunika Mgramara wa Chichewa*, says of ideophones:

> *Mchichewa muli mau ena amene katchulidwe kao ndi mamvekedwe awo amapereka tanthauzo ndi kulimbikitsa zomwe tiri kunena.*[62]

Loga, in *Muni*, has similar statements to make.[63] Although Chadza, in *Tiphunzire Chichewa*, has a chapter on ideophones, only examples are given.[64] More work needs to be done on this category, and on the following category too.

11. Zifanifani/Ntchedzero

---

[59] S.Y. Ntara, *Mau Okuluwika m'Cinyanja* (1964) (Lusaka: NECZAM, 1972), p. 5.

[60] Nankwenya, *Zofunika Mgramara wa Chichewa*, p. 132.

[61] Loga, *Muni wa Chichewa*, p. 169

[62] Nankwenya, *Zofunika Mgramara wa Chichewa*, p. 113.

[63] Loga, *Muni wa Chichewa*, p. 49

[64] E.J. Chadza, *Tiphunzire Chichewa* (Blantyre: CLAIM, n.d.), pp. 31-32.

At least one writer treats similes as another verbal art. Gwengwe, in *Chimangirizo ndi Chifupikitso*, devotes a whole chapter to popular similes and clichés.[65] Unfortunately, the examples are not accompanied by any definitions or descriptions of why the similes deserve separate treatment.

Other Major Forms

In a reclassification of the verbal arts, the eleven forms above would be recognised in their own right, with the meanings attached to them by the writers. However, forms like *nthanthi* (*ntanti*), which do not appear in the literature, would be subcategories of other major genres. In this case, *nthanthi* would be unsung folk-narrative, thus retaining its dictionary meaning and its relation to *nthano*. *Nkhani* retains its meaning as used by the writers. Gray's *luso*, *luntha* and *ndota* have been eliminated since they are not verbal skills.

12. Chisimo/Zisimo

This term appears in Gray's formulation and also in Scott's dictionary as custom and proverb.[66] In popular usage, it tends more towards proverb than custom as such. It can also refer to a parable or fable. Hence it is better to retain it as a subcategory of *mwambi* or *nthano*.

13. Ndawi/Ngaji/Ndagi/Chilape

Scott appears to equate *ndawi* with narrative forms.[67] Gray's collection of riddles recognises *ndawi* and its synonyms as riddles (conundrums, enigma, etc.)[68] It is suggested that *ndawi* is Yao and that the more popular *chilape* or *ndagi* be the major terms here.

14. Fanizo

The dictionary definition gives *fanizo* as parable or tale.[69]

---

[65] J.W. Gwengwe, *Chimangirizo ndi Chifupikitso* (1968) (Nairobi: Oxford University Press, 1970).

[66] Scott and Hetherwick, *Dictionary of the Chichewa Language*, p. 370.

[67] Scott and Hetherwick, *Dictionary of the Chichewa Language*, p. 370.

[68] Ernest Gray, "Some Riddles of the Nyanja People," *Bantu Studies*, 13 (December 1939), p. 253.

[69] Scott and Hetherwick, *Dictionary of the Chichewa Language*, p. 128.

15. Nthabwala/Kusereula

This term does not appear in the Chichewa literature or in the diction-naries, although in popular usage it refers to pranks, tricks and jokes.

16. Maloto

Chichewa writers sometimes devote sections, if not chapters, to a discussion of dreams and their meanings, e.g. Gwengwe's *Kukula Ndi Mwambo*.[70] In fiction, too, dreams occupy quite a substantial part, e.g. Ntara's *Nthondo* and even Gwengwe's *Sikusinja ndi Gwenembe*.[71]

Minor Verbal Arts

Although this writer would relegate *nkhani*, *mkuluwiko*, ideophones and *zifani-fani* to minor categories of the verbal arts, they have been singled out because Chichewa recognises their integrity and internal consistency, and they form a large proportion of the people's verbal arts. What the above writers have not identified as forming part of the verbal arts are the minor forms grouped below:

17. Formulaic Forms

Kutemberera (to curse), *kulumbirira* (to make an oath), *tamando* panegyric), *kutukwana* (to swear).

18. Ritualistic Forms

Mapemphero (prayers), *kupembedza* (to worship), *kuombedza* (to divine), *kulodza* (to bewitch), *kulogolola* (to exorcisw), *dalitso* (blessing), *nsembe* (sacrifice).

19. Naming

Dzina (name or nickname), *mfunda* (kinship term/clan name).

---

[70] Gwengwe, *Kukula ndi Mwambo*, p. 112.

[71] Ntara, *Nthondo*, and J.W. Gwengwe, *Sikusinja ndi Gwenembe* (1965) (Limbe: Malawi Publications and Literature Bureau, 1969).

20. Conversational Forms

Bodza (gossip), *langizo* (instruction), *kularika* (to preach), *kunyoza* (to insult), *kutonza* (ro tease), *kulonjera* (to greet), *kutsazika* (to say goodbye).

In this reclassification, sixteen major and four minor verbal arts have been isolated. In Chapter Three, *"Ulimbaso,* an Integrated Theory of Art," we discuss how all the arts are interrelated and unified under one comprehensive system. This could be done only after clearing the mystification shrouding the vernacular terms.

CHAPTER TWO:
PROBLEMS IN COLLECTING ORAL LITERATURE

The following quotation summarises the major problems facing researchers collecting oral literature in Malawi:

> I was once walking along a native path with a little boy, and when the conversation began to flag I proposed a native riddle for him. He turned round with a very peculiar look, and asked me if we recited riddles at our home. "Yes," was the reply, "and you do it too." Then he asked, "Do you do it at mid-day?" And by and by, after smothering many conflicting thoughts and some irresolution, he began to explain that the old people said that "if boys recited riddles at mid-day, horns would grow on their foreheads!" Tales and conundrums are generally recited after sunset. While asleep, as our companions thought, in a tent beside the camp fires, we have often lain almost bursting with suppressed laughter, as we listened to the tales and conundrums that went round.[1]

The first problem revealed is the collection of folklore material out of context. Duff Macdonald thought he could elicit riddles from the informant while walking at mid-day along a village or forest path. The second problem is one of attitudes: Macdonald took riddles to be conversation fillers: if there is a gap in the conversation, riddles are a form of entertainment to pass the time. They might be, in their proper context, like the camp fires or *bwalo* fires at night. However, they might also serve other more serious functions than he realised. The third problem is one of ignorance of forms and, as in this case, taboos or myths surrounding particular performances or occasions. And, as Macdonald is informed, oral literature of the kind he sought is only performed at night. The fourth problem is the choice of informants as sources of folklore items. In this case, a "little boy," the age is a factor to consider in the collection of data. The fifth problem is the manner of collection. In the quotation,

---

[1] Macdonald, *Africana*, Vol. 1, pp. 121-122.

eavesdropping is the mode, with the collectors divided socially and psychologically from the performers. The tent is a physical barrier that separates both parties. The final problem arises from the fourth and fifth: the resultant text is a fragment or distortion of the original. This chapter then, is an examination of the collections, contexts, informants and texts which have hitherto been the sources of oral literature study in the country.

Although the question of language does not appear in the above quotation, and is the subject of another chapter, a brief excursion will also be made into the problem of translation, not only by collectors but also by informants who provide the data in a language not their own.

Out of Context: "Induced" Contexts

Although the legitimacy of induced contexts for oral literature performance has only lately been recognised, some of the "induced" contexts which elicited Malawian data were not experimental, they were the method available for the collectors.[2] Material collected from Malawian slaves or freed slaves abroad, for example, are suspect.

Edward Steere, the first collector of Yao riddles, had two Yao slave informants supplying him the data in Zanzibar, East Africa.

> I began with the help of a young slave ... I found at last a really good teacher in a man called by the very common name of Mabruki. I heard afterwards that his original name was Mpanda. He had been a slave employed by his master in trading journeys to and from his own tribe. His master had by his will given him his freedom, and he then got a living by selling small ventures in one of the markets in Zanzibar.[3]

---

[2]   All the publications discussed in this chapter were published before 1960, i.e. prior to the phenomenon of "induced" contexts.

[3]   Edward Steere, *Collections for a Handbook of the Yao Language* (London: Society for Promoting Christian Knowledge, 1871), pp. v-vi.

Itinerant informants include servants or children of servants working for white masters outside the country. Madeleine Holland's informant is a case in point.

> In the year 1906, shortly before leaving Salisbury, the capital of Mashonaland and Southern Rhodesia, I overheard a young Manyanja boy telling my little son what appeared to be the old tale of Brer Rabbit and the Tar Baby.[4]

"Induced" contexts on the other hand were also possible, for example, with western educated Malawians studying or resident abroad. Hallowell had the following to say:

> In February, 1920, the following Yao texts were recorded from the dictation of Dr. Daniel Malekebu [sic], an educated Bantu, who was then living in Philadelphia.[5]

In this category, we include collections done in the country but in unnatural contexts. The class or lecture room, for example, has been used by several collectors as the sole source of data. One of the earliest is Cullen Young:

> Several of these Fables were heard in a Village School at different dates, being told by an old African teacher during the weekly period set apart for "Moral Lesson."[6]

(In this case the performer had the right intentions in the new context!) Most of Gray's collections of proverbs and riddles were also collected in this manner.[7]

The examples above are extreme and, taking into consideration the circumstances of the informants and collectors alike, perhaps the only means of collecting the data. Some of the collectors above, who were

---

[4] Madeleine Holland, "Folklore of the Banyanja," *Folklore*, XXVII (1916), p. 116.

[5] A. Irving Hallowell, "Two Folktales from Nyasaland," *Journal of American Folklore*, XXXV (July-September 1922), p. 216.

[6] Cullen Young, *Notes on the Customs and Folklore of the Tumbuka-Kamanga Peoples*, p. 179.

[7] Gray, "Some Riddles of the Nyanja People," pp. 251-291, and "Some Proverbs of the Nyanja People," pp. 101-128.

either not professionals or had other interests to be discussed later, were not aware of the problems created by the change of context. Other collectors were only too aware of the issues. Gray confessed in discussing the problems of collecting proverbs:

> They are not commonly on the tongues of young people, neither are they used for amusement or as a pass-time. The ideal way therefore—though it is a very slow one—is to be constantly on the alert for their cropping up in the course of ordinary conversation, when the circumstances in which they are used can also be noted. The ideal place to collect proverbs is in the courtyard, whether ecclesiastical or secular. If proverbs are solicited care must be taken to ask other reliable informants if the proverbs so collected are known to them and recognised as such.[8]

This method of collecting genuine folk material was also recognised by Cullen Young.[9]

Other collectors who employed informants made doubly sure also that the information did not come only from the informant's knowledge but was also verified from other sources. Sanderson, for example, expressed:

> indebtedness to Mr. Robert Mandere of Karonga who supplied the material, partly from his own knowledge and partly after painstaking enquiry among the old people of Nkhamanga.[10]

Sanderson himself did not only employ an informant, he worked with the people from whom the material came.

The problems of collecting material out of context are several. The greatest problem is one in which the context is not even mentioned, only the text given. But contexts also become anonymous: "a village school" (Cullen Young); "a market in Zanzibar" (StAfricaneere); "a tent beside the

---

[8] Gray, "Some Proverbs of the Nyanja People," p. 101.

[9] Cullen Young's publications come from close contact with the people. See any citation below.

[10] G.M. Sanderson, "Tumbuka Proverbs," *The Nyasaland Journal*, 5, 1 (January 1952), p. 38.

camp fires" (Macdonald); "ecclesiastical or secular courtyards" (Gray); in "Philadelphia" (Hallowell) or:

> Ms. collected at Blantyre, from a boy whose home was in the neighbourhood of the Murchison Falls, on the Shire River.[11]

The problem of anonymity will be raised again when discussing informants. The fragmented, incomplete, or distorted texts which result from the unnatural contexts will be discussed below. However, the unnatural texts lacking in "orality" are among the worst plagues afflicting the products. Finally, the contexts discussed above produce informants who themselves, are uprooted from their natural setting: they cannot reproduce the genuine texts which only "authentic" folk could produce. As Cullen Young confessed of his old school teacher,

> these tales represent the fable as retained and used by the modern, or "changing" African.[12]

The question of detribalised informants is related to language which will be dealt with later.

Attitudes

Stannus had this to say on Christian missionaries-as-collectors:

> one cannot help feeling that the ethnological character of his [Macdonald's] book suffers from the attitude which he, in common with most missionaries, takes in regard to many native customs. I believe that if missionaries, instead of turning away their faces in horror, had regarded these practices with an open mind, they would have found that their veiled statements were exaggerations of the truth, and that the old social code of the Yao native would compare favourably with the order of things in most civilised countries.[13]

---

[11]   Alice Werner, *Introductory Sketch of the Bantu Languages* (London: Kegan Paul, Trench, Trubner and Co. Ltd., 1919), p. 272.

[12]   Cullen Young, *Notes on the Customs*, p. 179.

[13]   Hugh Stannus, "The Wayao of Nyasaland," *Harvard African Studies*, III (1922), p. 230.

Although there are no direct expressions of horror or disgust from most collectors, one has a strong feeling that the material suffers from various attitudes: prudery resulting in censorship, exoticism or superiority.

Taylor interrupted one of Saka's stories told to her child:

> The story was stopped for juvenile ears at this point, as the climax was obvious. A *precis* of the sequel is as follows.[14]

Parts of the story were not only censored but truncated to suit the tastes of the audience. The truncation of folklore material is discussed further in another section; collectors thus also slant their material to particular age groups. Phyllis Savory is another example:

> This, an addition to the series of African Bantu Folk Tales, deals with a collection of stories better suited to the older generation, than were those of the "FIRESIDE" tales. Some of them are slightly more crude in their presentation ...[15]

In the same introduction, she tries to explain or apologise for the material to her readers:

> ... we should all endeavour not only to understand, but also to accept, in an effort to sympathise more deeply, with the background of the African himself.[16]

She also introduces the element of exoticism in her apologia:

> It should be realised that many of these beliefs and fables of antiquity were also our own, in the past far distant ages, before civilisation came to the European races, and long before the earliest African records).[17]

In the earlier publication the apologia-exoticism comes out just as strongly:

---

[14]   Margaret Taylor, "Angoni Stories," *NADA*, 4 (December 1926), p. 76.

[15]   Phyllis Savory, *Tales from Africa* (Cape Town: Howard Timms, 1968), p. 11.

[16]   Savory, *Tales from Africa*, p. 11.

[17]   Savory, *Tales from Africa*, p. 11.

> Some of the sense of humour in these animal stories may be thought to be of rather a distorted kind, but that is the way of Bantu fun—and who are we to condemn it? ... These animals are foreign to our soil.[18]

It is clear that Savory's readers are western readers. When the collector is not doing the pandering, it is sometimes reviewers who do it:

> The atmosphere of this collection arises from a landscape both physically and mentally *exotic*, where the drums beat for full-moon feasts in the mountains, in the plains, in the woods and in the marshes. *[researcher's emphasis]*[19]

In all these examples, the picture of a primitive world is the one the reader is supposed to be fascinated by. As one publisher put it:

> These tales have the atmosphere of primitive Africa with its unpredictable changes from laughter to sudden menace and danger ...[20]

The idea of exoticism and primitivism is sometimes related to the collectors' perceptions of their own informants. Madeleine Holland seemed to be surprised at the intelligence and artistic qualities of her informants, who happened to be her own servants:

> I think he *[her informant]* and his own brothers ... were particularly intelligent. Of those who worked for me one had a good ear for music and sang well; the other had a gift for speech-making.[21]

The master-servant relationship was particularly surprising to the collector since

> During the two years he *[the informant]* had been with us he had been a very silent boy, though gentle and amiable. Now that we

---

[18]   Phyllis Savory, *Fireside Tales of the Hare and His Friends* (Cape Town: Howard Timms, 1965), Introduction.

[19]   Quoted on the back cover of Elliot's *Where the Leopard Passes*, from *The Times Literary Supplement*. Full citation in note 23 below.

[20]   Publisher's blurb for Elliot's *The Hunter's Cave*. Full citation in note 24 below.

[21]   Holland, "Folklore of the Banyanja," p. 117.

were leaving the country he seemed able to reveal his store of tales; but he was rather shy.[22]

The effect of the reticence of most master-servant relationships on the quality of the items collected is revealed by the style of the form and content of the fifty-six stories Elliot collected.

Language

The language of oral literature is paramount in a discussion of problems of collection. Ideally, the vernacular language should be preserved as the only authentic rendering of the original. However, oral literature has been translated, retold, 'improved" upon, to obey the different demands made upon it. Even the audience or readers can form influential pressure groups to transform original material, as Miss Elliot discovered.

> Shortly after *The Long Grass Whispers* was published, I met a very charming old lady. "My dear," she said, gently patting my hand, "that book of yours! Dreadful!" My heart sank, but she went on. "It is not the tales—they are delightful and the children love them. It is the *names* of the animals. Quite unpronounceable! You ought to have thought of the Grandmothers and Aunts and Uncles who have to read the stories aloud!"[23]

Miss Elliot must be commended for retaining the vernacular names with the English translations. However, she still succumbed to the pressures of her readers in her next publication. The Hunter's Cave has a "Postscript: The Unpronounceable Names."[24]

Some of the problems of language are a result of the informants performing in a foreign language. Miss Holland, for example, gives an interesting case.

---

[22] Holland, "Folklore of the Banyanja," p. 116.

[23] Geraldine Elliot, *Where the Leopard Passes* (London: Routledge and Kegan Paul, 1949), p. vii.

[24] Geraldine Elliot, *The Hunter's Cave* (London: Routledge and Kegan Paul, 1951), pp. 173-174.

> [The informant] told me all fifty-six stories, using, not his own native Chinyanja speech (a dialect of Central Africa), but the broken-down Zulu so widely spoken in South Africa from Natal to the Zambezi. [25]

Why the informant could not tell the stories in his own language was not explained.

Another interesting case of language problems similar to the above is Saka's "Angoni" stories given in "pidgin" English. We are fortunate that whereas the original texts were not given in the Holland collection, Miss Taylor reproduced Saka's idiolect and dialect faithfully. For the full flavour to be appreciated extracts from two different performances are given below:

Angoni Stories

> Look, one day Labbit he go speak to Poptomansi. He say, "Me want to pull you, Mr. Poptomansi." Poptomansi he say, "You, Mr. Labbit, you very little boy; you not pull me." Now Labbit say, "All right; me come to-morrow." [26]

More Angoni Stories

> Mr. Otter and Mr. Badger they make friend. One day Mr. Otter is catchi too much fish. Is go give friendi for him. Another day Mr. Badger get plenty honey. He say, "I want to give my friend." Mr. Otter he say ... [27]

Mr. Saka's pidgin stories are the only printed samples of their kind. Most collectors give straight translations. Some straight translations, for example, are given side by side with the vernacular versions, making it easy to appraise the quality of the exercise. Other straight translations suffer from going through several hands.

---

[25] Holland, "Folklore of the Banyanja," p. 116.

[26] Taylor, "Angoni Stories," p. 75.

[27] Margaret Taylor, "More Angoni Stories," NADA, 5 (December 1927), p. 40.

The English translations Macdonald had altered and revised several times, and it is evident that he would have made further revision upon the text before publishing, had he had the opportunity. The corrections to the Yao stories submitted by Mr. Bowman have been inserted in the text, the original readings being indicated in each case in footnotes.[28]

It is not only the quality of the translation at issue here. It is how many alterations and revisions had been made to "disfigure" the original or pull it out of shape.

Some collectors confess that they have "retold" or "improved" the stories apart from translating them. Miss Elliot:

> The stories in this book are all based on genuine African Folktales.[29]

Or Miss Savory:

> I have set out to retell these age-old tales as they were told to me, by the people to whom they belong.[30]

Other collectors attempt to reproduce the texts as literally as possible. Miss Holland declares:

> I did not alter nor add to nor in any way shape the stories, endeavouring to take them down as literally as possible.[31]

Other honest collectors confess their inability to do full justice to the text. Hallowell declares:

> No claim to further accuracy can be made, however; and the writer is unqualified to offer any detailed linguistic analysis.[32]

Miss Werner appeals to readers for

---

[28]   C.M. Doke, Introduction to Duff Macdonald's "Yao and Nyanja Tales," *Bantu Studies*, 12, 4 (1938), p. 251.

[29]   Elliot, *Where the Leopard Passes*, p. vii.

[30]   Savory, *Fireside Tales*, Introduction.

[31]   Holland, "Folklore of the Banyanja," p. 116.

[32]   Hallowell, "Two Folktales from Nyasaland," p. 216.

any suggestions as to the translation of the obscurer parts; ... any information as to the word *nchokoti*, and the thing denoted by it ... The words in italics I can make nothing of, though the tentative translation which follows offers a conjectural rendering ...[33]

Most collections give "free" translations of the texts. However, there is also the phenomenon of "inter-linear translation" which needs discussing. Cullen Young explains what interlinear translation is:

an inter-linear translation is given showing exactly how the sense desired by the teller is built up out of the grammatical material at his disposal ... It should be enough to study the word and idea-building exhibited in the first two tales for some idea to be gained as to what it is that the African actually hears as a story is built up before his eyes through the skilled use of "words."[34]

The examples below of inter-linear translation are from Tumbuka and Nyanja narratives by different narrators and from different collectors.

The Youth and his Parents

Youth he-did-take woman coming with-her at parents his, and at-day one that child he-did-differ with father, and he-did-them-hit all and mother also he-said, To-day we-have-differed.[35]

The Story of the Cock and the Swallow

Cock and swallow they made-with-each-other friendship, and swallow he said, 'But you (must) come to our (house). And Cock he went ...[36]

It is interesting to compare this deliberate inter-linear word-for-word translation by native speakers of English with Saka's pidgin tales. In both

[33] Werner, "A 'Hare' Story," pp. 139-140.

[34] Cullen Young, *Notes on the Customs*, p. 179.

[35] Cullen Young, *Notes on the Customs*, p. 186.

[36] Werner, *Introductory Sketch*, p. 272.

cases it is arguable whether or not his is what the African actually hears when the text is in his own native Chitumbuka or Chinyanja!

Inter-linear translations are found in collections where interest was primarily in linguistic study of the language. Word for word and literal translations are obviously for lexical and syntactical comparisons. However, the transcription of such collections brings in the problems of punctuation. Oral performance has pauses, stress, pitch, i.e. suprasegmental features, to indicate different aspects of the oral performance. These markers are not possible in print. Some collectors have addressed themselves to this problem directly. Below is an example of the problem:

The story of Kalikalanje

There were people long ago in a village, where it was that village there was a woman, and that woman was pregnant, and the pregnancy was in the tenth month, now she was longing for eggs, and one day she was going to pay a visit to another village, and before she reached the village, on the way, she met a *Lisimu* (a monster, animal in form, usually male, may be well or ill-disposed to humans), when she met him she saw he was carrying eggs, when she saw those eggs she said Grandfather Lisumu *[sic]*, sir, I too (would like) eggs ...[37]

As can be seen it is possible to go on and on with only commas to punctuate the pauses and indicate phrase or clause boundaries. But closer examination will also reveal that the punctuation is purely arbitrary and can be erratic. Whiteley confesses,

The placing of sentence boundaries is clearly a somewhat arbitrary device, since both Mandunda and Kevin [the informants and transcribers] when reading the text subsequently tended to break it up rather differently.[38]

---

[37] W.H. Whiteley, *A Study of Yao Sentences* (London: Oxford University Press, 1966), p. 273.

[38] Whiteley, *A Study of Yao Sentences*, p. 261.

The problem of how to punctuate oral narrative is related to the mode of collection.

Mode of Collection

Collections out of context, from anonymous informants, by collectors who thought they were superior to the natives, can produce unsatisfactory versions. The matter is compounded by the mode of collection. In the latter part of the 19th century and the first half of the 20th, all collections were done by dictation. Macdonald, Werner, Hallowell and Taylor all had to go through the laborious and tiresome task of taking down oral narrative performances by hand. As Werner confessed, her collections were

> written down, as well as I could, from Mbuya's dictation—which is manifestly incomplete.[39]

forcing her to appeal to the *Journal of the African Society* to supply her with "a better text." The mode of collection is not a problem apparently with "retold"/"improved" versions of fragments.

Unfamiliar Forms

Some of the problems of collection are related to the collectors' unfamiliarity with conventions they were coming upon for the first time. Savory, for instance, confessed,

> I have found many different beginnings and endings to a number of these tales, varying no doubt, according to the tribe that tells them, and to the memory and humour of the tellers. Sometimes, too, I have found the well-known end of a folk tale, tacked on to the beginning of another favourite. This may have occurred when the memory of extreme old age (for the narrators are invariably the grand or great-grand mothers) begins to fail ...[40]

---

39   Werner, "A 'Hare' Story," p. 139.

40   Savory, *Fireside Tales*, Introduction.

Although Savory recognises the variables: tribe, memory and humour of the performers, the problem is whether or not the beginnings or endings were formally or structurally detachable narrative units, i.e. part of the narrative plot, or formulas marking the beginnings or endings of any narrative. From the quotation it is clear that these were narrative units; however, it is the nature of oral performance and folk narrative to behave in this manner, depending also on the variables mentioned above.

Unfamiliarity with conventions sometimes reached the extreme of actual suppression of some performances. Macdonald is a case in point.

> When I was writing to his dictation my private study became a small theatre. In vain I reminded [the narrator] that the nursery was near! His voice was audible in the outside, scores of yards from the house. School children stopped their games, and came giggling about, and demure old natives would turn off the public highway and advance in amazement. Yet even so my old man was not satisfied—his enthusiasm, he thought, fell short of the occasion, and he introduced two young women to sing responses to the chants. The natives do not speak of "telling a tale," but of "singing a tale" (*kwimba ndawi*).[41]

Belatedly, Macdonald realised that singing a tale meant not only vocal rendition but also performing. Oral narrative performance is also "theatre," and suppressing the theatrical elements as above is equivalent to censoring verbal elements. The manner of performance is essential to "live" performance. Miss Werner, discussed in the next section, was guilty of the same ignorance when she rejected several stories because the narrator adopted "a dirge-like tone" and "droned out stories which, apparently, had no end or beginning."

Stories which apparently had no beginning or end are again due to the collector's unfamiliarity with narrative performance. Miss Werner's problem is similar to Miss Savory's frustration with beginnings and endings which were tacked on to different narratives she met not only from different tribes but also the same or different performers. Although

---

[41] Macdonald, *Africana*, Vol. I, p. 48.

certain conventions are observed, the forms are flexible enough to accumulate new or other narrative strands apart from interpretations by different narrators.

Fragments or Retold Versions

It was remarked above that incomplete versions were collected. Miss Werner's appeal was not only to the readers of the *Journal of the African Society*. She wrote a desperate letter to *NADA* a few years later:

> I have meant for a long time to send you the enclosed for insertion in *NADA*, in the hope that some of your readers might be able to supply complete versions of these tales ...[42]

The incompleteness of Miss Werner's texts might have been due to the nature of the informants or the context of the performance or the mode of collection.

In some instances, summaries were deliberately given for the more repetitious versions. Miss Taylor's *precis* has been mentioned in the context of censorship. In a later publication, she not only summarises, she rejects material for its repetitiousness:

> In collecting more Angoni stories for *NADA*, I had to reject several ... The narrator, adopting a dirge-like tone, droned out stories which, apparently, had no end or beginning, and which I think must have been valued in the kraal chiefly for their soporific qualities.[43]

The manner of telling, i.e. the performance, as grounds for rejecting material, is due in large part to the collector's ignorance of the narrative forms. This aspect is elaborated on in a later section.

Madeleine Holland is also to blame for falling into the same trap:

---

[42] Alice Werner, "'Ngoni' Stories," *NADA*, 5 (December 1927), p. 100.

[43] Taylor, "More Angoni Stories," p. 39.

> Sometimes, however, in the case of the tedious repetitions in the manner of "The House that Jack Built" I have condensed them into a phrase. This will be apparent.[44]

This is a case of the collector recognising the form from a different culture yet not admitting that the repetitiousness is integral to the structural arrangement of the narrative. Miss Taylor was likewise aware of the formal aspects of the stories she rejected when she compared the rejects to ones she was familiar with from her own culture.

> This type might be compared with some English bedtime stories after the style of "And another grasshopper came and brought another blade of grass."[45]

Informants

It is also crucial to consider informants' age, sex, education, etc. if accurate renderings are aimed at. In some cases, collectors did not seem to mind the age of informants. Gray, for example, could say:

> The collecting of Bantu riddles is comparatively easy. It is only necessary to gain the confidence of a group of boys and start asking riddles oneself to set the ball rolling.[46]

Although riddles might best be collected from "boys," not all genres are most accurately, skillfully and even artistically rendered by youth. A case in point is Holland's 56 stories narrated by "a lad whose voice was just beginning to break."[47] Alice Werner's informants on several occasions were either boys or girls.

> All these stories were related ... by the same girl, Mbuya (afterwards Lucy), daughter of a "Ngoni" (Nyanja) father ...[48]

---

44 Holland, "Folklore of the Banyanja," p. 117.

45 Taylor, "More Angoni Stories," p. 39.

46 Gray, "Some Proverbs of the Nyanja People," p. 101.

47 Holland, "Folklore of the Banyanja," p. 117.

48 Werner, "'Ngoni' Stories," p. 101. See also Werner, "A 'Hare' Story," p. 139.

One of the effects of using young boys or girls as informants is that incomplete texts are given. This point is elaborated upon in another section. Perhaps the most hazardous deterrent is the one noted by Werner herself on another occasion. Not only would the young informants have incomplete knowledge of some of the material, they might introduce irrelevant or extraneous data out of pure mischief.

> A small boy who assisted in the revision of my notes at Blantyre, would have it that it was *momba matako*: this *may* be right ..., or it may have been a wicked attempt to entrap me into writing down *ku tukwana* [swear] words—such an attempt as was, on a different occasion, defeated by another small boy of more fastidious feelings.[49]

One wonders why Miss Werner had a penchant for small boys and girls as informants. Not all collectors, though, had such tendencies, as the examples in the other sections demonstrate. Even Geraldine Elliot, who was collecting and writing especially for children, got some of the materials from older members of the society. "An old Ngoni told these animal adventures."[50]

Another inherent effect of not taking age into consideration is that the informants tend to remain anonymous. Some of the informants are only "boys," "lads," "girls" or "old Ngonis." As is the case with material taken out of context, the items supplied by anonymous informants lose individuality, naturalness and even authenticity, since no signatures are seen or heard. Why the informants' names and backgrounds were not given could be a function of the attitudes of the collectors towards them or, in some cases at least, due to sheer amateur ignorance of the documentation of research items. Even Macdonald, who has the largest collection of folklore items, is content to acknowledge his sources with:

---

49 Werner, "A 'Hare' Story," p. 140.

50 Quoted from *The Observer* on the back cover of Geraldine Elliot, *The Long Grass Whispers* (London: Routledge and Kegan Paul, 1949).

Our contributors represented a wide district. My list included Wayao, Machinga, Anyasa, Angulu, Achipeta, Achikunda, and Awisa. But the tales seemed to be common to all these tribes.[51]

No names of actual informants, age or sex; no names of districts or villages; no context, occasion or purpose are given.

The Fluidity of Verbal Arts

The terminological problems of having, for example, *mwambi* refer to folk narrative, proverb, or riddle in Chichewa extend to the content and form of the verbal arts genres. This section examines the fluidity or variability of Chichewa verbal arts, in which an item behaves as if it were of a particular genre, yet is found in content to belong to other types of folklore in the same language. Towards the end, we offer possible solutions on the formal level.

The problem can best be introduced with actual examples:

1. Riddles: Song or Song-Riddle?

> Leader: *Banja ndi chiyani?*
> Chorus: *Banja ndi malichero.*
> (What is a family?
> A family is a lot of winnowing baskets, my friend.)[52]

The question-and-answer form places the item in the riddle category: the interrogative part is posed by one party, while the response is supplied by another.

2. Proverb: Song or Proverb?

> a. *Tsoka likalimba*
> *Omakana obvula-bvula olire*

---

51 Macdonald, *Africana*, Vol. I, p. 57.

52 From an examination script, E2015, *University of Malawi*, 1982.

(When misfortune persists [a woman] refuses even when she has already undressed.)[53]

This is a straight proverb in form and content. However, it is also a *mganda* song, with the same call and response form observed in the example above.

> b. *Amayi anga anandiuza*
> *Ukayenda uzisiya phazi*
> *Koma ukadzasiya mlomo*
> *Mlomo udzakutsatira.*
> (My mother told me
> If you go visiting leave your foot
> But when you leave your mouth
> Your mouth will follow you.)[54]

The original proverb is *Ukayenda siya phazi; ukasiya mlomo udzakutsatira* (If you go visiting, leave your foot behind; if you leave your mouth, it will follow you). In this case, it is not only the proverb that has been used, the song incorporates the mother as the source of the worldly wisdom that if you leave slander or gossip, it will return to you; however, if you leave only kind words, they will, like the footprint, remain with the listeners you gave them to, without any repercussions. This proverb-song is a more extended borrowing than the first one. It also reveals the nature of items which live in two worlds, as it were: song and proverb, and being comfortable in both.

The last example is a more disturbing one, since it cannot be said with certainty whether or not the item is just as comfortable in both worlds:

3. Proverb-Riddle or Riddle-Proverb?

> R: *Kansinde kokoma kakagonera*
> (A maize stalk that is sweet when it is overdue.)

---

53   Mrs. Mwale, personal communication, 13 May 1981.

54   Jessie Sagawa, "Some Malawian Jokes," unpublished manuscript, 1983.

A: *Mau aakulu*
     (Old men's counsel.)[55]

As in the first example above, the question-and-answer form places the item formally in the riddle tradition. However, there is a proverb *Mau aakulu akoma akagonera* (The words of the elders are only appreciated when they have been long established by tradition). *Kansinde kokoma*, is only added to the riddle as a distractor.

The disturbing feature about the last example, in fact about all the examples, is that one can never ascertain in which direction the item is moving: towards one or the other form. The problem can be illustrated by Figure 2, below. Only the major verbal art forms have been given. Other minor ones could be given. For example, in item 2b, the first two lines belong to *mwambo*, i.e. instructions given at initiation ceremonies.

FIGURE 2: THE FLUIDITY OF VERBAL ARTS

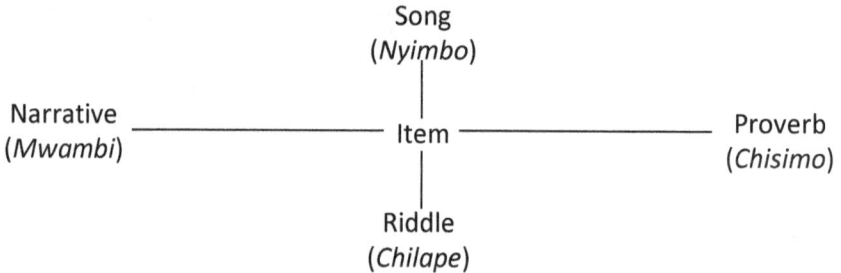

Song
(*Nyimbo*)

Narrative ———————— Item ———————— Proverb
(*Mwambi*)   (*Chisimo*)

Riddle
(*Chilape*)

In the ambiguous cases, it is both form and context (occasion or purpose) that largely determine how an item is classified. Initial, internal and terminal formulas for example are clear indicators of form for the major verbal arts. The easiest to identify is a song. Riddles have *chilape/nachize* to signal them, proverbs have *akulu adati* (the elders said). Folk narratives have *padangotero* (it once happened) to open them, the chorus as the

---

55 Enoch Timpunza Mvula, "Introducing Malawian Riddles," Supplement to Kalulu, 1, 1 (June 1976), p. 20.

internal punctuation and *Basi mpamene idathera* (that's where/how it ended), as the commonest formulas. Within the society, then, discrimination of form is facilitated in these formal ways.

Conclusion

The problems isolated in this chapter are those of collecting out of context, cross-cultural perspectives on form and content, dubious sources of information, crude methods of collection resulting in distortions of the texts, and the fluidity of the verbal arts themselves. These problems are surmountable by proper training of researchers, change in attitudes and respect for the integrity of original sources and material.

CHAPTER THREE:
ULIMBASO: AN INTEGRATED THEORY OF ART

Malawian art and aesthetics seem to be confounded by conflicting statements on them by the early colonial administrators and missionaries. In 1903, an administrator said:

> The sense of beauty is, of course [sic], very defective in the Central Africans. Beyond their few personal ornaments, there is nothing which they seem to cherish on account of its appearance only, or on the decoration of which they bestow any pains. The sublimest scenery leaves them totally unmoved. The most brilliant flowers are without any attraction for them and are neither cultivated in their gardens nor plucked in a wild state from the woods. Nothing in the beauty of animate creatures touches them. In the work of their own hands, again, there is hardly a trace of any effort to realise even the rudest conception of the beautiful. Their houses are mere shelters of grass and mud. Their implements and utensils are of the plainest description. As for pretty and interesting curios, they are almost entirely absent and even the few specimens of woodcarving, bead-work, and so forth, which one sees from time to time, are manufactured as a rule for sale to Europeans. The truth is that the point of view of pure aesthetics is unintelligible to these natives. They can understand well enough that a plant should be grown for the sake of its fruit, that a tree should be spared because it happens to shade a man's hut, that birds and animals should be preserved and bred in order to provide food. Also, they perceive well enough (though they are much too lazy to attempt anything of the kind themselves) why white men take the trouble to build brick houses, and to invent and construct appliances which take the place of manual labour or minister to personal comfort. But to prize any natural object as a thing of beauty apart from and above its material value, or to devote time and intense labour to the creation of merely beautiful things, or to the elaboration of purely aesthetic details in articles of everyday use, would strike them as

ridiculous, if they ever gave the subject serious thought, which I hardly believe they do.[1]

The report contains several contradictions, for a few pages later pottery is described as exhibiting "very pleasing tones of colour, ranging from pale terra-cotta to lustrous browns and blacks."[2] The people are shown to have "weapons of a superior kind, strong, delicate, well-balanced, well-wrought."[3]

> It is … as workers in metal that the Central Africans show to best advantage; and really, considering the lack of facilities, much of their work is very creditable.[4]

And after reviling the people for their functional uses of art and crafts he concedes that "For purely decorative purposes brass is more used than any other metal."[5]

Some missionaries were equally unsympathetic to indigenous art and aesthetics:

> [T]he remarkable thing about these arts and crafts is their failure to develop at all. Hints and suggestions were there continually; yet nothing ever came of them. Iron was digged [sic], smelted, and made into tools, yet no better tool for digging the ironstone itself was thought of than the hoe. Cloth was widely made on native looms before the advent of inferior trade goods, and needles, with eyes, for sewing mats; but the idea of sewn garments did not penetrate the native mind. Burned clay pipes were made to direct the wind from the skin bellows into the blacksmith's fire, but no one received from these pipes a hint of other possibilities. The idea of the wheel, with its boundless possibilities, did not suggest itself to the Konde mind, nor, so far as I know, to the Bantu mind anywhere,

---

[1] Hector Duff, *Nyasaland Under the Foreign Office* (1903) (New York: Negro Universities Press, 1969), pp. 281-282.

[2] Duff, *Nyasaland Under the Foreign Office*, p. 305.

[3] Duff, *Nyasaland Under the Foreign Office*, p. 307.

[4] Duff, *Nyasaland Under the Foreign Office*, p. 306.

[5] Duff, *Nyasaland Under the Foreign Office*, p. 309.

although hints of it were lying about, especially in the round tree trunks which were used as rollers when a canoe had to be dragged some distance from the forest to the water.[6]

Yet the same missionary could observe how "the more artistic potters work patterns in red"[7] and notice leather work "pleasingly decorated with shells," or bead work that had been "strung into pleasing patterns by using various colours."[8]

Not all colonial administrators or missionaries denigrated indigenous arts and aesthetics. Around the same period others could talk about the "beautiful design" and "considerable skill" in discussing pottery,[9] or the Yao people's "natural feeling for shape."[10] This can be contrasted with the administrator quoted earlier, who condemned the Konde for being "so very poor [in] their sense of form and order ..." that they suffer from a real and complete lack of ... "the prehensile eye."[11]

Another missionary in the same Central African context would highly commend the locals:

> The African constantly uses all his five senses; these all seem to be more highly developed individually than ours. He is able to detect many details which escape our perception ... This keen sense of observation gives him an intimate knowledge of natural phenomena ...[12]

It is partly due to these conflicting statements about Malawian art and aesthetics by non-Malawians that this book was written. The other reason for making this preliminary excursion into the field is the lack of any articulation of it by Malawians themselves. This chapter, then, is an

---

[6] D.R. Mackenzie, *The Spirit-ridden Konde* (London: Seeley Service and Co. Ltd., 1925), pp. 146-147.

[7] Mackenzie, *The Spirit-ridden Konde*, p. 152.

[8] Mackenzie, *The Spirit-ridden Konde*, p. 154.

[9] James Macdonald, "East Central African Customs," *Man*, 22 (1982), p. 118.

[10] Stannus, "The Wayao of Nyasaland."

[11] Duff, *Nyasaland Under the Foreign Office*, pp. 282-283.

[12] Salaun, "Initiation to Malawi," unpaginated manuscript.

investigation into the classification of existing linguistic terms related to the Chewa people's responses to art objects.

Some anthropologists actually addressed themselves, albeit briefly, to the question of values and aesthetics in the peoples they studied.

Margaret Read, after describing *ingoma* competitions under "The Art of Dancing," has this to say:

> the adults of the home village were the audience and the judges, deciding, after both teams had performed, which one had "danced most strongly" ... The points of excellence, as judged by the spectators, were the perfect timing of girls and youths, together, and the strong beating of the youths' feet on the dry dung floor of the kraal. When the verdict was announced, the leader of the defeated team went up to the leader of the victorious team and shook hands in Ngoni fashion, saying "Yes, we are defeated. Your *ngoma* was stronger."[13]

These remarks are a step in the right direction. As starting points they are, of course, invaluable. However, they are, like those of previous scholars, too brief to be useful.

Towards an Indigenous Aesthetic

Work on indigenous aesthetics is in its embryonic state in Malawi. There is a scarcity of artists, writers or critics who address themselves, whether in the vernacular or in English, to this currently urgent issue. It is not so much that there is no "language of aesthetics" as that it is only after recent trends in black scholarship (African and Afro-American) that local academics have started looking in this direction.[14] Only one or two writers

---

13   Margaret Read, *Children of their Fathers* (London: Methuen and Co. Ltd., 1959), p. 147.

14   Works on black aesthetics include Addison Gayle, Jr., ed., *The Black Aesthetic* (Garden City, NY: Doubleday, 1971), Gurr and Zirimu, eds., *Black Aesthetics*, and Johnson, ed., *Toward Defining the African Aesthetic*. Locally, an attempt to examine the "metrics" of Chichewa poetry was made by S.A. Mchombo, *Mapande: A Study of Chichewa Metrics* (London: n.p., 1977). Other general works are the review articles by Anthony Nazombe, "African and Afro-American Approaches to a Black Aesthetic," Paper presented to the Third Symposium of American Studies in Africa, University of Botswana, Gaborone, 4-7 September 1986, and Watson J. Msosa, "On

state in a phrase or two in their prefaces where or how they got their inspiration.[15] Before getting to the preliminary taxonomy let us examine what other Malawians have written so far on local arts.

Narrative Performance

So far only one folklorist has made a brief comment on the appreciation of oral narrative performance:

> Among the same audience there is the smaller group of people who are able to judge the correctness of the folk narrative and the style of singing the songs. These people who are well versed in the folk narratives and techniques of storytelling comment as the story is being told. A narrator who substitutes details in some stories with those from other narratives is corrected. The audience makes interjections such as *Satero! Mwalakwa! Mwasokoneza nthano!* 'That's not the way the story goes! You are wrong there! You have mixed stories!' After the performance of the narrative the audience comments on the good or bad performance.[16]

It will be noticed that emphasis here is on the "correctness" and the "style" of the details of the plot and the songs. The interjections are made either during the actual performances or at the end. The final comments are whether the performance was "good" or "bad." For our purposes, it would have been helpful had the actual evaluative terms been quoted. However, the important point made is that the audience *knows* whether or not a narrative is the authentic or original unified text, distorted or adapted and well or badly told, even though the criteria are not given.

Devising an African Poetics," unpublished manuscript (Zomba: Department of English, Chancellor College, n.d.).

[15] For example, Gumbi, in *Tili Tonse*, "*Amayiwa adandiphunzitsa luntha lopeka nthano za matanthauzo ndiponso kuyimba kumene,*" p. iv; and Zingani, *Madzi Akatayika*, "*... kuti ndipitirize ndi luso la zolembalemba,*" p. v.

[16] Mvula, "Chewa Folk Narrative Performance," pp. 35-36.

Songs: Vocal Quality

In a review article surveying research on music, there is a footnote referring to indigenous evaluation of a singer's vocal quality. Fortunately, in spite of the brevity, there were attempts to classify different kinds of voices:

1. *Timawu ta see*: ("A voice without grains" i.e., a voice smooth as nsima without any granular matter. Terms that suggest "sweetness" in taste, Dziko said, are similarly used to describe "sweetness" in sound.)

2. *Timawu tonga ngoli*: ("A voice like a finely tuned instrument.")

3. *Mawu a manzenene*: ("A voice that trembles.")[17]

Apart from classifying the different voice qualities there is an implied scale moving from the highly positive to the extremely negative. It is a pity that this first attempt at grading sound quality is not only brief but appears as a note. Are there intermediate grades? Are there other grades above or below the three given above? The paper does not address this issue.

Musical Instruments: Drum Quality

The same footnote above goes on to describe in a single sentence the sound quality of a drum: *"Ng'oma yolira"* ("A drum that cries like a baby.")[18] There is no scale to make any comparisons and the questions raised above also arise here, since there are different makes and sizes of drums and kinds of drum accompaniment to music.

Dancing Quality

The above paper is useful also in that the same footnote gives four categories of a good dancer:

1. *Wowuluka pobvina*: ("One who flies as he dances")

---

17   Mitchell Strumpf, "Ethnomusicology in African Studies," Staff Seminar Paper No. 28, February 1983, Chancellor College, Zomba, footnote 13, p. 5.

18   Strumpf, "Ethnomusicology," p. 5.

2. *Wopepuka miyendo*: ("One with light feet")

3. *Wothifuka*: ("One who bends but does not break")

4. *Wopanda mafupa*: ("One who has no bones")[19]

The next footnote gives the fifth category:

5. *Dama* ("Smartness or stylishness")[20]

Although five categories are given, the questions raised under voice quality above are pertinent here, too. Furthermore, the above are only positive qualities of a good dancer. What about a bad or mediocre dancer?

In spite of the brevity of the two notes, the paper mentioned above is invaluable. It has examined three important artistic areas in music: voice, drum and dance. It is also the first of its kind in print and gives us a good starting point for the kind of expansion needed in this area.

Ulimbaso

-Ul-: A Theory of Inspiration

-Ul-, from *ula* or *laula*, is the centre or the source of creativity or inspiration in the arts. In the dictionary definition of the word *laula* is:

> to speak words by the spirits; of trees and voices supposed unnaturally to speak ... also to prophesy ...[21]

By this definition, supernatural forces inspire the individual to utter prophetic words, moved by the spirits. The forces are powerful enough to infuse trees and other inanimate objects with the power of speech. In other words, then, the forces are the creative spirit which is at the centre of the world.

In this fomulation, at the bottom end of the scale of inspiration is *lankhula* (talk) or *chula* (say/pronounce). The next stage is *ulula* (reveal something

---

19 Strumpf, "Ethnomusicology," p. 5.

20 Strumpf, "Ethnomusicology," footnote 14, p. 6.

21 Scott and Hetherwick, *Dictionary of the Chichewa Language*, p. 232.

hidden), from which comes *ulutsa* (modern techniques of broadcasting over the radio). It is also related to *bvumbulutsa*, from which comes the Biblical *chibvumbulutso* (the Revelation). The third aspect, *lakatula*, is more relevant, since by definition it is also more closely related to divine inspiration:

> to utter oracular words ... be inspired, compose poems.[22]

Lakatula is related to *nang'amula* (the art of making up songs and jokes). However, *lakatula* is taken to be a more serious form of inspiration since it produces more substantial compositions.

The -*ul*- cluster is also related to other art forms like *sula* (metalwork, or by extension the art of curing a barren or sterile person), *gule* (dance forms) and *luka* (weaving), and constructions like *ulalo* (bridge).

If -*ul*- is related to -*ula* (casting lots) then there is also the link with the -*mb*- group (to be discussed next) through *ombedza* (the art of divining through casting lots). *Omba* or *umba*, as we have seen, is pottery, sculpture, etc., and *ombedza* is to consult an oracle, to learn about hidden or secret knowledge. *Omba* is also related to the art of beating drums used in *chamba* (dance). *Chamba*, interestingly enough, is used interchangeably with *gule* for any dance art, thereby linking it to -*ul*-. *Lankhula* is also used interchangeably with *kamba* (speak). Specifically, *lembula* (from *lemba* engraving, carving, designing, etc.) is linked in a similar manner.

As the foregoing has demonstrated, the -*ul*- inspiration theory is linked etymologically to the verbal and visual arts. (See Figure 3, below.)

-mb-: A Theory of Genres

All the arts are unified under -*mb*-, as Figure 4, below, illustrates. Significantly, *(y)amba* is start or begin, i.e. the origin of anything. In this formulation, *zokamba* (the spoken forms—also *zolankhula*, as discussed in the above section on inspiration) are on the *mwambi/mwambo* axis. The subcategories have already been discussed. The *zoyimba* (sung forms) are on the *nyimbo/chamba* axis. As we have seen also, *chamba*, as the

---

22   Scott and Hetherwick, *Dictionary of the Chichewa Language*, p. 228.

performing arts, are developments of the dance/drama forms with *sewero* as their modern term. The *zoumba* forms are on the *choumba/cholemba* axis. All the visual (plastic) arts come on this axis.

FIGURE 3: ORIGINS OF INSPIRATION

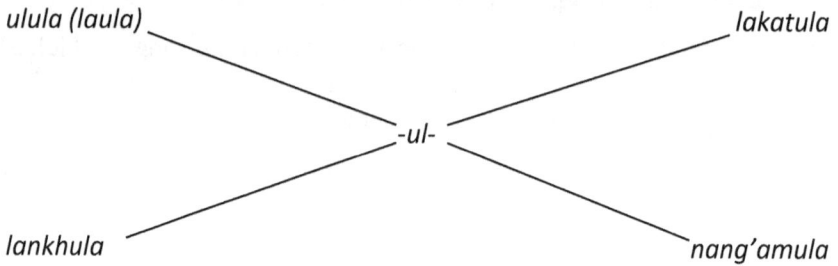

ulula (laula)   *lakatula*

-ul-

lankhula   *nang'amula*

FIGURE 4: INTEGRATION OF THE ARTS

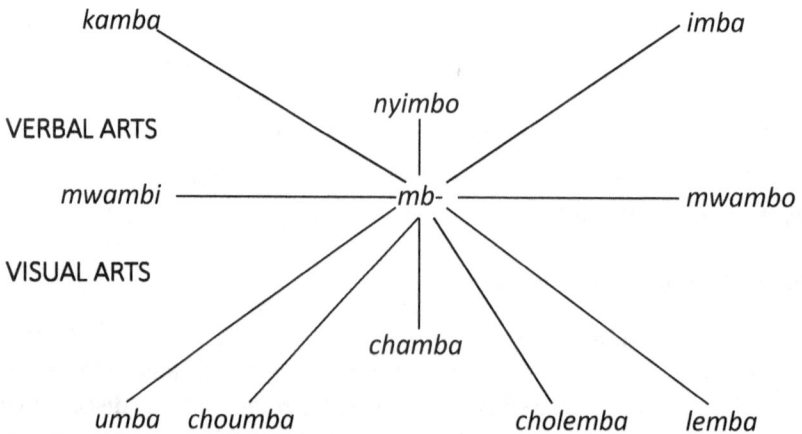

kamba   *imba*

nyimbo

VERBAL ARTS

mwambi ——————— *-mb-* ——————— *mwambo*

VISUAL ARTS

chamba

umba   *choumba*   *cholemba*   *lemba*

It is clear also from Figure 4 that once -mb- is taken as the unifying factor, all the distinctions between and relationships of the arts can be seen. If generic distinctions are made, then one need only find the axis on which the form is located. Furthermore, with this kind of interrelatedness it is not just a single axis that can be taken into consideration. Account must be taken of all the other -mb- axes. For example, *mwambi* (a story) is not only *kamba* (narrated), it is *yimba* (sung), it is *chamba* (performed), it needs *choumba* or *cholemba* (decorated masks or carvings or woven costumes) for its full realisation. It will be seen in the section below on *-so* art appreciation, that the appreciation of a single genre is also a unified sensibility.

-so: A Theory of Art Appreciation

In a discussion of the arts, a distinction is made between purely functional and artistic forms. The artist and the viewer share certain intuitions on an invisible scale, in which certain forms are deemed to belong to the lower or upper rungs of artistic expression. In *zokamba* (the spoken forms), *chima* (grunt under great effort) is at the bottom, while *mwambi* (a narrative) is at the top. In *zoyimba* (the sung forms), *vuma* (hum) is low and *(y)imba* (sing) high on the scale. In *zochita* (performances), the scale is between *tsanza* (imitate) and *sewero* (a play). Finally, the *zopanga* (visual arts) scale moves from *panga* (make) to *umba* or *omba* (mould/sculpture) and *lembula* (carve).

If the -mb- arts are so unified, it seems that the five or six human senses are also reduced to two basic organs: hearing and seeing. *Mwambi/mwambo* and *nyimbo/chamba* are apprehended largely through the ear. *Choumba* and *cholemba* are visual. In this case, however, since all the -mb- forms are performed, both the auditory and visual senses combine to appreciate them. Table 1, below, shows how the senses are reduced linguistically to two. The four senses of hearing, touching, tasting and feeling can be reduced to *-mva* in the expressions *-mva kukoma* etc. (feel nice to the touch, etc.). Furthermore, as can be seen, all art forms can be described with the two terms *-koma* (pleasant, positive) and *-sakoma* or *-ipa* (unpleasant, negative).

TABLE 1: REDUCTION OF FIVE SENSES TO TWO

SENSE	POSITIVE	NEGATIVE
-ona (see)	-komera kuona (nice, sweet, pleasant to look at)	-sakoma kuona; -ipa kuona (unpleasant to look at)
-mva (hear)	Komera kumva (pleasant to hear)	-sakoma kumva; -ipa kumva (unpleasant to hear)
-gwira (touch)	-kumva kukoma (feel nice, pleasant to the touch)	-samva kukoma (unpleasant to touch)
-lawa (taste)	as above	as above
-mva (feel)	as above	as above

Art exists on a *luso* (artistic expression) and *kaso* (artistic appreciation) scale as Figure 5 below shows. *Luso* and *kaso* share -*so* as the common denominator. In this formulation, *luso* is the process of the artist creating an art object, on the one hand and *kaso* is the viewer appreciating the artistry that went into the creation of the art object, on the other. Both the artist and viewer share some feelings of whether or not the -*mb*- art work is -*koma* (good) or -*ipa* (bad).

FIGURE 5: ART CREATION AND APPRECIATION

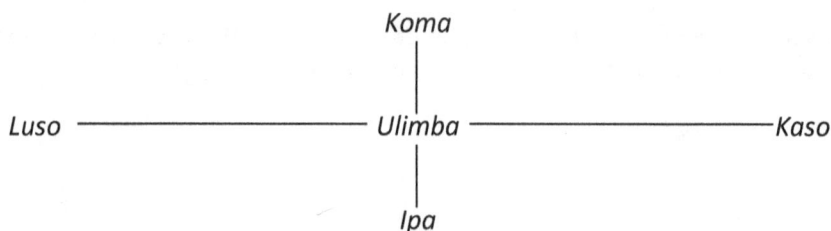

```
                         Koma
                          |
                          |
                          |
Luso ──────────────── Ulimba ──────────────── Kaso
                          |
                          |
                         Ipa
```

That *ulimba-* is a function of *luso* and *kaso* is supported also by usage. *Luso* refers to talent, skill, cleverness, experience or wisdom, i.e. the process of creating or fashioning a work of art. Hence:

> *munthu wa luso*: an artistic/creative person
> *luso lochitira zinthu*: skill in doing something

Kaso on the other hand refers to beauty, excellence, pleasure, neatness or admiration in viewing the product:

> *kuchita kaso ndi chinthu*: to be fascinated by an object
> *kaso kache*: its fascination

The above creation and appreciation of art can be demonstrated diagrammatically as in Figure 5, below. The artist, inspired by *-ul-*, creates a *-mb-* art work with *luso* which is going to be appreciated by the recipient as with *kaso*, i.e. *-koma* (pleasing) or without *kaso*, i.e. *-ipa* (displeasing). In other words, *ul-imb-aso*.

Ulimbaso: Art and Religion

Ulimbaso theory of art is related to religion at the same etymological level, as Figure 6 summarises. A person in the grips of *-ul-* inspiration is *mlauli*, a prophet: "one who utters things from the other world," as seen above. However, *-ul-* can be extended to *Mulungu*, God the creator. *–Mb-* is also related to the rituals of religion in the following: *nsembe* (sacrifice), *pemba* (worship), or *ombedza* (divination) on the positive side. On the negative side, it is related to *tamba* (witches' transmogrification for the purposes of telekinesis or teleportation or simply witches' dancing). Other negative relations are *temberera* (curse) and *lumbirira* (swear an oath). Finally, *-so* is related to *diso* (eye) or *maso* (eyes), whose functions are *ona* (see). *Ona* is in turn related to *M'bona* (or *Mbona*), the prophet or guardian spirit of the Mang'anja in the southern region. *Mlauli* of *-ul-* is any prophet (i.e., in the general sense), while *Mbona* is the specific prophet of the people themselves.

FIGURE 6: THE RELATIONSHIP BETWEEN ART AND RELIGION

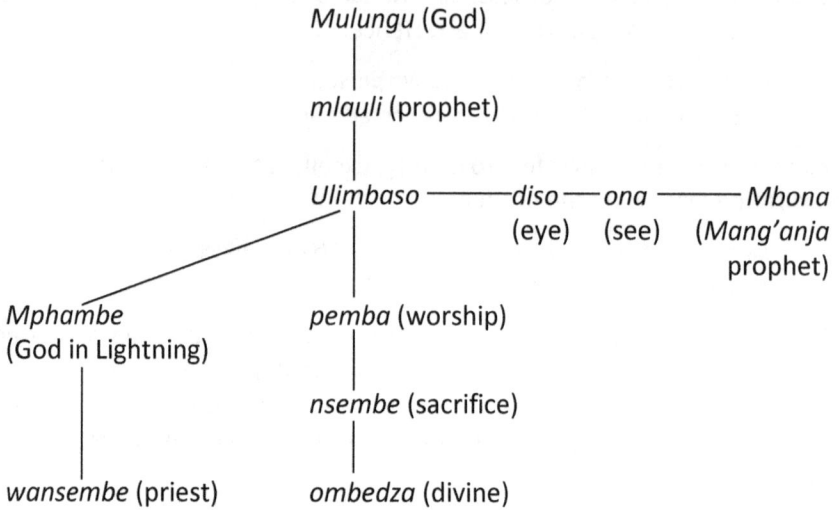

Mulungu (God)

mlauli (prophet)

Ulimbaso ——— *diso* — *ona* ——— *Mbona*
(eye) (see) (*Mang'anja*
prophet)

Mphambe   *pemba* (worship)
(God in Lightning)

nsembe (sacrifice)

wansembe (priest)   *ombedza* (divine)

The Artist (M'misiri)

The artist (*m'misiri*) is the possessor of special skills (*luso*) and is set aside (*wa zake*). The term *m'misiri* is general for any artist, artisan, craftsman, etc. However, there are different degrees of artistry, and in evaluating the artist the terms move up an invisible scale, from the more common *katswiri*, *chiphaka*, or *chikhwaya* to idiomatic slang and sometimes dialectal epithets: *dolo*, *namatetule* or *gandule*. The artist is also *mtengo* (tree, general) or *m'banga* (specific tree) on this evaluative scale.

The evaluative terms are bestowed upon the artist since he possesses some special skill(s). *Luso* is also a general term for talent, skill, etc. It is used interchangeably with *luntha*. Whereas *nzeru* (wisdom) is also a general term for skill in doing or making something, *luso* is specific to art works. *Ndota* on this invisible scale would be the well-seasoned artist with long experience behind him. In order of artistry, then, *nzeru* comes at the top. These persons are so-called or so evaluated because not only do they have the skills above but also, they are *ochenjera manja* (have clever hands for plastic artists) or *ochenjera pa kamwa* (have a clever mouth, for verbal artists).

76

The artist has these special accomplishments (*anatsiriza*) because he has eaten (*anadyera*) or drunk (*anamwera*) some (magical) potion that sets him apart from the rest of mankind.[23]

The artist is conceived as residing somewhere beyond, *pataidya* (beyond the river) or above, *pamtunda* (on a rise, peak etc.). When he is not beyond or above his fellows, he is considered as residing in the great depth *wakuya* or *wozama* ("he is very deep"). He is there because *anafikapo* he arrived) or *anapitapo* (he went there). The ordinary person cannot reach (*osamfika*), find (*osampeza*), handle (*osamutha*) or own (*osampata*) him. On the evaluative scale, *patsidya* or *pamtunda* are unmeasurable. So are *wakuya* and *wozama*. They, like the rest of the terms, are not quantifiable, although people "know" how skilled one artist is as opposed to the other.

The Audience as Critic

The consumer of the artistic product is filled with *kaso* or *chidwi* in viewing the art object or listening to the verbal arts. To describe his responses, he can use positive or negative terms as in Table 2, below.

Sometimes black and white are used positively and negatively:

> -*yera* (white) vs -*da (kuda)* (black)

The most recent usage is "bo":

> -*bo* (pleasant, good) vs -*bowa* (dull, boring)

---

[23] The earliest statement was made about the Yao in 1882: "Men of considerable skill are called *alupa* or *apalu* and are believed to have strong medicine or charms," Macdonald, *Africana*, Vol. 1, p. 39. Note also Chinyanja, *"Mpalu, a skilled man; artificer or hunter,"* Scott and Hetherwick, *Dictionary of the Chichewa Language*, p. 319. In Khonde society, "among the purely native arts that of the blacksmith is held in highest esteem; and the blacksmith himself is a man feared as well as honoured; and joked about as much as he is feared," Mackenzie, *The Spirit-ridden Konde*, p. 148. Among the Ngoni,

> The art of words used with music in songs was regarded as a special gift and those who possessed it were encouraged to develop it. Inspiration for words and music ... came "from the chest" and was regarded almost as if it was a special kind of breathing. Some used this gift to sing with a solo instrument such as a stringed lyre. Others used it to compose new songs for *ngoma* dances. Others again wrote Christian hymns and composed music for them, or set them to traditional Ngoni tunes. (Read, *Children of their Fathers*, p. 146).

TABLE 2: POSITIVE AND NEGATIVE RESPONSES TO ART

		POSITIVE ADJECTIVES	NEGATIVE ADJECTIVES
Referring to	all five senses	*-bwino* (good)	*-sakhala bwino: -ipa* (not good; bad)
		-sangalatsa (able to make happy/nice)	*-sasangalatsa* (unable to make happy/nice)
		-kondweletsa (able to please)	*-sakondweletsa* (unable to please)
	touch/ taste	*-salala* (touch, see: smooth)	*-sasalala* (touch, see: not smooth)
		-sapweteka (touch, feel: not painful)	*-pweteka* (touch, feel: painful)
		-wawa (taste, feel: not bitter)	*-wawa* (taste, feel: bitter)
	sight	*-kongola* (beautiful)	*-sakongola / -nyansa* (not beautiful; ugly/disgusting)

It is not yet clear whether or not the positive term is loaned from the Portuguese "bon" and when and how it came into use. However, "bowa" is an English loan from "to bore" or "to be boring."

If the terms above do not indicate the various degrees or kinds of aesthetic responses, the adverbial intensifiers below are unambiguous. It is, in fact, through such intensifiers that an evaluation scale can be constructed. The intensifiers listed in Table 3, below, are shared with all the senses.

TABLE 3: INTENSIFIERS IN RESPONSES TO ART

POSITIVE	COMPARATIVE	SUPERLATIVE
pang'ono (a little/a few)	*kwambiri* (much/more)	*kopambana* (most/excellent)
pang'ono zedi (very little)	*kwambiri zedi* (very much)	*kopambana zedi* (as above)

Various degrees of quality are permissible with *pang'ono* and *kwambiri*, while *zedi* serves to emphasise the intensifier:

1. *pang'ono kwambiri* (very little)
2. *kwambiri pang'ono* (a little much/more)
3. *kopambana pang'ono* (a little excellent)
4. *kopambana kwambiri/zedi* (most excellent)

The -mb- Art Object

A unified theory of the arts was formulated above. In summary, then, all the arts are unified under -mb- linguistically (or etymologically). In this integrated theory, spoken forms are on the *mwambi/mwambo* axis; sung forms (including performing arts) are on the *nyimbo/chamba* axis; and the plastic or visual arts on the *choumba/cholemba* axis.

The art object, regardless of its external manifestation or genre, is -mb-, neutral, but it can be judged positively or negatively by both artificer or critic. Once concepts of value, quality, worth, or skill, are operating on -mb-, we move to the aesthetics shared by both the artist and his audience.

What is an Indigenous Aesthetic?

Following the general principles laid out at the beginning of this discussion, a definition of an indigenous aesthetic can be attempted. In this formulation, an indigenous aesthetic is a unified response to or feeling for art forms or objects within a clearly defined ethnolinguistic context. A Chewa (Nyanja and Mang'anja) aesthetic, for example, is how the people living in this culture and speaking the same language respond to the art created by their own artists. This ethnocentric aesthetic assumes that within that culture itself there are clearly recognisable forms or objects considered to be skilful creations (regardless of function) and that there is a cluster of linguistic terms to describe the feelings aroused by their apprehension.

Ulimbaso, then, is an integrated theory for the creation and appreciation of indigenous Chichewa art. The advantages of this unified theory are the disappearance of incomprehensiveness, inconsistency, variability of form, performance, and viewers. Any art form, local or foreign, can be appreciated using the *ulimbaso* formula. There are other areas, however, which need refinement. There is more work to be done on the aesthetic terms and critical tools in more general use. Another area suggested in the principles laid out initially is the move from the ethnocentrism of *ulimbaso* to its application to other cultures, Bantu and non-Bantu alike.

PART TWO

APPLICATION: FOLK NARRATIVES

i

CHAPTER FOUR:
ORAL NARRATIVE PERFORMANCE

No comprehensive study of the dynamics of oral narrative performance is available in Malawi.[1] Yet from the early 1900s to the 1980s, large collections of narratives have been published by anthropologists, linguists, missionaries, administrators, and the like working in the country. These collections from scholars and amateurs alike, as we saw, are unsatisfactory in several respects: most of them are wrested from their meaningful context; some of them form parts of larger studies so that the narratives are not examined in their own right; other narratives are revised, modernised and transfigured beyond recognition; and some of them are only bare plots, stripped of their precious flesh. Thus, the published versions of the narratives do not give any indications of the processes of oral delivery as found in a live performance, thereby ignoring a crucial element in this genre: the audience and its interaction with the narrator.

This chapter attempts to give a more comprehensive analysis of the processes involved in oral narrative performance, based on actual attendance at sessions among the Nyanja (Chewa) and the Yao of Malawi. It is only by analyzing a matrix of the processes of a live delivery that the dynamics of this powerful mode of communication can be fully appreciated. Furthermore, an analysis of this nature is a closer approximation of the original performance than the published collections. For oral narrative is not only a matter of presenting the plot to the audience or collector. It is a two-way process involving the narrator and the audience so intimately that the narrative's very existence depends on this relationship being established from the outset.

---

[1]   The only relevant studies so far are the following. Steve Chimombo, "The Dramatic Experience in Malawian Folklore," *Outlook*, 2 (1975), pp. 19-26; Steve Chimombo, "Folk Story Analysis: Basic Approaches," *Kalulu*, 1, 1 (1976), pp. 35-51; J.A.C. Mapanje, "The Use of Traditional Literary Forms in Modern Malawian Writing" (unpublished M. Phil. Thesis, University of London, 1975); Mvula, "Chewa Folk Narrative Performance," pp. 32-45.

In this discussion, "narrative" covers such areas as tale, folk story and fable. Although the terms are used interchangeably here they refer to *nthano* as defined by the Nyanja speakers themselves, or *ndano* by the Yao speakers. *Nthano* is defined under *Nthanu [sic]* as:

> a story or custom ... mwambi.[2]
> Mwambi: a story ... tradition, true narration ...[3]

Although this definition is very misleading, we are going to use it all the same as covering the essential genres this discussion examines. For our present purposes, the processes we are analyzing are found in *nthano*. "Performance" here also refers to face-to-face oral presentation of a text to one or more persons by a single narrator.

The earliest attempt to look at the processes of oral narrative performance was made in 1906. As mentioned earlier, Werner gave an unsatisfactory account of "methods of storytelling." She devotes only two paragraphs to this. As it is the earliest examination and the closest we had in mind, we shall quote in full the two paragraphs:

> We have mentioned that one of the great amusements, both of children and grown-up people, is story-telling—*ku imba ntanu. [sic]* This means literally 'to sing a story,' and points to the way in which tales are usually told. Most of them contain short pieces which are sung, and are known to every one—so that, when the narrator comes to them, the audience all join in ...
>
> Another curious point is that, when a man is telling a story late at night—say, beside the camp-fire or on a journey—at every pause in his narrative the hearers exclaim in chorus, 'We are all here!' As the tale goes on, the responses become fewer and fewer, and at last, when no one is left awake to answer, the recitation stops.[4]

---

2   Scott and Hetherwick, *Dictionary of the Chichewa Language*, p. 410.

3   Scott and Hetherwick, *Dictionary of the Chichewa Language*, p. 353.

4   A. Werner, *The Natives of British Central Africa* (London: Archibald Constable and Co., 1906), p. 230.

As will be seen below, the process is not as simple as Werner puts it. Indeed, most of the narratives have singing accompaniment but the event is more complex than the quotation suggests. Werner calls the responses a "curious" point and does not explain why it is curious. Furthermore, the response, *Tili tonse*, as our discussion shows, is better translated as "We are together!" and not "we are all here!" It would indeed be curious in the context to exclaim "We are all here!" Finally, the response is one of the devices to ensure that the audience does not go to sleep when the session is late at night.

The second attempt to examine the process of oral narrative performance is made by Jack Mapanje. Although Mapanje examines more closely than Werner the salient features of oral delivery the study has a few unsatisfactory features. Mapanje does not examine the narratives he discusses in their ethnic contexts. Furthermore, the study is marred by the primary purpose, which was to study modern Malawian short stories which use some of the narrative features found in folklore. Therefore the folk narrative is not examined in its own right and no clear picture emerges of the processes we are going to examine here.

The most relevant studies for our purposes are the author's own works. In an earlier article, "The Dramatic Experience in Malawian Folklore," we give a general outline of the lines of communication and the processes observed in most Malawian story-telling sessions. The article was unsatisfactory for our present purpose in that the same objections we have raised for Jack Mapanje's work could be raised here. The second article, "Folk Story Analysis: Basic Approaches," is reproduced below. In it we concentrate on a single narrative, narrator and audience and give a step by step analysis of the features of performance. Although the analysis was of a single performance, we have examined several Nyanja and Yao narratives, narrators and audiences in their settings to give here a comprehensive model of the processes involved.[5]

---

[5] Although the discussion is restricted to Nyanja and Yao groups in Zomba, the author is also familiar with the Chewa of the central region. The patterns are similar.

A Model of Oral Narrative Performance

Generally speaking, Nyanja oral narratives embody most of the oral traditions found in the society. The riddle, proverb, song and dance are all here. As the Werner quotation above points out, the people talk of *ku(y)imba nthano* (singing a story), which is what happens in the actual performance. Below are the observable features of oral narrative performance. The framework is diagrammed also, for ease of reference.

Opening Formula

The narrator has three possible ways of signalling or establishing that he is about to tell a story. First, he might "throw" a riddle to which the audience is required to respond by giving the correct answer. If the audience cannot provide the answer, the audience "pays" a number of imaginary cows, and when the number is satisfactory to the riddler, he reveals what the answer is. For example:

Riddler:	*Chilape!* (Riddle)
Audience:	*Nachize* or *Jize* (Let it come!)
Riddler:	*Ndimati ndichimenye, koma chandimenya* (I wanted to hit it, but instead it hit me)
Audience:	*Madzi* (water)
Riddler:	*Eee* (Yes)

Among the Yao the form is the same:

Riddler:	*Ndagi* or *Ndawi* (Riddle)
Audience etc.:	*Jize* (Let it come!)

The riddle session might take a few minutes or more with some members of the audience throwing their own riddles.

The second method of calling the tale takes the form of song. Normally, the song is specific to a particular narrative, i.e. the song serves as a "title" to the story so that the audience knows in advance what the story will be. The audience gives antiphonal responses to the song. If they do not know the refrain the narrator spends a few minutes teaching them. For example:

Narrator:	*Tiponde madzi*	Let's dig for water
Audience:	*Pali lowe*	It's wet [here]
Narrator:	*Tiponde madzi*	Let's dig for water
Audience:	*Pali lowe*	It's wet here
Narrator:	*Kunadza mvula, Pali lowe Tiponde madzi*	It rained. It's wet [here] Let's dig for water
Audience:	*Pali lowe*	It's wet [here]
Narrator:	*Pali lowe*	It's wet [here]

This song is tale-specific; however, other songs are non-tale-specific but may also serve as a way of opening a narrative.

When riddles or songs do not act as a signal to a narrative, the narrator might simply go through the third method below:

Narrator:	*Nthano! Nthano!*	Story! Story!
Audience:	*Eee! or Inde!*	Yes!

A more elaborate form is found among the Yao, where the call is more extended and is actually sung. Although this form should appropriately come under the song formula it has been isolated for its special features:

Narrator:	*Ndano! Ndano!*	Stories! Stories!
Audience:	*Ndano!*	Stories!
Narrator:	*Achakulungwa watiji, Ndano!*	The elders said, Stories!
	Nkasaiwalaga ndano!	Don't forget stories!
Audience	*Ndano!*	Stories!
Narrator	*Ndano!*	Stories!

This example establishes the importance of narratives: the elder's injunction not to forget the stories becomes the *raison d'être* of story-telling, hence the narrator with the backing of the forefathers establishes his right, as well as authority, to tell a story.

86

The three forms discussed above are preliminary to any narrative. However, not all three are included by any single narrator, although at least one of them must be observed for the audience to be physically and psychologically prepared for the event. It must be emphasised that the forms come before the usual opening formula *Padangotero* (Once upon a time). The formula for the story proper and the audience response for the Nyanja is:

| Narrator: | *Padangotero* | It once happened |
| Audience: | *Tili tonse* | We're together |

A variation observed among the Yao is:

Narrator:	*Adisi njo!*	Untranslatable
Audience:	*Adisi njo!*	
Narrator:	*Paliji …!*	

The stage is set for the narrative to begin. Once this step has been taken there are no more preambles. The narrator plunges into the story.

However, before we continue, the audience's response needs comment here: *Tili tonse* establishes the fact that the performance is not a one-man show; it is as much the audience's as the narrator's. Hence the audience functions as the chorus, aiding the development of the performance. Implied in the *Tili tonse* also is the act of submission to the narrator, who holds the reins and manipulates the audience's feelings.

Internal Features

Within the narrative itself the two-way process is maintained. It is no exaggeration to state that at almost every pause by the narrator the audience interjects *Tili tonse* (Nyanja) or *Go!* (Yao ideophone, an extension of which is *gogodera*).

Apart from giving the unified rhythmic chant the narrative may require song accompaniment by supplying the appropriate antiphonal responses. As stated earlier the song might be narrative-specific, i.e. thematically part of the narrative. Again, it might not be. The narrator might incorporate an irrelevant song to liven up the performance especially if he notes that the audience is sleepy or losing interest.

A phenomenon observed among the Yao is that of *Kutengulera*. This term can be loosely translated as "harmonising." Loosely because as the illustration below shows it has a complex structure:

    a.   Narrator sings a narrative-specific song.
        Audience sings antiphonal responses; however, a selected member might "blend" with the narrator's melodic line to give an entirely different tune.

    b.   Narrator sings a narrative-specific song.
        A selected member of the Audience sings a completely different song but one which is also narrative-specific, i.e. the narrative has more than one song sung by different characters and, therefore, requiring a different voice.

One example comes from the story of the orphan boy who was tricked by his slave to switch roles so that when the two went to live with the boy's kin it was the slave who was honoured. The orphan boy was given the work of scaring birds from the rice-fields while the slave was feasted sumptuously at home. The orphan boy used to sing a "work-song" while in the fields:

Narrator:	*Aah! Mbalame!*	Aah! Bird!
Audience:	*Njenjereretu! Njenjereretu!*	[Ideophone]
Narrator:	*Amai anandiuza*	Mother told me
Audience:	*Njenjereretu! Njenjereretu!*	[Ideophone]
Narrator:	*Udzanke kwa abale ako*	You should go to your kin
Audience:	*Njenjereretu! Njenjereretu!*	[Ideophone]
Narrator:	*Kadimba mkazi Luli*	Kadimba and his wife Luli

Audience:	Njenjereretu!	[Ideophone]
	Njenjereretu!	
Narrator:	Aah! mbalame!	Aah! bird!
Audience:	Njenjereretu!	[Ideophone]
	Njenjereretu!	

As the orphan boy sang in the fields there used to come an answering song from the village graveyard. The answering song is sung by the orphan boy's mother's spirit singing in the form and with the voice of a dove. When this happens, the narrator automatically abdicates his role and becomes part of the audience for the time being: he responds to the refrain from the second song along with the audience. The song of the dove is the following:

Member of the audience:	Guku! Guku! Nanjiwa	[Bird song] Dove!
Audience:	Nanjiwa!	Dove!
Members of the audience:	Mwaleka mwana wanu	You have rejected your own child
Audience:	Nanjiwa[6]	Dove!

After the member of the audience has finished the song of the dove, he relinquishes his prominent role and rejoins his group. The narrator resumes his role and continues the story. The roles are switched each time the songs are required in the same narrative.

a. Narrator sings a narrative-specific song.
b. A member of the Audience may sing a completely different song, unrelated to the narrative.

This feature was observed in the session where the story of the orphan boy was told. A member of the audience, touched by the injustice perpetrated on the orphan-boy spontaneously burst out into a solo lament:

---

[6] The two songs were sung in Nyanja, not in Yao.

| Member of | *None ngulira* | I am also weeping |
| the audience: | *None ngulira* | I am also weeping |

The narrator and the rest of the audience waited for the soloist to vent her grief before the narration continued.

Non-Verbal Features

Dramatic elements of oral delivery have already been too well described by various commentators for them to detain us here. Facial expressions, gestures, voice modulation, etc., are part of the narrator's repertoire. Acting is another two-way process in which both narrator and audience take part, especially when members of the audience are selected to take parts.

Other non-verbal elements are clapping, drumming and dancing, which come into play when songs are sung. Those members who are not content to respond vocally, or get carried away by the mood of the narrative clap, stamp their feet or get up and dance (including the narrator, who sometimes takes the lead in such developments).

Extra-Textual Features

In this mode, where direct narrator-audience confrontation, participation and interaction are the basic requirements, certain features belong directly to the ongoing activity, i.e. the performance, and are not inherent to the text of the narrative itself. Interpolation is one of these features. The narrator leaves the text, suspends the action of the narrative, and explains some points to the audience. A member of the audience can also come in as an interpolator, for example to explain current human behaviour touched by the narrative.

Harangues are also two-way. The audience can comment on, or object to, the way the narrative is told. An example from the author's experience is that of a mother directing her son to cut short the episodes in an extremely repetitious story. The narrator might even remark on irrelevant matter. For example, he can pose the question of whether or not the potatoes which were roasting are ready for eating.

Within the narrative itself too, the narrator or audience might wish to dramatise an episode by taking part and improvising. An example of this has already been given, when a member of the audience took the part of the orphan-boy's mother's spirit and sang the song of the dove.

Closing Formula

The briefest closing formula observed here is a simple statement: *Basi, mpamene idathera* (Nyanja) or *Yamalire papopo* (Yao). Both mean "that is where the story ended." This might or might not be followed by a moral statement on the narrative.

The closing signal is followed by other formuals some of which, but not all, closely duplicate the opening form The narrative might be brought to a close by another riddle session. When this is done it is also a signal that someone else or even the same narrator can tell another story.

The narrator might close with a song that had opened or accompanied the narrative. Here again the option is left open: the song might or might not be narrative specific. The author was given an insight into the range of this feature at one session where the narrator brought a narrative to a close by improvising a song commenting on the ongoing scene:

Narrator:	*Nawo Achimwenewa*	Now our brother here
	kutitengera chitsulochi	brought us this machine
	kutitola mau.	to record our voices.
	Eeh!	Eeh! Eeh!

This, of course, referred to the author coming to the performance with a tape recorder.

Normally a set formula brings the narrative to a close. The following examples illustrate the variations:

Narrator:	*Chiphyele-phyele*	[Onomatopoeia] at the
	kumwendo phwetekere	legs, tomatoes have
	mbuu wamera	sprouted
Audience:	[No response]	

The above is Chewa. An alternative is the following:

| Narrator: | *Kandiphulileni mbatata pamotopo* | Take the potato from the fire for me. |
| Audience: | *Yaphyerera* | It is burnt! |

(This is a set formula, since it is given even where there are literally no potatoes on the fire.)

Another version from a published source is given below:

> I have ground the bean soup, on my knees, before the door and I
> enter : Take the potatoes from the fire : they're burning. [sic][7]

The example above is another illustration of how unsatisfactory the published versions of narratives can be. The formula does not state which parts are given by the narrator or the audience. In the author's experience it is always the audience which supplies the part about potatoes burning.

The final example of a formulaic ending is from the Yao:

| Narrator: | *Ajokole katolo* | [Untranslatable?] |
| Audience: | *Kate kumunga, aNkolokosa wawe!* | It was a smell of burning, Nkolokosa died! |

As can be seen from the foregoing discussion, narrator and audience form a ritual field in which, from the opening formula, step-by-step the two come closer and closer in performance, so that both are inseparable—almost inextricable—then gradually, ritualistically draw apart.

The next section gives the transcript of *'Kalulu ndi Chitsime'* and its translation, 'The Hare and the Well', the popular trickster tale, as narrated orally and recorded by the author. Analyses follow.

---

[7]   J. Rothenberg, *Technicians of the Sacred* (New York: Doubleday, 1986), p. 181.

TABLE 4: A MODEL OF ORAL PERFORMANCE

PERFORMANCE	NARRATOR (Artist)		AUDIENCE (Chorus)	AUDIENCE
OPENING FORMULA - Riddle - Song - Formula/Call			**OPENING FORMULA** - Riddle response - Song refrain - Formula response	
INTERNAL FEATURES - Narrative - Song refrain	**INTERNAL FEATURES** **NON-VERBAL** - Acting - Clapping - Dancing		**INTERNAL FEATURES** - Narrative response/chant - Song refrain	
CLOSING FORMULA - Riddle - Song - Formula	**EXTRATEXTUAL** - Extrapolation - Harangue - Improvisation		**CLOSING FORMULA** - Riddle response - Song refrain - Formula response	
COMPOSITION				**CONTENT**

93

Kalulu ndi Chitsime

Panali chaka china chake. Mvula kunalibe ngakhale dontho. Ndiye mitsinje yonse idauma. Basi, kungopatula kunyanja kokha ndiye kunali madzi. Tsopano nyama zimene zinali kukhala kumtunda kwambiri kumene kunalibe nyanja, ngati ku Mulanje uku, zinali kubvutika. Ndiye nyama zinapangana kuti zikakumbe chitsime. Ndiye anapita mbali yakudambo kumene kunali dambo labwino kwambiri kukhala ngati kuja amati kuLimphasa ku Nkhotakota, kokhala ngati kumene kuja basi, ndiye nyama zinasonkhana. Mfumu yake njobvu. Ali, "Ooh, koma tikumbe chitsime monga mukuona kuti tikubvutika kwambiri tikusowa madzi." Tsopano pamsonkhano paja zinalipo nyama zonse. Koma mkatimo munali kalulu ndiye paja mumadziwa kuti kalulu ndi wochenjera, iih, anangobvomera akanena kuti: "Ah, mukuganiza kuti akhala woyang'anira ntchito akhala ndani?" Iye basi: "Ah, ndinene ine, ah, koma akhale uje uyu, mkango akhale woyang'anira ntchitoyi." Basi adzingonena choncho. Ndiye basi lakwana tsiku loti ayambe ntchito yokumba chitsime chija. Zinasonkhana nyama zonse, koma kalulu sanabwerepo. Kungonamizira kuti, "Iai kalulu sanabwere, akuti mkazache mpaka anache onse amene mpaka iye amene, akudwala onse amene." Ndiye mfumu njobvu kumva zimenezi: "Ah, koma zingakhale zoona zimenezi kuti iye wadwala, mpaka anache onse, mpaka mkazache? Ameneyi ayenera akukhala akuzemba ntchitoyi. Iwe amene walandira mthengawu wamuona kaluluyo akudwaladi?" Ndiye akuti: "Iai, koma anadzandipatsira ndi kamwana kache kakang'ono. Inenso ndikudabwa kuti iyeyo akunena kuti akudwala iye ndi ana ache onse. Nanga ameneyo bwanji sanadwale, ndiye akhala bwanji kuti ana onse akudwala?" Basi akuti: "Ooh, chabwino, musiyeni. Tikadzakumba chitsime chathuchi iye sadzamwa nao madzi." Ndiye basi pamene paja ayamba kukumba chitsime chija. Ndiye popeza nyama zilibe zida zao zokumbira chitsime ndiye ankangoponda madothi ndi miyendo kuti dothi lija likamafewa likamati bukatibuka chonchi basi ndi kumapalasa, kumaponya kumtunda. Ndebasi m'mene amaponda amaimbira nyimbo yao, paja munthu ukamagwira ntchito umaimbira nyimbo kuti usatope iai. Ndiye amati:

Tiponde madzi, pali lowe. Tiponde madzi, pali lowe
Tiponde madzi, pali lowe. Tiponde madzi, pali lowe

The Hare and the Well

There was once a year, there was no rain, not even a drop, so all the rivers dried up, that is all, except at the lake, there, alone, there was water. Then the animals which were living in the highlands where there was no lake, like in Mulanje this way, were having problems. So the animals planned to go and dig a well. So they went to the place where there was a very good dambo like what they call Limphasa dam in Nkhotakota, like that place. There the animals gathered. The chief was the elephant. He said, "Ooh, but we should dig a well, as you can see that we are in great difficulty, we need water." Now at the meeting all the animals were there. But in the midst was the hare, and you know that the hare is clever. Iih, he just answered as they said, "Ah, who do you think is going to supervise the work?" He then said, "Ah, let me speak, ah, but it should be, what's his name, the lion should be the supervisor of this work." That's all he would say, like that. And then the day came for them to start the work of digging the well. All the animals were gathered except the hare. He just pretended, "No, the hare has not turned up, he says his wife even all his children, even he himself, all of them are sick." Then when Chief Elephant heard this: "Oh, but do you think this is true, that he is sick, even all his children, even his wife? He is just malingering to escape this work. You, the one who received the message, did you see that the hare was really sick?" And he said, "No, but the one who gave it to me is his youngest child. I am also surprised that he says that he is sick and all his children. What about him, why then is he not sick when all the children are sick?" Then he said, "Ooh, all right, leave him. When we have dug our well he shall not drink the water with us." There and then they started digging the well. Since animals do not have tools for digging wells they just stamped the earth with their feet so that when the earth softened and was ground to dust like this, they scooped it out and threw it on top. As they were stamping they were singing their song accompaniment: as you know, when a person is working, he likes to sing an accompanying song so he won't get tired, no. So they sang:

Let's stamp water, it's damp. Let's stamp water, it's damp
Let's stamp water, it's damp. Let's stamp water, it's damp

Tikuzunzika, pali lowe. Tiponde madzi, pali lowe.
Kudadza dzuwa, pali lowe. Tiponde madzi, pali lowe.
Tiponde madzi, pali lowe.

Nde basi kutibula kwabasi, kuponda pamene paja, kuponda, kuponda, mpakana kutopa. Nde kukhala kaye kupumira. Popeza chinali chaka chadzuwa ndiye anali kusowa choti adye choncho ena amangoti akatola kena kache angoponya choncho kuti kaya choncho, koma onse ndithu analimbikira kuti madzi apezeke kaye choyamba. Nde basi akapumapuma basi kubwereranso pantchito pawopo:

> *Tiponde madzi, pali lowe. Tiponde madzi, etc.*

Nde basi kugwira ntchito, kugwira ntchito, kugwira ntchito, mpaka dzuwa kulowa. Aweruka, ulendo kunyumba kukagona. M'mawa kwacha, abweranso kudzayambiranso ntchito yao. Mfumu Njobvu kutenga lejisitala yao kuitana anthu onse amene. N'kupeza kuti kalulu palibe. Kuwafunsa amene amakhala kwao kumodzi ndi kalulu kuti: "Kodi kalulu bwanji?" Ali, "Iai kalulu lero sitinamuone." Khazi khazi, akuti, munthu wina wache akuti: "Iai koma ine wandipatsira kalata." Kulandira amfumu: "Pepani sinditha kubwera kuntchitoko, chifukwa ndikudwalabe kwabasi." Ndiye Ali, "Ooh, chabwino ameneyo tsopano tidzangomutumizira munthu kuti akamuone kunyumba kwacheko. Koma ife tiyeni tidzigwira ntchito." Basi ayamba:

> *Tiponde madzi, etc.*

Ndiye basi. Akugwira ntchito, agwira ntchito, mpaka dzuwa kulowa. Iih, chitsime tsopano m'menemo chakwana iih, kapena chakwana fifite fiti. Iai, chachitali kwabasi. Nde basi aweluka ulendo kunyumba kukagona. Munthu wina anamtuma mthenga a mfumu a njobvu kuti mupite mukamuone kalulu. Kupita kuja adampeza kalulu basi akusewera msikwa: mvii! mvii! Mkazache ali uko, iye ali kuno, tiana tina tiwiri tili uko, tina tiwiri till kuno. Basi akusewera. Kalulu adzangoyang'ana basi, waona alendo Ali, "Oh! oh! Kodi mwabwera? Iai pepani ndithu, lero ndiye limene tikuyesa kupeza bwino. Ndiye tili paja poti paja amati ekesesaizi nde kulimbitsa thupi tati koma ndisewereko pang'ono. Koma kuti kutereku tangodzuka pamphasa posachedwapa, ndithu mphasa zili m'nyumbamu." Nde uja wa mthenga uja

We're tortured, it's damp. Let's stamp water, it's damp.
The sun came, it's damp. Let's stamp water, it's damp.
Let's stamp water, it's damp.

Then grinding very much, stamping there, stamping, stamping until the animals got tired. Then they sat down to rest a while. Because it was a year of drought they lacked what to eat but all the same, some just, if they picked up anything, they just threw it (in the mouth) like that, saying, I don't know, but all of them tried hard that the water should first of all be found. So when they had rested they returned to their work.

Let's stamp, it's damp, let's stamp water, etc.

And then working, working, working, until the sun set. They knocked off work, went home to sleep. The following morning, they returned to resume their work. Chief Elephant took his register, called all the people and found that the hare was not there. Asking those whose homes were near the hare's, "What about the hare?" they said: "No, we did not see the hare today." Soon, they said, a certain person said, "No, but he gave me a letter." The chief received it: "I am sorry I cannot come to work because I am very sick." And so he said: "Ooh, all right, now we shall just send a person to go and see him at his house tomorrow. But we ourselves we shall work." Then they started.

Let's stamp water, etc.

Then, that's all. They worked, they worked, until the sun set. Iih, the well now had reached, iih, perhaps it had reached fifty feet. Not [i.e. really] very deep. So, then, they knocked off work, went home to sleep. Someone was sent a message by Chief Elephant that you [he] should go and see the hare. Reaching there he found the hare playing *msikwa: mvii! mvii!* His wife is over there, he is here, two kids over there, two kids here. Then they were playing. The hare just glanced up, then he saw the visitors and said: "Oh! you have come? No, sorry, indeed, it's only today that we feel well. And we said since they say exercises strengthen the body we decided to play a bit. But even though we are like this we have really just got up from the mat, the mats are in the house." Then the messenger said, "Oh! Ah! All right, thank ali, "Ahee! Aa! Chabwino iai zikomo, amangoti ndidzakuoneni." Nde kucha m'mawa amfumu aNjobvu kuitana palejisitala pao anthu onse kupeza kuti kalulu sanabwere. Kumufunsa munthu uja wotenga mthenga uja n'kumanena kuti, "Koma kalulu ndinampeza dzulo akusewera msikwa ndi mkazache ndi anache. Ndiye amati imeneyo inali ekesesaizi kulimbitsa thupi chifukwa atangopeza bwino pang'ono kwa tsiku limenelo." Nyama zonse kubvomereza kuti, "No! munthu ameneyu basi akunama." "Chabwino tiyeni tipitirize kugwira ntchito yokumba chitsime. Koma ameneyu madzi athuwa asadzamwe nao, iai." Nde onse kubvomereza. "Oh! Eee! Inde! Inde!" Basi atachita choncho, basi yambani ntchito.

>Tiponde madzi, etc.

Nde basi kuponda, kuponda chitsime, kutaya dothi kunja, mpakana chitsime chidakwana mafiti kaya mahandiledi angati. Koma chakula kwambiri. Mpaka kupeza madzi nde basi, "Ah! Koma madziwa tiyese kukumbanso kwambiri kuti mpaka madziwa okhawa kapena madzi okhawa kaya mafiti kapena sikisite fiti." Yambaninso ntchito:

>Tiponde madzi, etc.

Basi, mpaka kutsiriza. Amfumu aNjobvu kubwera ndi chindodo chao chachitali kuyesa madzi aja kuona m'mene atalikira, ah! Iai, ndithu okwana! Ah! Nde basi adafuna timitengo tao kuika-ika pamene paja kuikapo chingwe, kuikapo chikho chotungira kuti kumatsitsa m'chitsime muja ngati chitsime chathu chapanochi basi. Kutunga madzi basi ndi chikho nyama iliyonse ndi kumamwa. Nde basi atachita chonchija akuti, "Koma tsopano pamenepa tiikepo londa chifukwa kalulu ndi munthu wochenjera akhoza kumadzamwa nao madziwa. Ndiye kuyambira lero yambani kaye mwakafuna zakudya tiikepo londa pano, londayo adzidya zakudyazo." Ndiye wina wache waliwiro, gwape, ndi kuthamanga kukafunafuna zakudya n'kubwera nazo kudzaikapo. Ali, "Tsopano londa woyamba akhale fisi adzilonda chitsimechi." Nde fisi nkukhala kumalonda chitsime chija. Nyama zitabalalikana kupita m'makwao. Popeza kalulu sanali yekha anzache analipo ofuna kum'thandiza, ndiye anapita kukamuuza kuti, "Madzi tapeza ndiponso ambili kwabasi ndiye aikapo londa, londa wache fisi." Nde kalulu kuganiza Ali, "Ah! Ai chabwino." Kwacha tsiku lina basi, anamuuza ndi nthawi yomwe nyama zidzikamwa madzi nthawi yakutiyakuti. Nde basi kalulu basi ndi kupita kuchitsime nthawi imene nyama you, they just said I should look you up." Then when morning broke, Chief Elephant called on his register all the people and found that the hare had not come. Asking the person who took the message, he just said, "But I found the hare yesterday playing *msikwa* with his wife and children. He said that he was exercising to strengthen the body because it was only that day that they felt well." All the animals agreed: "No, this person is lying, that's all." "Allright, let's continue the work of digging the well. But he is not to drink our water." Then everyone agreed, "Oh! yes! yes! yes!" Then when they had done so, the work started.

> Let's stamp water, etc.

That's all, stamping, stamping the well, digging, throwing the earth outside, until the well reached, I don't know, how many hundred feet, but it was very deep until water was found. And, then, "Aah, but this water, let's try to dig more, until the water perhaps, the water only perhaps, is sixty feet." Work started again.

> Let's stamp water, etc.

That's all, until it was completed. Chief Elephant came with a long big stick to measure how deep the water was. Ah! There was enough water! Ah! Then they found sticks and placed them there, put a rope, put a gourd for lowering it down the well, like our own well here. That's all, drawing water, that's all, with the gourd, for each animal to drink. Then when they had done that, they said, "But, now, we should place a guard here because the hare is a clever person. He can come to drink this water. So from today start with finding food to put here for the guard to eat the food." Then one quick person, the buck, ran and found food and came back and placed it at the well. They said, "Now the first guard should be hyena, he should guard the well." Then the hyena sat there guarding the well. The animals dispersed going to their homes. And because the hare was not alone, he had friends who wanted to help him, they went and told him: "We have found water and it is very plentiful, but they have placed a guard, the hyena is the guard." Then the hare thought and said: "Ah! All right." Came another day, then, they had even told him the times, that the animals were going to be drinking at such and such a time. Then the hare went to the well at the time that the

zina zisanabwere. Iye basi wapha nkhuku yache. Nanga sianatenga nkhuku ija kufika kufupi ndi kuchitsime kuja? "Odi! Odi!" Fisi ali, "Eh, ndani iwe?" Ali, "Ine kalulu." Ali, "Andiuza kuti na ukangobwera pano basi ndiwe ndiwo." Ali, "Iai, bwana tabwerani mudzaone, ndatenga nkhuku yoocha." "Aha! Nkhuku yoocha! Ndidikire kaye! Chabwino ndikubwera ndimayesa masewera." Ali, Iai, si zamasewera, iai." Basi kubwera. Kufika kuja. Fisi kuyang'ana nkhuku iih, dovu nju, nju! Ali, "Iai, koma pano pali kudya pano, kukhwasula." Basi kukhala nao pamene paja kudya nkhuku. Ali, "Koma tsono, bwanatu, ine nde nkhukuyo ndadya kale, ndakhuta ndi mkazanga. Koma tsopano inu dzidyani. Ine ndikubwera kaye ndikayambe ndaimirira." Kalulu uja zyee! wazemba. Anabisa chidebe chache pena pache pathengo. Wakatenga chidebe basi kubwera pachitsime paja. Tungani madzi, tungani madzi, chidebe thoo! Kukasiya panjira. Kukatenganso china kudzatunganso madzi kudzasiya panjira paja. Basi uku fisi akudyabe nkhuku. Anamusiyira si imodzi koma zinali ziwiri. Nde polimbikira kuti nkhuku ija, iai, ndiye ndikhute ndimvetsetse nde kudya ndi mafupa omwe malinga ndi njala ya masika. Kalulu kunyamula kunjira kuja kunali mkazache, kunyamula chinachi. Chidebe chinachi kunyamula mwana wache wamkulu kupita nao madzi kunyumba. Basi wabwerera msangamsanga kalulu kukampeza fisi kuthengo kumene amadyela nkhuku. "Bwana mwadya nkhuku?" Ali, "Eee, ah, iai, aisee, iih, wachita zabwino kwabasi. Koma tsopano adzayamba kutunga madzi anthu ena ache pamene paja. Ndikupita." Fisi waiwala kuti madziwa m'mene anamuuza kuti adzilonda madzi amati adzilonda chifukwa kuti kalulu asatunge. Tsopano iyeyo akupusitsidwa ndi kalulu yemweyo. Ndiye basi n'kubwerera kuchitsime ndi kukangoonako ndi kumalondela chitsimecho mpaka nyama zabweranso nthawi ina yake kudzamwa madzi. Kufunsa, "Bwanji sanabwere?" Ali, "Ah, kalulu anabwera koma anangonditengera nkhuku iih, wandipatsa nkhuku ziwiri, m'moti ndadya kwabasi." Ali, "Ah, iwe ameneyo sanatunge madzi?" Ali, "Iai sanatunge madzi. M'mene ndimadya nkhuku basi anangoti ndikukaimirira apa nde anakaimirira anabweranso mosachedwa kwambiri, iai." Wapusitsidwa ndi nkhani yankhuku. Tsopano anthu amene amamudziwa kalulu aone kunyumba kwa kalulu aona mkazi wache akubwera ndi chidebe cha madzi. Mwana wache wamkulu wanyamu-lanso chidebe cha madzi. Nde, "Kodi amai akalulu mwanyamula chani?" Ali, "Aah! Iai, tinapita kuchigayo uku nde basi tanyamula zakudya zathu umu."

other animals were not coming. He killed his chicken. Then didn't he take the chicken and reach near the well? *"Odi! Odi!"* Hyena said," Who is that?" He said: "Me, the hare." He said, "They told me that if you so much as come here then you will be killed for food." He said, "No, sir, come and see, I have brought roast chicken." "Ah, roast chicken! Wait for me! All right, I'm coming, I thought it was just a joke." He said. "No, it's not a joke." Then he came, he got there. Hyena looked at the chicken, iih, salivating *nju! nju!* He said, "No, there is eating here, just eating." Then he sat there eating food. He said, "But now, sir, that chicken I have already eaten with my wife. I've had enough but you can eat it. I'm coming. I'm going for a piss." The hare went *zyee!* he sneaked off. He had hidden his bucket behind a certain bush, he took the bucket and came to the well. He drew the water, he drew the water, the whole bucket *thoo!* full, and level, and left it by the wayside. He got another bucket, came to draw more water, and left it by the wayside. This all while hyena was still eating the chicken. He had been left with not one, but two. So with concentrating on the chicken, so that it should fill him up, he ate it whole with the bones since there was hunger during that summer. The hare took to the wayside where his wife was, took the other [bucket]. The other bucket was taken by the oldest child going home with the water. Then the hare hurried back to find the hyena in the bush, where he was eating the chicken. "Have you finished the chicken, sir?" He said, "Yes, ah, no, my friend, iih, you have done a good job. But now someone might start drawing the water over there, I am going." Hyena forgot that this water, when they told him to guard the water, it was to prevent the hare from getting it. Now he is being duped by the same hare. Then he went back to the well and lay down, guarding the well until the animals came back later to drink. They asked, "How, now, didn't the hare come?" He said, "Ah, the hare came but he only brought me chicken, iih, he gave me two chickens, and I've really eaten." They said, "Aah, didn't he draw any water?" He said, "No, he didn't draw any water. When I was eating the chicken, he just said I am going for a piss here, that's all, and after the piss he came back quickly." He was fooled by the chicken. Now the people who knew the hare noticed at his home that the hare's wife was coming with a bucket of water, his oldest son also carried a bucket of water. Then, "By the way, mother hare, what's that you are carrying?" She said, "Ah, we went to the maize mill over there, and we are carrying our food in these, that's all."

"Eeh?" Koma tiana poti sitidziwa chinsisi basi tapita kukasewera ali, "Iih, Amai atunga madzi, atunga madzi." Nyama zina kufunsa, "Atunga kuti?" Ali, "Iih, anapita kukatunga ndi ababa." Nde basi anthu ena tsopano ayamba kudabwa kuti, "Pamene apa zikuyenda bwanji?" Nde basi tsiku lina amfumu aNjobvu anauzidwa kuti: "Koma kalulu akuti watunga madzi pano dzulo." "Watunga bwanji madzi? Iwe fisi, talongosola, kalulu anabwera?" All, "Eeh, anabwera, bwana." "Anadzatani?" "Aah, anafika ndithu amati kuti akumva nane chisoni, kuti ndingokhala ndi njala poti anzanganu tinapangana kuti mubwere thu koloko nde kuti m'mawa wonsewu ndingokhala ndi njala anandibweretsera yowamba ziwiri. Nkhuku ziwiri." "Tsopano atakupatsa nkhuku ndiye anachita bwanji? Ali, "Iai, anangoti ndikukaimilira apa. Ah, sanachedwe, bwana. Panali pafupi kwabasi." Ali, "Ah! no! anatenga nthawi ameneyo. Si ndiye nthawi imene anakatunga madziyo imeneyo? Iwe bwanji umalola kudyera nkhuku pathengo?" "Bwana, nanga sitimatsata pamasamba abwino pamaudzu poti kuwandawanda basi pamenepo basi nde kuyalika masamba abwino n'kumadyera nkhuku pamenepo?" Ali, "No! ameneyo anatunga madzi basi. Chabwino, lero upange shuwa kuti nangati abwerenso kaluluyo pano kaya akubweretsera zakudya udzidyera naye pachitsime pompano koma iyeyo asatunge madzi." Ali, "Ooh, chabwino zimenezo ndalola." Basi kalulu wakhalakhala nde waona kuti, "Iai, madzi aja tatunga aja tasambasamba tsopano ena taphikira ena tamwa tasowa zoti tichite." Watenga chakudya chinanso. Wawambawamba kanyama kambuzi basi ulendo nayo nyama ija. Kufika kuja, "Odi!" Fisi ali, "Eee. Ndani iwe?" Kalulu ali, "Ine, kalulu." "Ah, bwera konkuno." Ali, "Iih, koma mubwere kuno!" Ali, "Ah, bwera konkuno." Wafika pafupi basi ali, "Ndakutengerani nyama." Ali, "Oh, yesi. Lero ndidyera pompano." Ali, "Ooh? eeh?" "Eee." Nde fisi sadafune kuulula kuti ndamva kuti unatunga madzi iai, anaopa kuti achita manyazi. Nde kudyakudya nyama ija nde akuti, "Pamenepo koma, eh, nde madzi abwinotu." Kusuzumira ali, "Iih, eee, iai, akuonekanso kuti ndi okatakata opanda dothi." Ali, "Eee, madzi ndithu ndi amenewa nde popeza iwe siunagwire nao ntchito nde, ah, siutunga nao." Iye ali, "Ah, ine ndilibe nazo kanthu. Ine ndangobwera kuti ndikupatsenitu nyamayi kuti mudye chifukwa ndimadziwa kuti inu mumabvutika kwambiri kufuna nyama. Nanga inu mumadziwa kudya udzu ngati ife ngati?" Ali, "Ah, ife sitimadya maudzu, zoona. Iwe mwana wodziwa bwino kulemekeza akuluakulu." Kalulu pamene paja tsono wathedwa nzeru. Wachoka paja

102

"Eeh?" But the children, since they do not know how keep a secret, when they went to play, said, "Iih, mother drew water, drew water." The other animals asked, "From where did she draw it?" They said, "Iih, she went with father." Then the other people now started wondering, "What is going on here?" Then another day Chief Elephant was told the news: "The hare is said to have drawn water here yesterday." "How did he draw the water? You hyena, explain, did the hare come?" He said, "Yes, he came, sir." "What did he come to do?" "Aah, he came indeed to say he pitied me, that I'm just sitting here hungry when you, my friends, we had planned that you would come at two o'clock so the whole morning I was hungry. He brought me two roast chickens, two roast chickens." "Now, after he had given you the chicken, what did he do?" He said, "No, he just said, I'm going for a piss here. Ah, he didn't take long, sir. It was quite near." He said, "Ah! No! It took some time, isn't that the time he went to draw the water? Why did you agree to go to the bush to eat the chicken?" "Sir, weren't we looking for a leafy place and a grassy place to part and there to spread the what-is-it, the good leaves, then eat the chicken there?" He said, "No, that one drew the water. All right, today you must make sure that if the hare comes again here bringing you food you eat it here at the well but he must not draw the water." He said, "Ooh. All right, I accept." Then the hare, after a while, he saw that no, the water we drew we used for washing, some for cooking, some for drinking, now we don't know what to do. He took food again, he roasted goat's meat, then went with it. When he reached there: "*Odi!*" The hyena said, "Yes! Who is that?" The hare said, "Me, hare." "Ah, come here." He said, "Iih, but you should come here." He said, "Ah, come here." He came near, then said, "I brought you meat." He said "Oh, yes, today I will eat it here." He said, "Oh, eeh?" "Yes." Then the hyena did not want to reveal that I have heard that you drew some water, no, he was afraid of being embarrassed. There he ate the meat and said, "There's nice water here." He peeped in and said, "Iih, eeh, no, it looks also quite settled, no mud." He said, "Yes, that's the water, however, since you did not help in the work you are not going to draw any." He said, "Ah, that does not concern me, I just came to give you the meat because I know that you find great difficulties in finding meat. You don't even know how to eat grass like us." He said, "Ah, we don't eat grass, that's true, you little one you know how to treat elders." The hare was now at his wits' end. He left the place and went by the wayside. Then he said, "Oh, now

103

wapita kunjira. Basi ali, "Oh, tsopano koma apa ndibvula chikopa." Chikopa chakalulu chinali chomatheka kuchibvula n'kuchisiya pansi. Basi wachibvula chikopa kungotsala basi kamutu kokhaka. Wachibisa pa malo pache pabwinobwino. Angopanga shuwa kuti pasakhale nyerere zoti zingadye chikopachi. Wayenda wakaima cha uko! Basi ali, "Kanyama kosendasenda! Kanyama kosendasenda! Thawani! Thawani! Thawani!" Fisi kuyang'ana yiih! Walisesa! Kuthawa kwabasi, kuthawa. M'mene anathawa choncho basi kalulu kuthamanga kukatenga zidebe zache kumene anabisako kudzatunga madzi kukasiya kunjira. Kuthamanganso chidebe china. Tsiku limenelo ndiye anachita kutenga zidebe folo! Ndiye poti paja iye anali ndi ana folo mkazache ndi ana ache atatu ananyamula zidebe zija kumapita nazo. Iye basi kuzungulira kukachipezachikopa chache chija ndikuchibvalanso basi kudzafika pali fisi paja, "Ah! nyama ija mwadya?" "Eee, ndadya koma tsopano, mhn, ndikubvera posachedwa pompa. N'nathawa pano." "Munathawa chani?" Ali, "Panabwera kachinthu kena kache koma kubadwa kwache kanabadwa ngati kalulu koma tsono kofiira. Thupi lonseli magazi okhaokha moti ine m'mene kandiophyeza pano, iih. Koma kameneko ndichani tija, tiujeni? Kandondocha. Nde n'nathawa. Tsono m'mene n'naona kuti kakukhala ngati kachokapo nde basi ndabwerera." "Eaah? Ah, iai, pepani. Basi ine ndangoti ndikuchezetseni. Ndapita." Kalulu ndi ulendo. M'mawa kwacha akumvanso malipoti amfumu aNjobvu kuti, "Koma kalulu madzi sakumusowayi. Tsopano lero wafika mpakana pothilira m'galideni yamaluwa." Mfumu Njobvu akuti, "Iwe fisi nena tsopano zadzulo. Zinachitika n'zotani?" Akuti, "Iai bwana, dzulo ndithu ndinapanga shuwa kuti kalulu basi, nyama imene—anabweratu ndi nyamanso koma dzulo adabwera ndi yambuzi. Akuti iye basi wangokondwera kundithandiza ineyo chifukwa ine ndimam'chitira zabwino nthawi zina zache nde nyama ndinadyera pompano pachitsime. Asakunamizeni kuti ndinachoka bwana pepani ndithu koma ndatha kudya nyama ija kalulu wapita. Patatha nthawi panatuluka kandondocha mbali ya kumeneku—kukaona, bwana kongofiira thupi lonse ngati magazi. Ndiponso kamanena zina zache zokuti sindingathe kunena ine pano, iai. Bwana monga mukudziwa kuti ndondocha ndi zinthu zoopsya kwabasi ine ndiye ndinathawa. Nde n'tathawa basi. Ndakhala nthawi, ndakhala nthawi, ndinabwera kuntchito ngati kuwenda, kubisala chonchi, kuyang'ana, kuyang'ana, nde n'kupeza kuti, iai, kanthu kaja palibenso, iai. Basi nkudzakhalanso. Nde iai, nthawi yache imene ndinachoka ndi nthawi but here I will take off my skin." The hare's skin could be removed and left behind. Then he took it off, except the little head. He hid it in a good place. He just made sure that there were no ants which could have eaten the skin. He walked and stood over there, then he said, "A skinned animal! A skinned animal! Run! Run! Run!" The hyena saw it, iih! He ran, he ran fast, ran away. When he ran like that, then the hare ran to get his buckets where he had hidden them to draw water and leave them by the wayside. He ran again for another bucket. That day, he actually brought four buckets, and since he had four children, his wife and three children took the buckets and went with them. He then went round to find his skin, put it back on, then got to where the hyena was. "Ah! You have finished the meat?" "Yes, I have finished it, but, now, mhn, I have just returned. I ran away from this place." "What were you running away from?" He said, "There came something born like a hare, but red. The whole body is bloody and how it scared me, iih. But I think it was a ghost because it must be, what do they call them? A zombie. So I ran, then, when I saw that it had gone, then I returned." "Aah, is that so? Ah, I'm sorry. Now I just wanted to chat with you. I'm gone." The hare went. The morning broke and reports were heard again by chief Elephant that, "The hare does not lack any water. Today he has reached the stage of even watering his flower garden." Chief Elephant said, "You, you, hyena tell us now about yesterday, what happened?" He said, "No sir, yesterday I made sure that the hare, the meat—he came with meat again, but yesterday he brought goat's meat. He said he was glad to help me since I have done him good things in the past and I ate the meat right here by the well. They should not cheat you that I left the place, sir, please when I finished eating the meat the hare left. After a time there came a zombie from this side—but, sir, it was red the whole body like blood. And also, it was saying other things that I cannot say at all. Sir, you know that zombies are very spooky things, so I ran away. When I ran away, then, I stayed a while, I stayed a while, then, I came stealthily back to work, then hid like this. I looked, looked, then I found that, no, the thing was no longer there, no. Then I came and sat down again. Then, no, the time that I left this place is that time only when the zombie came. And it didn't even draw any water, no. So they shouldn't tell you that

yache yokhayo kanabwera kandondochako. Kutinso sikakanatunga madzi, iai. Ndiye basi asakuuzeni kuti kapena kalulu anatunga madzi, iai. Si zoona iai." Ali, "Ooh, eeh?" Ndiye Njobvu anaitanitsa msonkhano kuti, "Koma pulizi kukupezeka kuti kalulu akumapezabe madzi koma iye sanabvutike nao kukumba chitsime, iai. Nde zikuoneka malinga ndi dziko lonse kulibenso kungapezeke kuli madzi. Madzi ali kutali kwabasi kumene sangafike kalulu iai. Tichitepo chotheka kuti kaluluyi basi timugwire." Nde anaikapo tsopano ma "si-ai-di" [CID] oti afufuze nkhaniyi, aone m'mene zinakhalira. Atam'siya fisi kulondanso tsiku limeneli lachinai lacheli, kalulu anabweranso. Tsono wabwera ndi timakeke take tabwino zokhala ngati za Kirisimasi timadya kwa ankolo zija. Kuyang'ana zimene zija akuti basi, "Pulizi, ooh, aisee, wabwera ndi zakudya?" Nde kuti, "Eee." "Ah, koma tsono pano nde dzulo lija kanabwera kachinthu kena kache kanandiopsyeza. Ali, "Iih, aisee, zikhala zokuopsyezazo nde zako chifukwa m'mene m'mapangana inu ufiti wanuwo ndi chitsimechi ine sindikuzidziwa. Ine ndingofuna kukuthandiza iwe chifukwa ukufa ndi njala pano kudikira chitsime." Akuti, "Ooh, chabwino zikomo. Koma tsopano sungandiuze nzeru kuti katabwera ngati kameneko ndingachite bwanji?" Ali, "Iih, sindingakuuze." Tsono m'mene amachita choncho ma "si-ai-di" anaika Njobvu aja atabisalabisala m'thengomo n'kumayang'ana. Ndiye tsopano akuyang'ana chonchija kalulu nde anachoka ali, "Ooh! Zidyani makekewa, ine ndikubwera." Wapita kuseli kwina kwache wakachibvula chikopa chija. Basi wabwera pafupi. "Kanyama kosendasenda! Kanyama kosendasenda! Thawani kanyama kosendasenda!" Iih, fisi wayang'ana uko! Waliyala liwiro! Makeke aja kukwapatira ena m'khwapa chonchi kukadyera kutchile. Wakakhala kuja nthawi. Ma "si-ai-di" aja ankangoyang'ana akuti, "Ah, kanyama kosendasenda?" Ayang'anitsitse aona kuti kalulu wathamanga wakatenga zidebe zache folo akudzatunga madzi mkazache ndi ana atatu akuchokera kumadzi ulendo. Iye kalulu akukazungulira pofika kuja basi podzabweranso n'kuoneka kuti tsopano thupi linali lofiira lija basi wabvalanso chikopa chache bwinobwino. Ma "si-ai-di" aja ali, "Ooh chabwino." Tsopano sanamudziwitse ujeni uyu, fisiyu. Anangomusiya. Tsiku lachisanu ndi chimodzi lakwana kubwera amfuma aNjobvu nkuwauza ma "si-ai-di" aja ali, "Aah koma pano kanyama kamene akutiko ndi kandondocha kamafanana ngati kalulu. Akukhala ngati kalulu yemweyo koma, ofukozi. Koma zimene kakumanena kanyamako zosafanana ngati zimene zonena anthu wamba. Iai, kapena kangakhale kandondocha, sitidziwa, koma kali ndi mapilikaniro ngati kalulu,

106

perhaps the hare drew water, no. It's not true." He said, "Ooh, yeeh?" Then Elephant called for a meeting saying, "But, please, it is found that the hare still has access to water when he did not labour with us to dig a well, no. And it is obvious that there is no water found anywhere else in the whole country. The water is too far away for the hare to find it, no. We must do our best to capture this hare." So they now placed detectives to investigate this case to find out how it happened. When they left the hyena to guard that day again the fourth day, the hare came again. This time he came with his nice little cakes like the Christmas ones we were eating at uncle's place. Looking at them he then said, "Please, ooh, I say, you have come with food?" Then, "Yes." "Ah, but now yesterday there came here something that scared me." He said, "Iii, I say, the scary things are your own affair because when you were planning the witchcraft and the well, me I don't know. Me, I just want to help you because you are going to die of hunger guarding the well." He said, "Ooh, all right, thank you. But now couldn't you advise me on what to do when the thing comes again?" He said, "Iih I can't advise you." Then, when they were doing that the detectives Elephant had placed there hid themselves in the bushes, watching. Then when they were watching like that, the hare then left saying, "Oooh, go on eating the cakes, I'm coming." he went round another bush, took off his skin then came near. "A skinned animal! A skinned animal! Run! run! A skinned animal!" Iih, the hyena looked there. He ran. The cakes he put some under his armpits like this to eat in the bushes. He stayed there for a time. The detectives were just watching saying, "Ah, a skinned animal?" Watching closely, they saw that the hare had run to take his four buckets to draw water, his wife and three children came from the well on their way home. The hare himself went round and reaching the place then, it looked on his return that his body which was red he had now put back his skin nicely. The detectives said, "Oh, all right." Now they didn't inform who's this, the hyena, they just left him. When the sixth day came the chief Elephant was told by the detectives that, "Aah, but here the little animal that is said to be a zombie looks like the hare. It looks like the same hare but, of course. But what it says is not similar to what ordinary people say, no, perhaps it could be a zombie, we don't know, but it has ears like the hare all right but its body is skinless, red like blood." He said, "All right, now,

bwinobwino, koma thupi lache ndi lopanda chikopa, lofiira ngati magazi." Ali "Ooh, chabwino. Tsono ine poti munaona choncho tsopano mawa ma "si-ai-di" inu musakhale malo amodzi. Wina akabisale pakathengo kena kache. Wina pakathengo kena kache; makamaka, mbali zimene anafikira kaluluyu mudzikabisala kumeneko." Ali, "Ooh, chabwino, tikabisala." Tsono londa wa pachitsimepo n'kukhala fisi yemweyobe. Nde basi tsiku lachisanu n'chimodzi akhala pamene paja afisi akulonda. Kalulu wati kuganiza nanga si akunyada tsopano kunyumba kwache tsopano madzi akuthirira maluwa, akusamba bwinobwino. Madzi ena angotaya choncho. Koma ntchito anabvutikira ndi anthu ena. Waphikanso zakudya zache zina tsopano tsiku limenelo nde wangochita zokazinga m'mafuta. Zophika bwinobwino anyezi, zonunkhira, kaya inali nyama yankhumba, kaya. Waitenga, ulendo wakuchitsime. "Odi!" Fisi ali, "Eeh! Kodi ndani?" "Aah, ndine." Ali, "Kodi ndiwe kalulu? Ah, bwera, aisee, bwera. Wan'tengera chani mwana? Aah gudu, mphwanga munthu wabwino kwabasi. Chani chimenechi?" Ali, "Nkhumba imeneyi. Sosejesi." Ali, "Ooh, yesi, vere gudu. Zikomo kwambiri." Yambani kudya pamenepaja sosejesi. Ali, "Tsopano ndikupezani. Ndikuti ndikamuone mnzanga patsidyapa." Apita kuja wakabvula chikopa chache. Tsopano osadziwa kuti pamene akubvulirapa imodzi ya nyama ija anaziika "si-ai-di" ija ili pafupi. Ndiye anangowauza kuti mukamuona akubvuladi chikopa chache mukango-tenga chitedze mukapake. Ndiye basi iwo aja aona kalulu wachibvula chikopa wachisiya. Akukazungulira kuti adzikatunga madzi, kukafika kuchitsime kuja basi kukamuopsyeza fisi. Fisi ndi kuthawa. Iye kutungatunga madzi ndi mkazache basi. Mkazache akupita ndi madzi, iye kuzungulira uku wakafika pali chikopa chija koma tsopano chikopa wachitaya. "Aiihih!" Wayamba kufuula yekha akudzikanda kalulu. Koma kuyamba kufuula, "Fisi! Kuno ndikubvutika ine. Ndikubvutika!" Fisi wathamanga kusiya madzi aja tsopano kukamuyang'ana kalulu. "Kodi kalulu, wachita bwanji? Si chikopa chako ichi?" "Inde, aisee, koma usandidyere, pepa. Koma ndabvutika ine chitedze." "Aah watani nanga?" "Aah, iai." Basi a "si-ai-di" aja alumpha onse mthengo muja kubwera basi n'kudzam'gwira kalulu basi m'mangeni. Atam'manga basi n'kubwera amfumu aNjobvu. Basino anangom'kwapula koopsya ndi kum'manga ukaidi wa zaka khumi chifukwa cha zimene ankachita. Basi pamene inathera. Ajokole katolo, tatekumunga aNkolokosa wawe.[8]

---

[8]   Simika, December 1975.

since you saw that, tomorrow the detectives should not be in one place. One should hide in one bush. Another in another bush, especially the side from which the hare emerged, you should hide there." They said, "Ooh, all right, we will hide there." Now the guard for the well was still the hyena. So on the sixth day the hyena sat there guarding. The hare thought, now, isn't he boasting at home that he has water for watering his flowers, for bathing properly. Some water he is just throwing away like that. But the labour was done by others. He cooked another kind of food and on that day, he really fried it in oil. The food was cooked nicely with onions, smelling nicely, perhaps it was pork, perhaps. He took it to the well. "Odi!" The hyena said, "Eeh, who is that?" "Aah, it's me." The hyena said, "Is that you, hare? Ah come here, I say, come, what have you brought for me, my friend?" "Aah, good my young brother you are a very nice person, what is this?" He said, "It is pork sausages." He said, "Ooh yes, very good, thank you very much." He started eating the sausages there. He said, "Now I'll find you. I've got to go and see a friend on the other side of the river." He went there and took off his skin. Now, he did not know that the place he was taking his clothes off one of the detectives was nearby. They told them that if they saw him taking off his skin they should just apply itching beans to it. Then they saw the hare taking off his skin, leaving it. He goes round to draw water, reaching the well to scare the hyena off. The hyena ran away. Then he drew the water with his wife. When his wife was going away with the water he went round this way to where his skin was, but now itching beans had been applied inside, so he threw it away, "Aiihih!" Kalulu started shouting alone while scratching himself. But he started shouting, "Hyena! I'm being tortured here! Tortured!" Hyena ran, leaving the water to look for the hare. "Hey, hare, what has happened? Isn't this your skin?" "Yes, I say, but don't eat it, I implore you. But I'm being tortured by the itching beans." "Aah, what have you done?" "Ah no." Then the detectives jumped from the bush and grabbed the hare, then tied him up. When they had tied him, then chief Elephant came. So then they gave him a severe beating and imprisoned him for ten years for what he had done. That's all, that's where it ended. *Ajokole katolo, kate kununga aNkolokosa wawe.*

The Performance of "The Hare and the Well"

By the second pause, the narrator has already run through the complete vowel system of the vernacular (*a, e, i, o, u*). And most of the possible consonant combinations have been utilised by the sixth pause (*mv, ng, kh, th, nd, dz, kw, mb,* etc.). A frequency count will not be enumerated here, but what is important is that the vowel and consonant combinations enhance the musicality of the text. Consider, for example, the effect of the first utterance: *Chaka china chache*, or the fourth: *kungopatula kunyanja kokha … kunali …* Here, the alliteration is a result of the concordial requirements of the language—*ch* in the former example, and *k* in the latter. Musicality is further enhanced by the fact that the language is tonal.

We shall not attempt to comment at length on all the possible syntactic patterns which the text shows. If the reader/listener observed the first four utterances, he would be struck by the peculiar syntax. The transcriber put full stops to indicate long pauses, but dashes or strokes would have been more appropriate. It is a known fact that oral transmission does not indicate where the full stops, commas, exclamation marks and other punctuation marks are. This is only a barbarism of the printed word. The spoken form indicates these by pauses of varying lengths, tone of voice, stress, rhythm and intonation, which have no satisfactory equivalent in the written form. This might appear incidental, yet it is vital to the verbal arts. As we can see from the way the first four utterances are arranged: *Panali chaka china chake/Mvula kunalibe ngakhale dontho/Ndiye mitsinje yonse idauma basi, kungopatula kunyanja kokha ndiye kunali madzi.* A literal translation would render it as: "There was once a year. There was no rain, not a drop. Therefore, the rivers dried up. Except at the lake that is where there was water." It must be admitted that normal conversation does not follow this pattern. Yet it is permitted and expected that the structure of the utterances be in this form for this genre, and in this medium. A translation of a variant of this story has the following as the opening line: "Once upon a time, in the olden days, there was a drought throughout the world." [9] It will be noted that the rhythm of the vernacular version is lost

---

[9]   E. Singano and A.A. Roscoe, eds., *Tales of Old Malawi* (Limbe: Popular Publications, 1974), pp. 33-36.

in the translation. This is a point worth stating here: the oral transmission has perfect freedom to break the normal structure of sentences for the purposes of rhythm. This is also the case with poetry, of course, but that is a different genre.

It is not only in the syntactic licence that we can observe this mode departing from the norm. The examples quoted in the previous paragraphs will also serve to illustrate the ungrammaticality permitted. Throughout the story, the reader/listener is exposed to incomplete or "incorrect" sentences which the narrator modifies as he continues recounting the story. Certain words are frequently run together into phrases, not sentences or paragraphs. As will be observed, the transcriber ran into difficulties here, and got over the problem of paragraphing by mostly ignoring it, thereby violating one rule of written forms.

Another obvious grammatical feature which strikes the reader/listener is the vagueness of referents, especially where pronouns are concerned. The narrator, in dialogues, refers to all characters, whether Njobvu, Fisi, or Kalulu, as *ali* ("he said"). It is even more problematical when females are concerned, because the vernacular does not in fact differentiate between the genders in its use of pronouns.

A prominent feature of the story is the amount of repetition which exists not only at the word level, but also at phrase, sentence and episode levels. Repetition of incidents or events is a structural feature of the narrative and will be discussed later. Meanwhile, it might be worth observing that the rhetorical device, *Basi*, is repeated sixty-nine times in the twenty minutes that the story lasts. Some meaningful repetitions are scattered throughout the story: *kuponda, kugwira ntchito, tungani madzi, ndakhala nthawi, kuyang'ana*. These are meaningful in that they serve as intensifiers of an action. Others serve to show the passage of time. At the same time the musico-rhythmical features are heightened immensely.

Sentences and whole sections are repeated very often. There is repetition also through dialogue. For example, *Kalulu* says, "*Odi!*" and *Fisi* answers, "*Eee, ndani iwe?*" *Kalulu* goes on, "*Ndine Kalulu,*" to which *Fisi* replies, "*Aah, kodi ndiwe?*" etc. This happens in each of the six visits *Kalulu* makes to the well. There is also repetition through song. The work-song the animals sing is not telling the audience anything new. It is merely retelling them the purpose for digging the well, that is, there was drought and the only way to survive was to dig a well. Yet this song is sung six times. *Kalulu's Kanyama kosendasenda!* is another form of song and repetition.

Words, phrases, sentences and sections repeated so often form an intricate pattern of what in the written form would be dismissed as redundancy. But here the pattern is to consolidate names, places and events and to imprint them in the minds of the listeners, so that they will remember clearly what has gone before, what is happening, and what is going to happen. If there were no such system of repetition, no one would remember the account, seeing as it is the spoken medium only that is in use. Reception and retention are thus taken care of too. On a more subtle level, the effect of these repetitions is hypnotic,[10] drugging the listener into a passive acceptance of the events being narrated, however fantastic they are.

In the body of the text are also numerous examples of the narrator interrupting the flow of the narrative to explain what has happened, or to address the audience directly. When he says, *Fisi waiwala kuti madziwa m'mene anamuuza kuti adzilonda madzi amati adzilonda chifukwa kuti Kalulu asatunge. Tsopano iyeyo akupusitsidwa ndi Kalulu yemweyo*, this is only for the benefit of the audience (which included children of five, eight and ten years old.) It does not aid in the development of the story in any way.

Another feature which is not part of the basic transcribed text is the narrator's direct address to the audience. This happens twice in the story, when the narrator is making references to establish the setting more locally or when he is seeking verification of facts outside the story. Early in the story he breaks the narrative and says, *Ngati kuja amati ku chiani? ku*, and the audience supplies the missing word and the narrator continues, *Eee, ngati kumeneko*. A second time this happens is when *Kalulu* takes off his skin and the narrator forgets the name of an equivalent: *Amati chiani chija? ... Ndondocha.*

---

[10] The idea is as old as Plato.

These features are of course possible only in oral transmission and they belong to the level of Narrator vis-à-vis Audience, that is, the narrator's awareness of the audience immediately before him. On another subtle level, they belong to the psychological implications of oral transmission. Whereas repetitions serve as consolidators, these asides, interruptions, explanations, direct address, help the mind to relax a bit. Too much concentration would strain the mind. The breaks are provided for overtly through song participation, but covertly through this communication technique.

This awareness of the audience is an important aspect of the narrative because it regulates a large amount of inclusions which would have been absent had the story been in the written form. These inclusions are particularly meaningful when the narrator refers to the local environment or facts, attitudes, values, etc., which are within the common experience of both narrator and audience. The animals attach a string to a gourd for drawing the water from the well and the narrator says, *ngati chitsime chathu champompanochi* ("like our own well here"). Again, *ngati zapa Kirisimasi timadya kwa ankolo zija* ("like the food we ate on Christmas Day at uncle's"). Yet again, *ngati ku Mulanje uku* ("like in Mulanje over there"). The narrator is appealing to a common body of knowledge here. Admittedly, the examples are serving as comparisons with what the audience already knows. But when the narrator says, *wayenda wakaima chauko* ("he went and stood over there"); or *kanatuluka kandondocha mbali ya kumeneku* ("a zombie appeared from this direction"), we are coming closer to establishing the fact that the well the animals are digging is actually where the audience and narrator are. That is to say, the setting of the story is the setting of the story-telling, or vice-versa. The narrator's awareness of the audience is also clearly seen when he uses the demonstrative adjectives or locatives: *uku* ("there"), *apa* ("here"), *chonchi* ("like this").

Far more important, however, if we want to isolate a single aspect where the audience is in the narrator's mind, is the delivery or performance. The transcriber was present at the occasion on which the narrator told the story. There were elements of drama here: acting, gesticulation, change of facial expression and tone of voice. These important elements are not seen in the transcript as there is no method of representation which could be made apart from filming the performance.

We could start with the tone of voice. The inflection, tone and intonation, of course, varied between statement and question, but variations also occurred to include irony, humour, sarcasm, seriousness and mockery. We shall not go into where exactly this happened, as this would require apparatus for measuring and recording. Suffice it to say that the narrator's voice changed in quality and pitch in the dialogues. He had one voice for *Njobvu*: dignified and deliberate. *Fisi* had a hoarse, whining voice, where the narrator emphasised the nasality to portray the Hyena's dull-wittedness. *Kalulu* had a very distinctive voice: high, small, and delivered faster than any of the other animal's speech. This was especially so when *Kalulu* came to frighten *Fisi* with *Kanyama kosendasenda*. That is why we suggested earlier that this part functioned as a song as well. Mrs. *Kalulu's* and her children's voices were variations of *Kalulu's*.

With the change of voice for different characters came also the gestures, facial expressions and elements of acting. The narrator wore a very dignified air when he came to *Njobvu* to call for a meeting and interrogate *Fisi*, and a stupid air for *Fisi*. *Fisi* features prominently in the story and the narrator dwelt on him extensively, first a foolish and trusting friend, through a suspicious character, to a very greedy one. The narrator went through the motions *Fisi* made when eating the different kinds of food given to him by *Kalulu*.

It is in the gestures that the narrator excelled himself. He did not actually stand up and act, but was shifting and moving in considerable agitation as he got carried away with the role he was playing. This was especially so when he acted *Fisi* being frightened by *Kalulu* at the well. *Iih walisesa liwiro* ("Did he run fast!"), or *Waliyala Fisi* ("Hyena ran very fast"), and, coming slowly back to check that the zombie was gone: *ndinabwera kuntchito, kuchita ngati kuwenda, kubisala chonchi, kuyang'ana, kuyang'ana* ("so I came back stealthily, hiding like this, and I looked this way and that"). And again, *Fisi's* moral indignation when *Kalulu* is discovered: *kodi, Kalulu, wachita bwanji? Si chikopa chako ichi?* ("What have you done, hare? Isn't this your skin?")

114

The same level of dramatic presentation was observed with the other characters, especially when *Kalulu* was first discovered to be feigning sickness. The messenger came to his house to find not a sick family, but a happy one playing a game of *msikwa*. The embarrassed *Kalulu* has to cover up: *Oh, oh kodi mwabwera?* A translation of this into English would be nonsense ("Oh, you have come?"). The situation explains itself. *Kalulu* performs his tricks brilliantly even to the point of taking off his skin, when the itching beans are applied to it. The narrator underwent the violent motions of scratching himself all over from putting the skin back on. *Aiihi! Wayamba kufuula yekha akudzikanda Kalulu* (When Kalulu had put the skin back on, he immediately threw it away and started shouting, while scratching himself").

As the foregoing briefly shows, the narrator introjected himself into the story and identified himself with the various characters. What remains of great interest before we leave him is the narrator himself and his idiolect. We shall not go into the dialect he uses, but comment on the extensive use of Anglicisms or loan-words in the text. Some of the chichewalised words are: *ekesesaizi* (exercise), *lejisitala* (register), *galideni* (garden), *pulizi* (please), *shuwa* (sure), *lipoti* (report), ofukozi (of course), *vere gudu* (very good), *sosejesi* (sausages), and *yesi* (yes). This is interesting in itself. But it also illustrates the fact that not only can the narrator draw his verbal mannerisms from the whole world of traditional rhetorical devices, but also his western education is a stylistic feature in the rendering. It would be enlightening to have a narrator without the influence of western education narrate the same story.

Up to this point the discussion has directed attention at the narrator and the performance. This is as it should be: it is the narrator who brings the text into existence. But story-telling is a two-way process. On the one hand there is the narrator, on the other, the listeners, the audience, or, as some prefer to put it, the chorus. We have implied that the audience is a crucial factor in the story-telling, and have pointed out the areas where they are a controlling factor. If demands are made of the narrator, the same goes for the audience. In the story, the audience are also part of the narrative. Part of the manipulation by the narrator has its effect on the recipients, of course, but to heighten the dynamic relationship that exists between the two we have the audience participating with the expected responses.

The audience comes in right from the opening formula, *Padangotero* ("Once upon a time"), with the response, *Tili tonse* ("We are together"). The closing formula is a device that is found among the Yao—which goes to illustrate how many influences there are on the narrator. The narrator's closing formula extends beyond the *Basi pamene inathera* ("that is where the story ended"). He brings it formally to a close by *Ajokole katolo!* to which the audience reply, *kate kununga aNkolokosa wawe*.

Apart from providing the rhythmical response of *Tili tonse*, the audience joined in the song led by the narrator. This involved the audience and increased their degree of identification with the situation. The audience also came in directly when the narrator asked them questions. Here the audience was acting more or less as a sounding board, aiding the memory and development of the story. In other stories the harangues are known to take more elaborate forms than was observed here.

The Text as a Variant

Earlier we mentioned the fact that there are variants of the story. The variations are not only in the characters and plot but also in the songs sung for each one. The translated and published version mentioned does not include a song. However, a version in one variant is the following:

Tiponde! Tiponde!	Let's stamp! Let's stamp
Madzi adauma	Water dried up
Nanga lero!	What about today!
Nanga lero!	What about today!
Tionere a Njobvu	Let's watch the Elephant

Our version of the story has *Kalulu* being punished and put into prison. In other versions the hero suffers no such punishment. The point here is the fact that the narrator has used his freedom to introduce variations, to reshape and reorder episodes and to add not only new episodes, but also the words, phrases, sentences and stylistic devices which were at his disposal. Depending on which version came first, the narrator was also free to twist the ending and put a new one. This is not really a problem for us; it is one of the formal characteristics which the analyst may recognise and accept. It is a fact that folk stories are highly mobile, and each society and individual is free to impose their own creative pattern on them. This characteristic is not shared to the same degree with printed works.

What the narrator could not or did not tamper with is the other formal characteristics of formulae which we saw earlier, and of course the narrative technique. However much common knowledge and experience exists between narrator and audience, it is understood that certain steps in the rendition will be followed. It is only in very rare circumstances (although other models of folklore might permit this) that the omniscient authorial stance is violated. This of course depends on other factors such as occasion, composition of audience, branch of folklore and the narrator himself.

The Content of "The Hare and the Well"

Whichever variant one comes across, there are elements of the story that are recognisable and therefore analyzable: character, theme, plot and action, etc. The only problem is one of approaches and the tools to be used. If we approach the story from any angle, we are faced with certain difficulties as to the point of departure and where to go from there.

There are three prevailing theories of plot.[11] One theory states that plot consists of three elements: situations, thoughts and actions. To analyse the plot is to go through the story analyzing these elements. This constitutes isolating the central action or change in the thematic development of the story, and picking out the series of actions that led up to the change, and what follows after the change. What is not clear is what will be considered as the actions and situations to be counted as central to the plot.

Another theory of plot recognises two types: that which involves the modification of a situation and that which involves transgressions and punishment. This theory recognises three stages in the development of a story. The first is the initial situation. The second is an action which modifies or which is intended or threatens to modify the initial situation. And the third is the new situation which emerges as a result of the effects

---

[11]   Jonathan Culler, *Structuralist Poetics* (London: Routledge and Kegan Paul, 1975), pp. 205-224.

of the second on the first. The problem here again is that until something has taken place which tells us or signals the actual or prospective modification and its contributions, we are still not sure or do not know which are the important or relevant elements of the plot.

The third theory proposes that plot consists of actions which destroy equilibrium and actions which seek to restore equilibrium. The difficulty arises when you identify one action that manifests different functions.

Admittedly, these theories come in useful in literary criticism, which is precisely what we are trying to achieve. The scope of this discussion does not, however, allow us to argue the status of the folk story as literature. For our purposes, we take it for granted, and behave as if it were a work of art, and approach it as such.

In any case our exploration has given us a possible framework to use for analyzing the story. As can be observed, each of the plot themes above could be used for the present story, or all of them in fact. The most appropriate framework, however, would be the second. Here we are going to use a modified version, because the genre we are dealing with comes under the heading of "Trickster." Scholars recognise five stages in this type of story, which we will also modify as we go along: friendship, contract, violation of contract (deceit), discovery of violation, end of friendship (calamity or escape) or resolution.[12]

As we can see in the story, there is a crisis—drought—and all the animals including *Kalulu* agree at the meeting that they should dig a well. But *Kalulu* boycotts the actual labour, feigning illness, whereupon the rest of the animals resolve that he should not be allowed to drink from the well. Water is found, but *Kalulu*, despite the precautions to prevent him, enjoys the fruits of the other animals' labour. In the end, he is caught and punished. So we could categorise the plot under "Trickster Out-tricked or Out-witted," which, as we have already mentioned is a variant of the trickster tale. We do not need to go into the details of how this is done. The analysis of the structure of the story will illustrate the point.

---

[12] Lee Haring, "A Characteristic African Folktale Pattern," in Richard M. Dorson, ed., *African Folklore* (New York: Anchor Books, 1972), pp. 165-179.

The organising principle underlying the story is one of repetition. This point was made earlier, when we were analyzing the verbal elements. Although we seem to be carried progressively forward as the narrative continues, we find that the same or similar incidents recur in various ways. This is a structural repetition observable in most folk stories. Benison Gray, in *The Phenomenon of Literature*,[13] isolates four different methods of structural repetition which we will use here.

The first method consists of similar incidents happening to the same person or persons. The first half of the story consists of the same type of activity: waking up, going to dig the well, and going back home to sleep. The different stages of this activity are marked by the work song. The animals are engaged in this for four successive days, each day being described in the same manner by the narrator. After the stage has been set for the dénouement of the trickster, we find that *Kalulu* tricks *Fisi* six times in succession before being caught. There are variations in the method of trickery, of course, but each time it is a trick, regardless of how it is accomplished.

In a variant of the story, mentioned above, we have the second method of repetition, in which the same incidents happen to different protagonists. There we have *Kalulu* deceiving the monkey, the gazelle, and other animals, with the same trick, until he is caught by the tortoise.

The third method of repetition Benison Gray mentions is that of narration-repeating incident. Examples of this type are numerous. Very early in the story, we have the messenger, who had been sent on a fact-finding mission about *Kalulu's* sickness, reporting to *Njobvu* word for word what the listeners already know happened at *Kalulu's* home. Later on, *Fisi* reports five times the details of *Kalulu's* visits and the tricks performed. These the audience already know again, but the narrator insists on recounting verbatim.

Fourthly, we are exposed to repetition through future internal narration. This method consists of decisions being made on a future course of action, and in the narration, we see them being carried out in another account of

---

13   B. Gray, *The Phenomenon of Literature* (The Hague: Mouton, 1975), Chapter V.

what form this took. For example, the narrator at the beginning of the story tells us that there was a drought and all the animals decided to dig a well. When *Njobvu* directs the meeting, he says the same thing in direct speech. Consequently, we see and hear the animals carrying out the decision practically. This method also applies to instructions given to be executed. For example, *Njobvu* finally instructs the detectives to apply itching beans and capture the culprit when *Kalulu* divests himself of his skin. Again, we see the accomplishment of the directive in a detailed manner in the narration. It involves being told what is going to happen, then seeing it happen, and finally the developments from there on. As we can see, the verbal and structural devices are very important when discussing the unifying factors, modifying situations, or the development of the story from the initial situation to the final resolution.

Even the aspect of time is a significant element in the structure of the story. Certain things can only happen on certain days in the story. If an episode were changed from, say, the fifth day of the second section to the third or fourth, the whole story would have tremendous structural faults. The narrator himself emphasises this time-action-space aspect. We mention this because there are one or two instances when the narrator was confused about the days, but smoothly corrected his error without breaking the action-space relationships. Initially, there is a vague reference to time—a period of drought, a meeting held. But as soon as the decision to dig a well is taken unanimously, time begins to be important. The narrator specifies: first day, beginning of work; on the second day, the well is now fifty feet deep; on the third day, water is found one hundred feet down, but they decide to dig another sixty feet of water alone. *Kalulu* is informed that water has been found. Up to this time we might say the narrator has been setting the stage for certain actions to be performed.

The two parts of the story are so interrelated that the sequence of actions in the second could not happen without the first. The trap is then set and there is a break in the time sequence. The narrator talks about *tsiku lina* ("one day"). *Kalulu* makes a visit to the well. This marks the beginning of another set of days, and therefore sequence of events. In this part the narrator had difficulties in keeping track of the days but was still faithful to action-place, even though events were happening simultaneously in two or three, if not more, different places. For example: *Fisi* eating chicken

120

in the bush, *Kalulu* and family drawing water, people meeting *Kalulu*'s wife with a load on her head, and the children revealing to their mates that their father had drawn water. Narration of all these events made the narrator skip two days from the fourth to the sixth, but by the time he had explained he had recovered the two days, and confidently resolved the plot on the sixth day.

The first part of the story has a work song accompanying the labour. Earlier in this discussion we mentioned the fact that this song is a form of repetition because it is repeated five times. But here we can comment on the fact that it is also functioning as a structural device of serious repetition. The content of the song is repeating what the body of the narrative has already informed the listeners of, and also mentioned the purpose of digging the well: there was a drought, and this was the only way to survive. It is also a clever musical device for describing work-in-progress without boring but rather involving the audience.

Mention was also made of the fact that *Kalulu's kanyama kosendasenda* is playing the role of singing. Without stretching the point too far, so could the initial dialogue parts of the interchange between *Kalulu* and *Fisi*: "*Odi!*," "*Eee!*" etc., where the narrator adopted a chanting tone before the main dialogue ensued. So we might talk about "song equivalents" here.

The point is that the song and song equivalents are also marking the passage of time (days) and the enactment of certain episodes. Therefore, they are significant structural devices consolidating the other repetitions discussed above.

The Trickster and the Society

The first thing that strikes the reader/listener about the story is the fact that the story involves animal characters. On one level this is unreal, and, we might say, makes the story uninterpretable. To refer to Gray again:

> The point or meaning or theme of a work is understood when the event presented is recognised as being analogous to an aspect of human behaviour. This does not mean that the characters depicted have to be human, or even creatural. The particular kind of human behaviour to which the event is analogous is what provides the

> controlling idea, the organising principle, the theme of work ...
> When the reader or listener discerns the particular kind of human
> behaviour to which the fictional event is analogous, then he has
> interpreted the work.[14]

Which gives us a starting point. Even though the characters are animals, we seem to be familiar with their behaviour, actions, values, or situation. There are only a few instances in the story where animal nature is depicted as such, e.g. reference to hares eating vegetable matter, hyenas eating animal hide and certain animals digging the well with their hooves. Apart from these examples of animals behaving as animals, the rest of the story consists of animals behaving like humans. There are actual examples of the animals being referred to as persons.

In times of crisis like war, pestilence, drought, people meet together to deliberate and decide on a certain course of action. In this story, we have the animals meeting in a time of drought and deciding to dig a well. The whole community is involved in the actual labour, except of course the nonconformist trickster. Here we might note the structure of the society. *Njobvu*, the elephant, is the chief, and calls for the meeting. *Mkango*, the lion, is appointed leader of the work gang, or supervisor. Other divisions of labour could be cited where characters are appointed to specific tasks; for example, *Gwape* (antelope) was employed as food gatherer, and *Fisi* (hyena) as watchman at the well. As we can see, this structure is analogous with human society.

We also note with interest recreation, such as playing *msikwa*, or exercises being performed during convalescence. Punishment inflicted upon wrong-doers takes the form of whipping, application of itching beans on the body, and imprisonment.

The smallest unit in human society is the family. *Kalulu* has a family of five. Mrs. *Kalulu* takes care of the domestic side of life, such as drawing water from the well, and going to the grain mill. The family, like the rest of the animals, lives in a house. Material possessions include mats and buckets. The *Kalulu* family even has a flower garden needing constant watering.

---

[14] B. Gray, *The Phenomenon of Literature*, Chapter V.

Apart from these facts, we have the animals using water for drinking, washing and cooking. The types of food are also interesting: roast chicken and goat's meat, cakes, sausages fried with onions and tomatoes. The food is arranged in ascending order of attractiveness. This is to say the types of food selected for the story have great appeal for human appetites.

Perhaps the most important single aspect which informs the reader/listener that the story is not about animals is the use of speech for communication. The animals carry out discourse in normal, everyday language situations. We have already given instances of this. Here we might narrow down the examples to, say, forms of address. *Kalulu* and *Fisi* refer to each other as close friends *aisee, mphwanga, mwana*. When one is addressing the chief, *amfumu* and *bwana* are used as terms of respect.

We could give other examples of this kind of behaviour. Acts such as feigning sickness to be let off work, going to visit a friend across the river, or going behind a bush to answer a call of nature, sending the youngest member of the family to deliver messages early in the morning, work song and roll call at labour camps gives a very strong impression that this is a human world that the narrator has created.

This point also makes us work on the characterisation by human types: *Njobvu*—chiefly type; *Kalulu*—rogue type; *Gwape*—messenger type; *Mkango*—leader type; *Fisi*—stupid or greedy type. These characters are, of course, treated minimally in the text itself, but presented as life-like in the actual performance. This is the level at which delineation of character comes out most realistically, that is, when the narrator acts and lives the characters he is recounting.

These characters are not operating in a fantasy, animal world either. They have homes to go to after work, mats to sleep on, a well to draw water from. The time is a period of drought, therefore hot and dry. These animals lived on the slopes of a mountain like Mulanje, where they were worst hit by the drought, especially as the rivers had dried up. Their decision to dig a well in a *dambo* was reasonable. This is where one would expect to find water nearer the surface. We see the characters moving from their homes to their place of work in the *dambo* and back. With minimum physical description, a complete and recognisable world created for us in which certain events are taking place in space and time.

The devices for creating this microcosm have already been examined, so have the patterns of life. If these are recognisable to the audience it stands to reason that the narrator is recreating a world he knows, in this case his own and the audience's, and along with it the patterns of life, beliefs, customs, aesthetics of the society.

> In the tales of a people ... those incidents of everyday life that are of importance to them will appear either incidentally or as the basis of a plot. Most of the references to the mode of life of the people will be an accurate reflection of their habits. The development of the plot of the story, furthermore, will, on the whole, exhibit clearly what is considered right and what wrong.[15]

If we take the folk story as the "autobiography of the tribe" then a close study of the people's culture, beliefs and customs will emerge with startling clarity to enable us to form valid conclusions on what cultural imperatives dynamise that society.

The story we are analyzing gives us a profound insight into not only how the society is structured, but also the ties that govern it. Furthermore, we can see what interpersonal relationships or reciprocal behaviour exists between individuals, and what binds them to the society as a whole. In times of crises the society acts together as an organic whole. Yet the expected responses do not come from every individual. There are some members of the society who do not conform to the standards of behaviour expected of them.

It is interesting to observe closely the manner in which the trickster is outwitted and how the trickster type is depicted in the story.

We can telescope the events in any way we feel fit. If we want to be strict adherents of realism and work within the bounds of what can be achieved in a certain period of time, we will see the deep well could not have been dug in four days with hooves or paws. In this way, a day may represent a week, or a month, or even a year. Here we are going to take the narrator's word and state as recorded the fact that the story takes us through events

---

[15] F. Boas, quoted by J. Melville and Frances S. Herskovits, *Dahomean Narrative: A Cross-Cultural Analysis* (Evanston: Northwestern University Press, 1958), p. 70.

that happened between ten and fourteen days. Each day *Kalulu* produces a new trick to keep out of the contractual obligations imposed by customary institutions on the individual. This in itself creates suspense in the mind of the listener: Is he going to be caught, and how is this going to come about? And if not, why not? What is interesting, here, of course, is why the narrator makes *Kalulu* elude the forces of good for so long, and so cleverly too. All the time the narrator focusses attention on *Kalulu's* tricks and intelligent manoeuvres so that the listener identifies with the outlaw, and not the other characters or the society as such.

This obviously means that the society lays emphasis on, or admires and respects, intelligence and wit in the individual, such that he comes to terms with his situation, or for survival in general, i.e. this is the "basic paradox of folklore," in that

> friendship and contractual relationships are prominently displayed as cultural ideal norms but at the same time the narrator and audience can identify with the trickster who blatantly ignores these norms.[16]

This is one reason why the trickster is even allowed to escape punishment at the end of some variants of this story, i.e.,

> the fact that contracts are violated means that the folktale structure provides an outlet for protest against the binding nature of interpersonal obligations of the kind imposed by formal or quasi-formal institutional friendship pacts.[17]

On the other hand, we have also the fact that the institutions are too weak to bind him, and *Kalulu*, being what he is, can turn the situation to his own advantage.

---

[16] Alan Dundes, "The Making and Breaking of Friendship as a Structural Frame in African Folk Tales," in Pierre Maranda and Ellie Kongas Maranda, eds., *Structural Analysis of Oral Tradition* (Philadelphia: University of Pennsylvania Press, 1971), p. 180.

[17] Dundes, "The Making and Breaking of Friendship," p. 180.

There is clearly a certain amount of greed, exploitation and corruption in the story. *Kalulu* exploits *Fisi*'s greed and stupidity, bribing him six different times before he is brought to justice.

However, this variant ends badly for the protagonist: *Kalulu* is tortured and put into prison. (Incidentally, he is not killed, which implies that the trickster-hero must live on to perform other remarkable tricks on the society.) Therefore, another way of looking at it would be that the renegade or outlaw may succeed for a time, but the forces of good, or the institutions built to protect the society from such types, will always win in the end.

PART THREE

APPLICATION: FOLKSONGS, RITUAL, AND DANCE

CHAPTER FIVE:
LORE, LIFE AND RITUAL

In "The Hare and the Well," analogies were made between the animal world and human society: the animal activities duplicated human behaviour and the animal roles corresponded to the organisation of human society. In the discussion below, the correspondences drawn work in reverse: human behaviour seems to parallel the animal behaviour of "The Hare and the Well" with such closeness as to tempt such an analysis. The discussion focusses on the motifs of drought, attempts to find water, the location, guarding of the well, payment for drawing water, kinds of duplicity and modes of punishment. The underlying argument centers on the following quotation:

> at some early stage weather rites, initiation ceremonies and *nyau* constituted one magico-religious complex, which at a later stage separated into rain shrines on the one hand and *nyau* and initiation rites on the other.[1]

In other words, the discussion is on human behaviour during very critical stages of life: drought and rain-making; *rites de passage* (especially growth and death) and the role of *nyau* animal and human masks and structures in the later activity.

Drought and Rainmaking

In "The Hare and the Well," the critical situation is a drought. All the animals meet to decide on a course of action: digging a well on a *dambo*, low-lying marshy ground. The animals meet and dig a well to the accompaniment of a song. Water is found to the general satisfaction and joy of everyone. It is not difficult to find correspondences in human society: a drought always calls for a rainmaking ceremony, involving not

---

[1] N.E. Lindgren and J.M. Schoffeleers, *Rock Art and Nyau Symbolism in Malawi* (Malawi Government: Department of Antiquities Publication No. 18, 1978), p. 46.

only the rain priests but also the chiefs, the headman and the elders of the community.[2] They all process to the rain shrine, pray, sing and dance for rain. One rain song will suffice here:

Ku Msinja kanjerenjere adauma	At Msinja the maize has dried
Mvula kolole, Mvula kolole!	Rain wash away! Rain wash away!
Tikaone madzi minjira.	We shall see water on the way
Ndi aka! Ndi ako!	This little one! That little one!
Kadza mvula nkoti kamtambo	From which cloud will the rain come?
Ku Msinja kanjerenjere adauma	At Msinja the maize has dried
Mvula kolole, Mvula kolole!	Rain, wash away! Rain, wash away!
Patseni madzi, kumtima kwauma	Give me water, the heart is dry
Ndi aka! Ndi ako!	This little one! That little one!
Tiyeni tithawe! Tithawe! Tithawe!	Let's run! Let's run! Let's run![3]

The song mentions Msinja, the central Chewa rain shrine, where the maize, the staple food has dried in the drought. The suppliants pray for rain to drench the earth and their throats. As they run away from the shrine, it is with the firm belief that the hoped-for rain will fall before they get back home. Indeed, the rain clouds have already started forming.

It is interesting that the Msinja rain song is thematically similar to the work song of the animals in "The Hare and the Well."

---

[2] Important works on Malawi rain cults include W.H.J. Rangeley, "Two Nyasaland Rain Shrines," *The Nyasaland Journal*, 5, 2 (July 1952), pp. 31-50; W.H.J. Rangeley, "Mbona The Rainmaker," *The Nyasaland Journal*, 6, 1 (January 1953), pp. 8-27; and J.M. Schoffeleers, *M'bona the Guardian Spirit of the Mang'anja* (B. Litt. Thesis, Oxford University, 1966). The author is summarising from these works.

[3] J.M. Schoffeleers, *Symbolic and Social Aspects of Spirit Worship among the Mang'anja* (Ph.D. Thesis, Oxford University, 1968), pp. 228-229, as modified in S. Chimombo, *The Rainmaker* (Limbe: Popular Publications, 1978).

Tiponde madzi, pali lowe	Let's stamp water, it's damp
Tiponde madzi, pali lowe	Let's stamp water, it's damp
Tikuzunzika, pali lowe	We're tortured, it's damp
Tiponde madzi, pali lowe	Let's stamp water, it's damp
Kudadza dzuwa, pali lowe	The sun came, it's damp
Tiponde madzi, pali lowe	Let's stamp water, it's damp
Tiponde madzi, pali lowe	Let's stamp water, it's damp

The animals' work song centers on stamping or digging deep into the earth. However dry the ground is, the wish is that the earth is already getting damp, i.e. they are getting nearer to the water. In other words, regardless of the reality, it is the desired outcome that is envisioned as already coming to pass.

Both the animals' work song and the Msinja rain song are reflections of Chewa-Mang'anja-Nyanja history, which is punctuated by periodic droughts and famine.[4] In fact, historical time is also marked by famine, the last and worst being the one in 1949. It is not surprising, then, that the people's religion is closely tied to rain shrines, rain priests and rain calling. Nor is it surprising that the origins of the *nyau* secret society in one version, are traced back to a time of great famine.

> ... there was a great famine in the country and many people were going a long way to look for food. Nyanda [the founder] never ceased dancing, and people gave him food and he was not troubled with the famine. If Nyanda danced with three or four other people, they were given enough food to last them for several days ... Other men saw that Nyanda never lacked food and began to go with him at his dancing so that they might receive a share of the food ... and so all the young men began to learn the dances ... when the people saw that the famine had greatly increased, all those people who had no food went to dance with the *nyau*. Some of the young dancers, when they collected the food that was given to them, called the old

---

[4]   J.M. Schoffeleers and I. Linden, "The Resistance of the Nyau Societies to the Roman Catholic Mission in Colonial Malawi." I am using the original collected papers, p. 254; however, the article also appears in T.O. Ranger and I. Kimambo, eds., *The Historical Study of African Religions* (London: Heinemann, 1972), pp. 252-273.

men who had no food and so the old men also learned to dance *nyau*.[5]

Nyanda, the founder of *nyau* society, like *Kalulu* the hare in the folk story, used his special skills to survive the famine.

As in the folk story, the society paid or sustained him in food (maize, chicken, goat). This mode of survival was so successful that others joined him. In the folk story, however, the hare is punished in the end, whereas Nyanda is not only rewarded, with a large following, he ends up being installed the chief and he dies as one. This last aspect is the focus of the next section where *nyau* features greatly in funeral ceremonies.

Funerals

Droughts and famine bring about many deaths. It is hardly surprising, then, that originally, where there was a rain shrine, there was also a *nyau* society. *Nyau*, however, developed into a secret society for men performing at funerals for members only. How it first got associated with funerals is given in the same story above.

> Long long ago, *nyau* was never danced at funerals … When Nyanda died the people said, "We cannot stop dancing the dance of *nyau* at the funeral of Nyanda. We should go on dancing because the inventor liked these dances." And so, from that time, they started dancing *nyau* at funerals.[6]

The same story states that the members practised in the bush away from the non-initiates, women and the village. The dances were of two kinds: nocturnal and diurnal.

It is tempting to draw more parallels between "The Hare and the Well" and the *nyau* society. The well was dug on a *dambo*; the *nyau* society's meeting place is also called *dambo*, or more popularly *dambwe* or

---

5   W.H.J. Rangeley, "'Nyau' in Kotakota District," *The Nyasaland Journal*, 2, 2 (July 1949), pp. 36-37.

6   Rangeley, "'Nyau' in Kotakota District," p. 37.

kumadzi, at or near the water.[7] Like the animals' well the *dambwe* too is the most closely guarded place: non-members and strangers "would be severely manhandled, and long ago even killed."[8] Nowadays heavy fines are levied. Certain rituals similar to the hare's approach to the well are also strictly adhered to. The escort of a person to be initiated brings with him the fee, a chicken and the neophyte:

> Arrived at the *dambwe*, the *phungu* calls out, and the people of the *dambwe* tell him to enter with the initiate. Immediately the *phungu* and the initiate have entered the dambwe, the members of the *nyau* fall upon the *phungu* and beat him with sticks.[9]

In the folk story, the hare always brings a fee with him in the form of honey or some other attractive food, to be allowed entrance to and use of the well. He also earns a severe beating for himself in the end.

A motif worth exploring in some detail is the detachable skin. In "The Hare and the Well," the hare removes his skin several times to scare the guard away from the well. There are several ways of looking at this act. The *nyau* society uses masks and grass or leaf structures to hide their identities. One observation is that both the masks and structures "may be combined with measures to terrify or frighten people."[10] Some members chase anyone on sight whether or not initiated. Furthermore, some of the human figures come out naked (i.e. after detaching their external covering), with only the "red earth" covering their bodies (i.e. like the bloodied and skinless hare after he had divested himself of his skin). At each skinless appearance the guard and other witnesses believe the hare to be a spirit or a zombie. In this case the *nyau* in their animal structures are not only *zirombo* (beasts or animals) they are *mizimu* (spirits of the dead).

A related motif is the final punishment of being thrown on a heap of ashes (in one version) or bunch of grass (in another). Significantly the *nyau*

---

7   Rangeley, "'Nyau' in Kotakota District," p. 40.

8   Rangeley, "'Nyau' in Kotakota District," p. 40.

9   Rangeley, "'Nyau' in Kotakota District," pp. 40-41.

10   Rangeley, "'Nyau' in Kotakota District," p. 42. See also Part 2, p. 28, for the "red earth," cited fully in footnote 18 below.

animal structures, which are made of perishable materials like grass, leaves, etc., are never stored, but "burned in a hole dug in the ground, and the ashes are hidden or buried in this hole, or are thrown in a pool or stream."[11]

If the motifs discussed so far for resemblances are too farfetched to be acceptable, what cannot be dismissed is the fact that *nyau* uses the major animals found in "The Hare and the Well" for its masks and structures. Significantly there are two types of *dambwe*.

> The senior *dambwe* is *dambwe la Njobvu* (*dambwe* of the elephant), also known as *dambwe lalikulu* (the great *dambwe*) and at this *dambwe* only *Njobvu* (the elephant) and *Ajere* or *Abwenzi* (the hunters) are made.[12]

In other words, the senior *dambwe* itself is named after the chief of the animals in the folk story. Similarly, all the other animals are represented in their own masks or structures of *mkango* the lion, *kalisenjere* the leopard, *gandali* the giraffe, etc. As argued earlier, human beings here are playing at being *zirombo* animals in theory and practice. There is no pretence that they are doing anything else as they come to the dancing arena in the village starting with *Kalulu mtengo wa bwalo*, the hare mask.[13]

> *Nyau* is normally carried on for five days and on the sixth day ... *Njobvu* and *Ajere* appear, but not before. They comprise the climax of the *nyau* [14]

The rest of the animals come in between. One observer provides a fascinating account of the mingling between man and animal:

> The Great Spirit of Men sends a message to the Great Spirit of the Forests in his domains. He tells him that men are dancing every night by the light of the moon, that the earth is rejoicing, and that merriment and drunkenness reign supreme. He adds that he wants

---

11   Rangeley, "'Nyau' in Kotakota District," p. 43.

12   Rangeley, "'Nyau' in Kotakota District," p. 43.

13   Joseph Kuthemba Mwale, interviews by the author, 1976.

14   Rangeley, "'Nyau' in Kotakota District," p. 43.

a truce of a few days with his enemy. Men will lay down their arms, and the animals must pull in their horns and take off their claws. He invites the visitors from the forest to mix with men, and to drink and dance with them to the sound of the drum and by the light of the nocturnal luminary. The spirits of the Forests accept the invitation, and for the duration of the feasts he sends every day a few of his subjects.[15]

The same observer noted that there were three stages in the *nyau* performances: unmasked dancers, masked dancers and animal structures in the five- or six-day truce between man and animal.

What are these humans-as-animals playing at? Although the correspond-dences so far have been drawn between *nyau* and "The Hare and the Well," it is far back to the beginning of time that we have to go to find an explanation.

In the creation myth centering round Kaphiri-Ntiwa, man, animal and spirit (god) lived together in harmony. But man invented fire and drove spirit and animal from him. God (*Chiuta*) fled to the skies, the animal into the forest. Man seeks reunion with the godhead and animal. A perpetual harmony of all three is only possible in the sacred groves, e.g. *Msinja* or *Nkhulubvi*, although no one lives there permanently. However, there can be temporary reconciliation, and this is where *nyau* is significant:

> Temporary reconciliation is symbolically enacted in the *nyau* where masks and structures represent spirits and animals coming from the bush to the village to associate with men ... But the reconciliation is only temporary, because when the performance is finished, the animal structures are burned, and man symbolically repeats what happened at the time of the cataclysm. The *nyau* are thus to be seen as a mystery play which relates the story of the beginning of the world. But it is also a cosmic ritual ... It lifts basic everyday human experiences on to a higher plane, where it can exercise its cathartic function.[16]

---

[15]   E. Foa, quoted by Schoffeleers, *Symbolic and Social Aspects*, p. 313.

[16]   Schoffeleers, *Symbolic and Social Aspects*, pp. 413, 415.

The significance is in the thematic patterns revealed in the above quotation, the idea of enactment, the representational aspect of the masks and structures, the implicit conflict which is essential to drama, the form this performance takes, i.e. the appearance at the beginning and the disappearance at the end of the masks and structures. Here is drama, if not tragedy, exercising its cathartic function in the performance.

The *nyau* are known as *gule wamkulu* (the great, or big, dance). Throughout this section, the author has advisedly been talking about the *appearance* of the human and animal characters. True, it is a dance, executed in the most spectacular fashion, accompanied by singing and drumming. However, as Rangeley states: "Although the term 'dance' is used, these *gule* are really mimes or small plays."[17] But this would be looking at the parts or acts only, and not the whole. The pattern, although made up of small units, constitutes one indivisible whole: a dramatic performance.

There is a specific sequence in the appearance of the characters. This does not mean it is a carnival procession of humans, masked or unmasked, and animal structures. The characters are seriously acting the parts of different persons and animals. The dance involves acting the parts and not merely displaying the artefacts. A baboon mask imitates the action of a baboon. The human masks imitate people, including other ethnic groups. We might briefly describe the conflict between two characters in an episode to conclude this section. Rangeley describes the act of *Njobvu* (Elephant) and *Ajere* or *Abwenzi* (Hunter) in the following way:

> When approaching the *bwalo*, the *Ajere* call out "Bwenz, bwenz, bwenz" following *Njobvu*. At the *bwalo*, they act in pantomime the stalking, approach and hamstringing of *Njobvu* in the same way as the old-time hunters used to hunt elephants. When they attack *Njobvu*, they shout, "*Ndiyanga, ndiyanga, nyamazo, nyamazo*" (It is mine, it is mine, that animal, that animal). *[sic]*[18]

---

17   Rangeley, "'Nyau' in Kotakota District," p. 45. See also Part 2, cited in footnote below.

18   W.H.J. Rangeley, "'Nyau' in Kotakota District, Part 2," *The Nyasaland Journal*, 3, 2 (July 1950), p. 21.

These two characters always conclude the ceremony: man and animal symbolising the restoration of the original harmony that existed between the two before the cataclysm.

Social Control

The trickster figure is usually created by the society to dramatise or expose those areas of stress, strain or conflict which, in spite of its elaborate rules, values, checks and balances, it cannot somehow cover. It is in these gaps that the trickster figure emerges. The *nyau* society, in spite of the religious significance attached to it, also performs the role of the trickster figure to expose society in all its pettiness and weakness.

> The *Nyau* or *Zinyau* functions both as an instrument of social control and as an expression of reverence for and communication with the ancestors ... In the *Nyau*, social characteristics that are undesirable in Maravi society are personified and ridiculed with derisive and often earthy songs which accompany the dancers.[19]

The dramatisation of undesirable social characteristics is left to the *Kapoli*, the human masks or characters.[20]

Nailed, for example, is a *Kapoli* who depicts females in different roles: taking care of the home or children, for example. He is also their mouth piece in laughing at sterile husbands, as this song reveals:

Eeh amuna wanga	Eeh my husband
Gulani wailesi	Buy a wireless [radio]
Ndiyese mwana	So I can pretend it is a child
M'kacoka[21]	When you are away

Some figures depict certain human characteristics through the mask, the act or the songs sung by or to them. *Mfiti's* (witch's) mask depicts an ugly

---

[19]   Barbara Blackmun and Matthew Schoffeleers, "Masks of Malawi," *African Arts*, V, 4 (1972), pp. 36, 41.

[20]   The section on the *Kapoli*, their songs and routines, is a summary of interviews with Kuthemba Mwale.

[21]   Kuthemba Mwale, interviews.

or evil-looking person; *Kabvinasabwe* represents the poor, shabby, or by name, the "lousy." Other masks satirise ethnic groups. *Simoni Petulo* (Simon Peter), *Maliya* (Mary) and *Mzungu* (Whiteman), for example, satirise the white man and his religion. Below are a few examples of different figures.

Mwam'na wa Chilonda depicts the lame, crippled or deformed. The mask sings that these unfortunate people should not be laughed at or despised for one might have children similarly afflicted. In the first song below the *Kapoli* takes the role of a woman refusing to respond to one of these unfortunates:

Mwam'na wa chilonda	The man covered with sores
Toto kundiitana	Don't call me
Undiitanira chiani?[22]	Why do you call me?

In the second song, the mask takes the part of one of the unfortunates who, in this case, is attracted by the woman he is beckoning to:

Leka kundipenya	Don't look at me
Mtima uli paiwe	My heart is on you
Paiwe toto paiwe	Is on you, no, is on you
Leka kundipenya	Don't look at me
Mtima uli pa iwe[23]	My heart is on you

Another *Kapoli* sings of the deceased murdered by his relations, who pretend that it was a natural death:

Mwangupha dala	You have just killed deliberately
Kuti m'ziti n'Chauta	So you can say it is God
Eeh Chauta tsoka[24]	Eeh God, misfortune

The mask unmasks the truth of the situation by exposing the culprits.

---

[22] Kuthemba Mwale, interviews.

[23] Kuthemba Mwale, interviews.

[24] Kuthemba Mwale, interviews.

Themes taken up by the masks are those described above, as well as ones related to male/female relationships, responsibilities or lack of them. Some masks give *mwambo* instructions on daily and married life.

The role of *nyau* in social control needs to be extended to touch upon mother-in-law relationships, ethnocentrism and resistance to Christianisation. These are the focus of the rest of the discussion.

One way of viewing the origins of *nyau* is to see it as a *male* secret organisation created as an escape mechanism in a strictly matrilocal society.

> In such a system the husband remains essentially a stranger in the family of his wife. He has no authority over his children, but he is often held responsible for the sickness or death of his wife or children. His movements are no longer free. He is unable to improve his situation: i.e. to build a nice house or to acquire a rich plantation. The other people in the village would be jealous. At any moment he might be asked to return to his own village and abandon his wife and children; this is almost certain to happen at the death of his wife. Under such conditions his affection, his interest, his allegiance all tend toward his own relatives, his brothers and sisters and the children of his sisters, it will be these children whom he must defend and support because of his position as their tutor. But in his wife's village he remains simply the "mkamwini," the "munthu wa ganyu," a male whose sole duty is to work and provide children for the benefit of a family group to which he can never really belong.[25]

In such a society, husbands who are placed in the same unenviable position tend to draw closer and closer to each other for mutual support. That the system is fraught with antagonisms is illustrated by the fact that one of the first acts of an initiate is to steal his mother-in-law's chickens for the *dambwe*.[26]

---

[25] Salaun, "Initation to Malawi."

[26] Schoffeleers and Linden, "The Resistance of the Nyau Societies," p. 258.

The men in the *dambwe*, however, did not enjoy their autonomy for long. Women encroached into the *dambwe* and started making their own masks after those of the men.

> The members of *nyau*, if they know of this, and hear the *unamwali* drums beating, take their images away from their *dambwe* and hide them. But the *anamkungwi* know they are likely to do this, and so they hide near the *nyau dambwe* while the *nyau* is dancing at the village. When the *nyau* return to the *dambwe*, the *anamkungwi* are hidden watching and see where the *vinyau* are taken and hidden. When the men have hidden the *vinyau* and gone off, the *anamkungwi* come out and inspect them.[27]

With the passage of time it was no longer necessary to hide, women were admitted as members. The *nyau* too were invited to attend girls' initiation ceremonies to instruct or chastise the candidates. In fact, *nyau* became closely associated with boys' and girls' initiation ceremonies. Whenever there was a funeral or a commemoration of the dead, there would automatically be an initiation ceremony.

During the colonial times as more schools were opened by Christian missionaries it became a matter of competition who would get more candidates: the school or the *dambwe*. The more schools were opened the more open nyau became to younger and younger members of the society:

> But *nyau* has in the most degenerate areas become a boys' initiation ceremony within the last 60 years, and in some areas attempts are made to force every possible boy into membership. There is little doubt that this is a counterblast to the efforts of the missionaries, because the missionaries frown not only on *nyau* itself but on many of the traditional tribal practices of the aCewa.[28]

Earlier than the Christian missionaries, the *nyau* was the form of resistance to the fight for political supremacy between the rain shrines and *nyau*

---

[27] Rangeley, "'Nyau' in Kotakota District," p. 44.

[28] Rangeley, "'Nyau' in Kotakota District," pp. 48-49.

dancers, i.e. the original Phiri and Banda clans.[29] The *nyau* then was used later in the Ngoni/Chewa struggles for autonomy. The Christian missionaries joined in the foray in some areas to side with the Ngoni.

> ... the balance of power between the Ngoni, the Chewa, and the missionaries was so delicate and complex that the *Nyau* societies were able to survive through the colonial period and not only to survive but to articulate and defend Chewa identity.[30]

In the folk stories considered here, the trickster is never killed or completely eliminated. The *nyau* society managed to survive drought and famine, Phiri/Banda strife, Ngoni/Chewa struggles, and *nyau*/Christian battles to emerge into the post-independence period of the country. Like all trickster figures, however, they are not conducive to political control.

> ... the *Nyau* are not in modern terms politically minded or politically usable on any scale larger than the village or locality ... In the 1920s the Chewa chiefs were unable to exert their authority over *Nyau* to bring about reforms; the missionaries were unable to crush them in many districts; and pressure from the government today would certainly be counterproductive.[31]

---

[29] I. Linden, "Chewa Initiation Rites and Nyau Societies: The Use of Religious Institutions in Local Politics at Mua," in T.O. Ranger and J. Weller, eds., *Christian History of Central Africa* (London: Heinemann, 1975), p. 32.

[30] Linden, "Chewa Initiation Rites," p. 33.

[31] Linden, "Chewa Initiation Rites," p. 38.

CHAPTER SIX:
FOLK, FLORA AND FAUNA

The role of animals in folk stories has been extensively discussed. The trickster and the dupe are the most popular examples. In Malawian folklore, *Kalulu* the hare, as the trickster figure, has *Fisi* the hyena as his dupe. The other animals, in turn, play their supporting roles as dupes or other types: *Njobvu*, the elephant; *Mkango*, the lion; *Mvuu*, the hippo; *Nyalugwe*, the leopard, etc.[1] The use of animal figures and structures in initiation ceremonies has also received great attention.[2] Very little exploration, however, has been made on the relationship between folksongs and flora and fauna.[3] Yet flora and fauna play integral and symbolic roles in folksongs, especially those sung at critical times in the people's lives and history. This chapter is a preliminary excursion into the role of flora and fauna as depicted in the folksongs of the Chewa-Nyanja-Mang'anja-speaking peoples. The songs selected are those dealing with times of drought, funerals, initiation ceremonies and recreation. The underlying assumption is that there is indeed a relationship between man and his environment. In this assumption it is interesting to note such correspondences between the important animal figures remarked above and human activities and social organisation.

---

[1]   Some of the local examples are given in Steve Chimombo, "The Trickster and the Media," *Baraza*, 2 (June 1984), pp. 3-21, and Steve Chimombo, "The Dupe in a Modern Context," *Baraza*, 3 (April 1986), pp. 48-67.

[2]   Among the Chewa, there are several, the most important being Rangeley and Schoffeleers, cited fully in footnote 4 below. Makumbi's *Maliro ndi Miyambo ya Achewa* also deserves mention here. Among the Yao, Sanderson and Stannus are central. They are cited fully in Chapter Two, footnotes 10 and 13.

[3]   The statement refers to the absence of actual studies establishing that kind of relationship, not to collections, without comment, of songs connected with flora and fauna.

Famine

The religion of the Bantu-speaking peoples of southern Africa is intimately tied to rain shrines, rain priests or rain-callers. There are two important territorial rain shrines, of the Chewa at Msinja and of the Mang'anja at Nsanje.[4] Other small local shrines are found at or near hilltops like Michiru, for example. In times of drought and famine, all the important members of the community are involved: chiefs, headmen, and shrine functionaries, singing, dancing, drumming, etc., in procession to the shrine. All these: shrine priests, chiefs, functionaries, hold the strong belief that climatic conditions can be manipulated, following the proper rituals.

The rain songs and prayers themselves dwell on the drought, the people's plight, begging for forgiveness, if they have transgressed, and the hopes, if not demands, for rain to fall. The Msinja song quoted in the last chapter illustrates some of these themes.[5] The song appropriately mentions Msinja, the central Chewa rain shrine where the maize, the staple food, has dried in the drought. The people pray for rain to drench the earth and quench the dry throats. The suppliants leave the shrine running, so that the hoped-for rain does not drown them. The rain clouds, in the song, are already forming, hence the firm belief that they will meet the rain on their way back home.

At another level of interpretation, it is not only the maize which dried up, but all natural productivity. Sterility has also set in and all the world needs are the regenerative waters to bring back fecundity. The fact that it is the heart (and not the throat as in popular parlance) that has dried up makes it a very powerful figure of speech. The heart, as the centre of life, spells the death of mankind when it dries up.

The *Chisumphi* rain song below includes the priest officiating the ceremony:

---

[4] Central works used for this section are Rangeley, "Two Nyasaland Rain Shrines" and "Mbona The Rainmaker"; and Schoffeleers, *M'bona the Guardian Spirit of the Mang'anja*.

[5] See Chapter Five, footnote 3.

Wabwera Chisumphi	Chisumphi has come
Chiuta wamtaya	*Chiuta* let him loose
Bwerekeni khasu	Lend me a hoe
Chiuta wamtaya	*Chiuta* let him loose
N'khumbe nkhonde	To dig around the hut
Chiuta wamtaya	*Chiuta* let him loose
Madzi angalowe	Lest water flood in
Chiuta wamtaya[6]	*Chiuta* let him loose.

Chiuta Wamtaya (let him loose) is ambiguous. At the literal level it could be as the translation is: *Chiuta* (God) has freed or unchained *Chisumphi* the rain priest. It could also be that God has abandoned *Chisumphi*, hence the drought and the necessity for praying for rain. The third possibility is for *wamtaya* to be *wantaya* i.e. *wanditaya*, i.e. *Chiuta* has abandoned me the supplicant. Whichever meaning is taken, there is all hope that, now that *Chisumphi* is here, rain will come; hence, protective measures should be taken by digging around the shrine (a hut) to prevent the downpour from flooding it. The hut is a phallic symbol, with the digging of the surrounding area having symbolic significance too.

The third rain song talks about not only the drought condition but a significant tree:

Liwawa dzuwa	The sun is better
La m'nkhadzi.[7]	Under the *nkhadzi* tree

Although the song is short, it has greater significance than the condition it describes. Any sunshine under drought conditions is bound to be pitilessly hot; however, seeking refuge under a *nkhadzi* (euphorbia) tree is equally futile. The *nkhadzi* tree has no leaves to provide shade for the seeker, the sun will still beat directly on the refugee. The greater significance lies in the tree as the one selected to shade and hence provide eternal protection

---

6   Salaun, quoted by Schoffeleers, *M'bona the Guardian Spirit of the Mang'anja*, p. 248, as modified in Chimombo, *The Rainmaker*.

7   Sam Mchombo, "Msinja Tapes." The author is indebted to Dr. Mchombo for making the tapes accessible.

at grave yards. In other words, what does not protect the living is protecting the dead, who will not even feel the heat of the sun.

The song above is thematically similar to the one below:

Nyumba yaku Msinja	The house at Msinja
Ilibe chiundiro[8]	has no verandah/eaves

The house in this sense is again the rain shrine itself at Msinja. In spite of its sacred significance, it is always built without eaves or raised verandah, and hence, in the merciless sun, cannot protect the suppliants.

It is useful to conclude this section with a rain-song:

Mphambe Mphambe	Lightning Lightning Lightning
Mphambe	The fig tree is the home of birds
Kachere ndi mtunda wa	The m*njale*-tree is unclimbable
mbalame	Fireflames never sweep the
Mnjale sukwereka	anthill-top
M'chulu sumapita moto	Leaves of the sacred grove
Masamba akunsitu	Women never roll them into
Akazi sawazinga nkhata	headpads[9]

The interpretation below is more detailed than the original:

> This prayer is interesting on, at least, two accounts. First it does not really sound like a prayer, and, secondly, as a rainprayer-song it does not contain, in an explicit way, anything of relevance to asking for rain. Rain is neither mentioned nor even alluded to, and the connection between what is said and the invocation of rain, if it does exist, must be highly tenuous ... The message in this poem is expressed symbolically. The *mnjale*-tree was commonly found at shrines for rain-prayers. A tall tree without branches except at the very top, apparently, grows on ant-hills. On the other hand ant-hills normally do not have grass growing on them. The grass lies at the

---

[8]   The "Msinja Tapes."

[9]   This is Sam Mchombo's version, found in "Cryptic Meaning in Chichewa Poetry," *Kalulu*, 1, 1 (June 1976), p. 30, selected for reasons given in footnote 10 below.

base so that even when there is a bush fire, the fireflames will not sweep the ant-hill-top. The fire will die out at the base.

These two objects are used in this context as phallic symbols. The *mnjale*-tree always found at shrines acquired the air of a sacred tree, only to be approached on special occasions. In many ways it can be viewed as a phallic symbol. Fire too is commonly regarded as a symbol for lust, so that the two lines comment on men's abstinence from sexual meeting; something equally observed by women, for it is said that 'the leaves of the sacred grove are never rolled into headpads' (These headpads, usually made of grass, are circular with a hole in the middle). The act of placing the headpad on the head is itself highly symbolic of 'family union'. Thus the 'sacred grove', 'the leaves' and 'the headpads' can all be seen to be used symbolically, and the statement made is itself about the women's sexual abstinence ... It seems that this plays a dual role in this context. In the first place it was instituted that before going to pray for rain family activities must stop so that the people could appear in their pure state. The poem is therefore a statement on their purity, a necessary condition for communication with God, who has already been invoked in the first line. On the other hand it is a partial reflection of the situation with a hint at its consequences. The suspension of family activities reflects the suspension of the macrocosmic union between heaven and earth; the discontinuity of the human race implied by the abstinence reflects the consequences of severe drought—destruction and extinction of all God's creation, for the rain is the driving force behind life and fertility. Since God may not like to see His Creation completely destroyed, He may relent and provide the rain, for without it not only will the women never beget any more children, but at the same time the earth will have nobody to care for. This then gives an ironic twist to the line 'the fig tree is the home of birds.' If the earth, which is symbolised by the fig tree can no longer provide for its children, as the fig tree provides for the birds, then the children can no longer claim to have a home.[10]

The rain prayer echoes all the themes of the other songs discussed above. *Mphambe* lightning is the name of the god in rain, whilst *Chisumphi* is also one of the names of god. The fig tree (*Ficus dekdekana*), as the home of birds, echoes the *nkhadzi* tree and the Msinja shrine, which under drought cannot provide the needed protection. The *njala* tree (*Sterculia appendiculata*), as a sacred tree, is related to the *nkhadzi* tree, as special trees performing certain functions where they grow.[11] The rest of the prayer mentions in symbolic language the ritual observances in times of drought to ensure that the conditions for bringing rain are established.

In these examples it is clear that other human behaviour in the micro-cosm, like rain-calling, has got overt and symbolic significance for the macrocosm. Rain-calling starts with the cleansing of the human heart ("give me water, the heart is dry") for the rains in the clouds to be released ("from which cloud is the rain going to fall?").

Funerals, Flora and Fauna

The relationship between man and his environment has never been so intimately demonstrated on the physical and symbolic levels as in the *nyau* society:

> The *nyau* are a society of masked dancers who perform mainly at the closure of funeral rites … and at female initiation ceremonies.[12] *Nyau* was designed without doubt to ensure that the departed spirits ceased to worry the community. *Nyau* was to placate the spirits of the recently departed.[13]

---

[10] Schoffeleers, *Symbolic and Social Aspects*, pp. 225-228. Sam Mchombo's interpretation, in "Cryptic Meaning," pp. 30-31, is used here for the full significance of the prayer to be appreciated.

[11] The Latin names for trees are from Schoffeleers, *Symbolic and Social Aspects*.

[12] Lindgren and Schoffeleers, *Rock Art and Nyau Symbolism in Malawi*, p. 38.

[13] W.H.J. Rangeley, "'Nyau' in Kotakota District," p. 38.

The intimate relationship is seen not only in man imitating animals but also in the exploitation of all the natural resources around him, earth, water, plant, fire and air. A *nyau* performance combines all the human arts and professions: culinary, carving, medicinal, drumming, dancing and singing.

In one of the early accounts of the performers there is an actual invitation for the animals of the forests to come to the village to mingle with mankind for a period of harmony and festivities.[14] The animals come from the bush or the pool (hence the *dambwe*, of the water) to the village and back again to their places of abode. In local parlance, the expressions are *kukasaka nyama*, to hunt for forest animals, and *kusodza nyama* (literally 'to fish'), to hunt for some of the animal structures coming from the pools. The animals are brought to the village *bwalo* or the dancing area as if they were indeed from the forests and the pools: the elephant, the lion, the buffalo, the giraffe, etc.[15] Only a few of the animals are brought to mingle with man at a time for a period of up to six days. The Great Spirit of the Forests sends his subjects, starting with the jackal's *Bwe! Bwe!* announcing on the evening before the actual performance starts that the animals will commence accepting the invitation the following morning. The first day opens with *Kalulu mtengo wa bwalo* (the hare is the leader of the dancing arena).[16]

Not many songs mention the names or even describe the characteristics of the masks or animal structures they represent. The majority depend on the topicality of the themes, leaving the actual physical representations to speak for themselves. The song below is an example:

Kalulu mtengo wa bwalo x2	The hare is the leader of the arena
Bwandende bwandende	*Bwandende bwandende*
Kalulu mtengo wa bwalo [17]	The hare is the leader of the arena

---

14   See Chapter Five, footnote 15.

15   Kuthemba Mwale, interviews.

16   Kuthemba Mwale, interviews.

17   Kuthemba Mwale, interviews.

As will be noticed, apart from mentioning the hare, the animal itself does not feature in the song. What is of interest is its role in the arena not only as the leader but also as the *kalambula bwalo*, i.e. the one who clears the arena so that the rest can dance easily afterwards. It is the first *Kapoli* to appear and dance. Its dance routine resembles the short, swift movements of the animal it represents.

The truce, during which man and animal mingle, dance, drink, feast freely with each other for a week, ends with the real owner of the *dambwe*, *Njobvu* the elephant. The elephant's song below, also only mentions it by name. The song actually describes its inability to negotiate rises, inclines or hills because of its weight.

Njobvu idalema	The elephant got tired
Pokwera mtunda	When climbing the hill
Njobvu idalema[18]	The elephant got tired

The dance routine imitates the elephant's slow, dignified and ponderous steps.

In between the two animals, the hare and the elephant, come all the other masks of men and animals. Two kinds of animals are usually represented: animals hunted for food and animals whose meat is never eaten (e.g. lion or leopard).[19]

Some songs describe aspects of the animals they represent. The *Nthiwatiwa* song is an example:

Nthiwatiwa	The ostrich,
mbalame yakunyanja	the bird of the sea
Idamkonda kuyera, eee,	I loved its whiteness,
nthiwatiwa[20]	yes ostrich

Although strictly speaking the ostrich is neither aquatic nor lives near the sea, that is not the point of the song. It is more its beauty and the way it is

---

18   Kuthemba Mwale, interviews.

19   Blackmun and Schofferleers, "Masks of Malawi," p. 41.

20   Kuthemba Mwale, interviews.

represented physically that the composer of the song and constructor of the ostrich structures were interested in.

Another song describes the *Fikisa* bees and their honey.

Fikisa anamwali eh	*Fikisa* girls, eh
Fikisa anamwali ndi uchi eh	*Fikisa* girls are honey, eh
Fikisa za pa chulu[21]	*Fikisa* from the ant-hill

Fikisa are a kind of bee which build their nest in ant-hills. The honey is just as sweet as, if not sweeter than, that from ordinary bees. The song is ambiguous: it could be telling the girls what *fikisa* are, or it could be stating that the girls are *fikisa* and just as sweet. It is interesting that the song is sung to the *Simoni Petulo* (Simon Peter) and Mzungu (Whiteman) masks. *Simoni Petulo* himself is considered impotent and represents priests in general.[22]

The two songs below deal with the vegetable world:

Kholowa ndi mtambe	Potato leaves are climbers
Nakholowa ndiwo	Potato leaves are relish
Phikani gaga iai lero ae	Cook the maize husk porridge
Taleka ntakuomba nayo	today ae
Waombera kumodzi	Let me shoot you
n'mwana[23]	He has shot together with the child

The characteristics and uses of potato leaves have been described. They are especially delicious when eaten together with *nsima* from maize husk flour. The results are that the eater is energised to lustfulness. Unfortunately, a child got in the way.

The second one is a song about *chewe*, a small wild plant whose leaves have got a sticky consistency similar to okra:

---

[21] Kuthemba Mwale, interviews.

[22] Kuthemba Mwale, interviews.

[23] Kuthemba Mwale, interviews.

Chewe chewe	Chewe chewe
Mwamuna osampatsa chewe	A man should not be given *chewe*
Alin'chake[24]	He has got his own

An obvious point to make in concluding this section is that, although *nyau* is a funeral dance, very few of the songs and dances deal directly with death as such. The occasion for dancing is the mourning while the songs seem to direct attention elsewhere. The content of the songs themselves, the dance, the masks or the animal structures describe the whole universe involving man and his environment.

Initiations

A comparison could be made between the Chewa *nyau* as an initiation ceremony and the Yao *lupanda* and *chiputu* initiation ceremonies for boys and girls respectively. In the Yao ceremonies, direct instruction is given on animals, "their habits, whether they are good to eat, whether they are dangerous, etc., and all the stories about them."[25] During the initiation period the initiates are given animals' and birds' names. For example, at *chiputu*, the girls are given names like *Alitawala*, a kind of rat, or *Sanalyelye*, shrew.[26] At *lupanda*, the boys acquire names like *Alikule*, jackal, or *Achisuwi*, leopard.[27]

The Yao ceremonies have fewer masks or animal structures than the elaborate Chewa pageant. What animal representations they have are the picture models dug in the ground and patterned over with flour.[28] There is a direct interaction between man and the models in this context also. The *Nalungume* whale song below describes some of this interaction:

---

[24] Sam Mchombo, personal communication.

[25] Stannus, "The Wayao of Nyasaland."

[26] Stannus, "The Wayao of Nyasaland," p. 271.

[27] Stannus, "The Wayao of Nyasaland," p. 257.

[28] Another description, apart from the earlier Stannus study referred to in footnote 25 above, is given by G.M. Sanderson, "Inyago, The Picture Models of the Yao Initiation Ceremonies," *The Nyasaland Journal*, 8, 2 (July 1955), pp. 36-57.

Arrived at *nalumgumi* the *m'michila* sings:

"*Nalumgumi nalitanda, nalumgumi asiwile kuchiko!*"

"The whale in the pool, the whale has blocked the ford!"

after which he straddles the head of the whale while one of his assistants does the same at the tail and thus sitting, they do a kind of wriggling dance, singing to the time marked by clapping of hands:

"*Nalumgumi atundumula, eh! eh!* (repeat)

"The whale showed its back above the water, eh!

Apalapala wate kundema;

There it did fail me;

Apalapala wate kunumba;

There it did half break;"[29]

In the *lupanda* picture models, other animals might not receive such elaborate attention. The *Mbanda* zebra and *Mbalapi* sable antelope songs, for example, just mention the animals and the object pointed to in passing, as the *Sato* python song below illustrates:

"*Anasato kwajanji! yerere, eja! Yosepe Yekoto!*"

"You python come and answer! all (is) beautiful!"[30]

A certain amount of imitation or acting is also done in the *lupanda* dance. Some of it is done only by the instructors, in others the initiates join in. The *Pimbi* lemur song is done by the chief instructor and his assistants only.

"*Kapimbi'gwe ugwe sanga mtela!*"

"The little lemur, you jump from tree to tree!"[31]

The singers climb a tree with their backs to the trunk; at the top they turn upside down with their legs on top, looking down on the assembly below. The *Nampopo* lizard song is also acted by the instructor and his assistant:

"*Nampopo londola chisango amwali ku malembe kwendela kuwila!*"

"The lizard casts lots boys to graves as going to die!"

29   Stannus, "The Wayao of Nyasaland," p. 260.
30   Stannus, "The Wayao of Nyasaland," p. 261.
31   Stannus, "The Wayao of Nyasaland," p. 251.

The instructor sings the song while the assistant acts the part of the lizard: "The assistant lies on his belly and bobs his head and shoulders up and down, lifting himself on his hands."[32]

In the *Njati* buffalo song, the qualities of the animal are bestowed upon the initiates:

> "*Ananjati ndenga pa mtw'po tagani utandi, ankunga, ambiranje!*"
> "You of the buffalo (lit. feathers) on the head you put flour, ankunga call me!"

The chief instructor sings the song as he goes round sprinkling flour on the heads of the initiates, who

> with flour on their foreheads resemble buffalos which have white patches on their horns, and they will therefore be as strong as these beasts in the bush whither they are about to go.[33]

Fun and Frolic

It is tempting to start this section on children's songs with the equivalent of the "famine" or rain song which opened this chapter.[34] Pre-puberty children of both sexes go into the bush for a day to play house as adults do. The boys build houses while the girls collect firewood and cook food. This is known as *masanje*, children's games. After the game is over, they trail back to the village in procession singing various songs. One of the songs similar to the Msinja rain song is the following:

Ku Lilongwe njala x2	In Lilongwe there is famine
Ndikapempha kachimanga	I will go and beg some maize
Konyengela mwanayu njala	To give to the child, famine

---

[32] Stannus, "The Wayao of Nyasaland," p. 251.

[33] Stannus, "The Wayao of Nyasaland," p. 255.

[34] Unless indicated otherwise, the songs are from the author's own collection. See also S. Chimombo, "Functional Aspects of Children's Songs," *Kalulu*, 2 (June 1977), pp. 8-17.

The direct parallels between this song and the rain songs are numerous. The irony here is that the children have just been fed on their own cooking and are going to eat some more now that they have returned home.

Another parallel with the adult world occurs in the *nampopo* lizard song discussed under the Yao *lupanda* initiation ceremony above:

Nampopo, popola masamba	Lizard cut some leaves
Atamile alendo, nampopo[35]	for the visitors to sit on, lizard

When children see the blue-headed lizard, they squat, singing the song while undulating the trunk and nodding the head the way the reptile does. The *nampopo* lizard has been observed doing the same as if in counter-imitation. The song is meaningful not only because it is sung in another serious context, the initiation ceremony, but also because of the situation it refers to: where there are no mats or chairs available, the least one can do is to spread some leaves on the ground for visitors to sit on. At the same time the children are practising those very movements they will need when grown up.

Another children's song seems to echo "The Hare and the Well" motif of itching beans being applied to the trickster's skin so that he cannot put it back on:

Chitedze chandiyabwa	Itching beans have made me itch
jere jereje x2	*jere jereje*
Chitedze chandiyabwa!	Itching beans have made me itch!

The children go round in a ring singing the first line, then in the second, turn to one another at the left and right, demonstrating their scratching abilities. The fun comes in who can scratch oneself more furiously than the other. On a more serious note, again the song echoes some of the punitive practices at initiation ceremonies which feature the application of itching beans to the victim.

---

[35]   Mrs. Chitekesa, Samuel Makoka Village, personal communication.

Some of the songs do not seem to carry the double load of child and adult practice. The *bongololo* centipede song below seems to be purely descriptive.

Bongololo wafera panjira	The centipende died by the wayside
Miyendo khumi-khumi	With dozens and dozens of legs
Mafuta kunsana ng'ani ng'ani	And a shiny oily back

One cannot help wondering, however, if the song is not echoing the *mdondo* millipede song of the *nyau* animal structures.

Another centipede song actually imitates the progress and curling round of the creature:

Bongololo tiye! tiye!	*Centipede let's go! let's go!*
Bongololo tiye! tiye!	*Centipede let's go! let's go!*
Chisese se! se!	*Let's sweep! sweep! sweep!*

The children hold hands, pulling each other along in an erratic line. At the climax of the song, the line curls back upon itself like a disturbed centipede. After a while the ball uncurls again to resume its erratic course across the playground.

The example above gives us a smooth transition to the next point: certain animals are generally associated with certain conceptual phenomena. This is especially so in etiological, mythic or purely legendary cases where the association has to be clothed in concrete terms.

The examples following will revolve round the Chewa creation myths. For their significance to be felt, a brief outline of one of the myths will be given: *Chiuta* (god), man and animals lived happily together at Kaphiri-Ntiwa, "the cradle of mankind." The first man invented fire and drove god away into the skies while the animals fled into the forests. This action set into motion a whole series of reactions too numerous to enumerate here. But the relevant ones are that god's wrath brought mortality to man and the animals' anger meant that there would be no peace between man and animal.

The chameleon song below dramatises briefly one aspect of the myth—the advent of death:

Birimankhwe maso adatupa ninji?	Chameleon, why are your eyes swollen?
Kwathu maliro msamaseke ana inu	[There's] death in our home, don't laugh children.
Kwayera mbee, mbee, mbee.	It's empty, empty, empty.
Ine n'dzachoka pam'dzi pano	I shall leave this village.
Mutsale mumange pam'dzi pano	You [can] stay behind and build the village.
Taonani pakhomo pangapa	Look at my house:
Payera mbee, mbee, mbee.	It's empty, empty, empty.

The mythic imagination states that at the fall of man, god sent two messengers down to mankind. The message that man would live eternally was entrusted to the chameleon, and that he would die, to the lizard. The faster animal, lizard, arrived first, with the fatal message. Death was loosed upon mankind and man's wrath turned against the chameleon which arrived too late to save him. Up to this day, it is a common sight to see children reliving this eternal hatred by stuffing the chameleon's mouth with dust, snuff, tobacco, or pepper. This is an excellent illustration of how these songs are effective in inculcating societal attitudes.

Apart from the physical description of the chameleon: swollen eyes and mournful countenance, and the bare outlines of the myth, the song has other cultural implications. (Incidentally, it is not only a predilection of children to laugh at other people's exaggerated or distorted features. Modern cartoonists have made it a remunerative profession.) The song asks for the origin of things in general. The explanation of the chameleon's swollen eyes comes as a shock to the children's derision: excessive weeping over sucessive deaths in his household. When we move the context again and realise that it is children who kill most chameleons, the irony goes too deep for laughter. The children's persecution is forcing the chameleon to move house. A chameleon emigrating may not be such a remarkable loss, but there is a human parallel. When a household in the Chewa community is struck by too many deaths, the head of the family removes the surviving members to safety. There is another twist in the ending of the song. Abandoning the children to build the village will most certainly assure the collapse of the society.

As can be seen, the chameleon in the song acquires different layers of symbolic significance. Some of this significance relies heavily on the ambiguous role the animal plays from bringer of death to a vital source of reconstruction if not regeneration. This multiplicity of meaning demands that even children's verse carries a heavy burden of cultural imperatives worth exploring in the context in which they operate.

Belonging to the same circle of etiological songs is the *nalimvimvi* song. *Nalimvimvi* is a wingless insect and the folk imagination has sought to explain why this is so through song:

Analimvimvi tiyeni	Nalimvimvi let's go
Ulendo wanga uno	I am on my way
Wokamera mapiko	To grow wings
Anabwera nalira	He came back weeping
Anam'mana mapiko	He was denied wings

In one of the creation myths all the winged kind were going to *Namalenga* (the creator) to be given wings. Friends called upon *nalimvimvi* to join them, but he did not do so immediately because he said he had to eat first. As result, he arrived too late: the wings had run out.

In contrast to the slow, mournful rhythm of the chameleon song this one is lively. The children race across the playing field, elbows bent, hands flapping at the shoulders like wings.

As in the adult world, children's songs abound in bird and insect lore. There is, here too, the belief that one can influence events, objects or the environment by performing certain actions. The *chelule* chant is supposed to induce sleep in the bird of that name.

Chelule! gona! gona!	*Chelule!* go to sleep!
Chelule! gona! gona!	*Chelule!* go to sleep!

The words are chanted to the bird to hypnotise it to sleep so that it can be captured or killed easily.

156

The *nkhumbutera* song below works on the same belief:

Nkhumbutera! tera! tera!	Nkhumbutera! land! land!
Kwanu kulibe mtengo, eh!	There's no tree at your home! eh!

When the *nkhumbutera* insect (which is edible, but is also killed for its hard wings used for making a stringed musical instrument) hears the song it is supposed to alight on the nearest tree or grass since it will not be able to do so where it is going. Its destination has no landing facilities so rather than die in flight it has to land near the singer.

Some songs are sung purely for the joy of imitating the sound of birds. The *njiwa* wild dove song is a good example:

Amai!	Mother!
Adafa!	Died!
Ndi diwa!	In a trap!
Kuti! Uh! Uh!	She said: Uh! Uh!

It is a slow plaintive chant of the wild dove, bringing more of the tragic theme of death than joy in its rendition.

As noted above, the children's world is also full of correspondences, echoes and parallels being drawn between the human and non-human worlds around. In this way, certain relationships are established between man and his environment.

PART FOUR

APPLICATION: OLD AND NEW FORMS

CHAPTER SEVEN:
ART AND SOCIETY

If aesthetics in Malawi is confounded by both local and non-local commentators, the art objects are even more so. On one hand there are statements like:

> It is *mwiko* [*sic*, i.e. taboo] to go into a white man's house, for the pictures on his walls are the spirits of his ancestors, who are specially dangerous at night, when they may launch an unseen spear at the unlucky wight who has had the temerity to enter so dangerous a place.[1]

Among the Nkhonde, photographic representations are not only the spirits of the owner's ancestors, they are defendants of the descendants against any enemies. In this case, fear of the photographic representation is added to the fear of the whiteman in general, his house and other artefacts.

Another observer describes similar reactions among the Yao:

> These people have, of course, no writing. We met with many that had never seen a book before. The sight of pictures impressed them so much that their first impulse was to run away supposing that the little painted lion or leopard was dangerous. By and by someone in the crowd discovers that this lion is quite thin! He has looked at the back of the paper and found that the body of the lion is not there! Some of the boldest, after we assure them of safety, will even put their hands upon him. The attitude of old and young is one of utter, speechless amazement.[2]

In the Nkhonde quotation, above, the people were presumably responding to pictures of human beings. That the Yao here are responding

---

[1] D.R. Mackenzie, *The Spirit-ridden Konde* (London: Seeley Service and Co. Ltd., 1925), pp. 101-102.

[2] Macdonald, *Africana*, Vol. 1, p. 47.

to pictures of animals is by the way. What is at issue is that this art form was not only new to them, it was frightening.

Sculpture, it seems, was another new art form.

> Sculpture can hardly be said to be an art known to the Yao. The only piece of stone work I have ever seen was a granite boulder, on the surface of which cup-holes had been made for the game of Bau *[sic]* … The Yao, of course, make no idols … No native would allow any wooden figure to remain in his house for fear of ill luck; the women especially would look askance at them, fearing some misfortune in their next pregnancy.[3]

What is perplexing after reading such comments is the fact that the Yao and Nkhonde quoted above belong to the Bantu speaking group which also developed other pictorial art-forms handed down to posterity in rock paintings in caves and rock shelters. Furthermore, the Nkhonde could make "clay images of men and cattle,"[4] while the Yao themselves could make "little wooden figures of birds … affixed to the point of the hut roof."[5]

This chapter summarises the art history of Malawi as a way of introducing some of the modern developments in the visual arts. The two main strands since recorded history are the indigenous and non-indigenous. Sometimes the two strands, it will be seen, co-existed without influencing each other. The syncretic modern forms, however, are a fusion of both local and non-local styles. Furthermore, with the advent of modern technology there is a diversification of styles, apart from the emergence of new art forms, modes and content. That the new art forms and techniques are due to western civilisation need not be over-stressed; that there is also the indigenisation of foreign forms and a continuation of traditional forms, if not in spirit or declaration, will be the burden of the argument.

---

3   Stannus, "The Wayao of Nyasaland," p. 348.

4   Stannus, "The Wayao of Nyasaland," p. 348.

5   Stannus, "The Wayao of Nyasaland," p. 348.

Rock Art

Archaelogical findings in Malawi's pre-history indicate that Stone Age Man left implements and rock paintings in caves and rock shelters.[6] The Iron Age brought more advanced ironmongery, pottery and rock art. Subdividing these two eras is unnecessary for the purpose of this discussion. What is of note is the styles employed by both: geometric for the earlier and schematic for the later age. Although there was considerable overlap between the two eras it appears that there was no cross-fertilisation.

Early Stone Age man's tools were "simply split pebbles" from quartz and quartzite which developed into the hand axes, picks and scrapers (Karonga) of Middle Stone Age. These latter tools were "almost certainly carpenter's tools for making implements and recepticles from wood and bark."[7] Pottery (Cape Maclear and Monkey Bay) made its appearance in the Late Stone Age, with the Bantu.[8] The rock paintings from as far north as Mzimba to as far south as Blantyre date from the Late Stone Age. At least sixty rock paintings have been found at thirty-eight different sites.

As noted above, the two styles isolated were the geometric and the schematic. A description of a representative of the geometric style follows:

> Common designs found include series of parallel lines (usually vertical), concentric circles, sunbursts, empty ovals, ovals filled in with a few vertical lines or crossed lines to form gridirons, U shape empty loops, broad loops either supporting vertical lines or inverted loops suspending vertical lines, rows of dots or ovals or short strokes, long zigzag lines, ladder designs, and a whole range of less easily described designs.[9]

---

[6] Some useful studies are J. Desmond Clark, "Prehistory in Nyasaland," *The Nyasaland Journal*, 9, 1 (January 1956), pp. 92-119; the Editorial accompanying Margaret Metcalfe, "Some Rock Paintings in Nyasaland," *The Nyasaland Journal*, 9, 1 (January 1956), pp. 58-70; Lindgren and Schoffeleers, *Rock Art and Nyau Symbolism in Malawi*.

[7] Clark, "Prehistory in Nyasaland," pp. 95, 97.

[8] Clark, "Prehistory in Nyasaland," p. 97.

[9] Lindgren and Schoffeleers, *Rock Art and Nyau Symbolism in Malawi*, p. 1.

The schematic paintings are zoomorphic: "crude stylised drawings of animals, humans and 'snakes'."[10] More details are supplied elsewhere:

> One that is particularly curious is a horned skeleton figure apparently that of a man. One could recognise giraffe, leopard, crocodile, various birds and several curious reptiles.[11]

In speculating why the schematic style was adopted, an important observation was made:

> ... it is the reproduction in paint on rock of an engraving technique executed on wood or bark which latter is much more likely to have been of a schematic nature due to the difficulty of producing curved lines in such media.[12]

The significance occurs in contexts where the argument is that painting on canvas, and sculpture are not indigenous art forms. (Hence *Mwala-wolemba* from *lembula*, pictured or painted as a later development ushered in by western technology and techniques.)

The possible interpretation given for the schematic painting is that the symbols were associated with atmospheric or climatic conditions: sun, rain, clouds etc. Others might have been representations of an accountting system, whereas the U shapes were associated with initiation ceremonies. All in all, it is agreed that they may have had magico-religious meanings.[13]

Modern Art

Murals are a recent development noted at the opening of this century from Mponda and as far south as Mulanje.[14] Mural art is a recent form and

---

[10] Clark, "Prehistory in Nyasaland," p. 101.

[11] Metcalfe, "Some Rock Paintings in Nyasaland," p. 61.

[12] Clark, "Prehistory in Nyasaland," pp. 104-105.

[13] Lindgren and Schoffeleers, *Rock Art and Nyau Symbolism in Malawi*, p. 46. See Chapter Five, footnote 1, for the extract quoted.

[14] A. Werner, "A Native Painting from Nyasaland," *Journal of the African Society*, VIII, XXX (January 1909), pp. 190-192.

due to western influences since "natives themselves state that none was done before the advent of the 'white man'".[15]

By now:

> Wall-art is a major, and fascinating feature of Malawian life, and well worth watching out for. Examples are not hard to spot, as they are everywhere ... Ready-designed, and original, murals jostle side-by-side ... [H]ouseholders decorate the plaster walls of their home with wonderful patterns—geometrical, naturalistic, surrealistic.[16]

Mural artists fall into two groups: the commercial and, therefore, professional artist and the amateur who learns by observing others at work: "It is the non-professionals, however, who create some of the loveliest wall-art in Malawi."[17]

Elaborate art forms seem not to be indigenous. Prior to the advent of the white man or Arab and Swahili culture, decoration consisted of geometrical patterns on tools, weapons, domestic goods and other personal belongs.[18] As an observer put it:

> As for arts, manufactures, industries, little variety of beauty need be looked for in this direction, seeing that the principle which the native constantly holds in view is the avoidance of superfluous aesthetic detail and the reduction of indispensable adjuncts to their rudest and least enduring forms ... These slight decorations ... seem to be almost the only concession which they make to aesthetics in the manufacture of articles, other than those intended for personal adornment or for sale to Europeans.[19]

Modern art then is inextricably intertwined with western influences. A comment on the Nkhonde is relevant here:

---

[15] Hugh Stannus, "Native Paintings in Nyasaland," *Journal of the African Society*, IX, XXXIV (January 1910), p. 187.

[16] Barbara Snow, "Street Art in Malawi," *Focus on Malawi* (September 1984), pp. 17, 19.

[17] Snow, "Street Art in Malawi," p. 19.

[18] Stannus, "The Wayao of Nyasaland," p. 349.

[19] Duff, *Nyasaland Under the Foreign Office*, pp. 304, 306.

At every point the native mind seems to have been waiting for the stimulus which was to come with the white man, and which has led to an awakening, the full extent of which is not realised except by thoughtful persons.[20]

In this view, then, there is an upsurge of new art forms or the reshaping of old ones. For example, among the Nkhonde:

A new development of this industry [basketry] is the making of articles to European, or native, order ... there is a good trade [in weaving] ... for the European market.[21]

Among the Yao, to give another example of the extent of this influence, another observer noted:

Of late years, individuals here and there have begun carving wooden figures of men and animals ... I should think that this art has sprung up within the past twelve or thirteen years, that is to say, since there has been a market for them among European residents.[22]

Similar developments were observed in the Chewa society, where *nyau* man masks, figures and other structures incorporated western personages or objects in secular or sacred life: *Maliya ndi Yosefe* (Mary and Joseph), D.C. (the district commissioner), or *galimoto* (motor car) in the 1930s and 1940s.[23] One could compare other developments in literacy, numeracy and the other arts like dancing, singing and theatre which make up the subjects for separate studies.

Some Malawian artists themselves confess to this strong western influence. Cuthbert Mede, sculptor and painter for over twenty years and owner of "Galerie Africaine" includes in his influences the following: cubism, fauvism, pointillism, surrealism, futurism and naturalism. He

---

20 Mackenzie, *The Spirit-ridden Konde*, p. 147.

21 Mackenzie, *The Spirit-ridden Konde*, pp. 152, 153.

22 Stannus, "The Wayao of Nyasaland," p. 348.

23 "Central Africa," *African Affairs*, 50, 200 (July 1951), p. 213.

admires Picasso, Bracque and Henry Moore.[24] Brian Hara, a cartoonist for over twenty years, admits the early influences of *The Saturday Evening Post's* Golden Age of Illustration. In Norman Rockwell, the cartoonist found "the visual world that was neither fantasy nor total escape." Other influences were comic strips like "Blondie" by Chic Young and "Rip Kirby" by Alex Raymond (of 'Flash Gordon' fame). The cartoonist "marvelled at the sheer beauty of draftsmanship both artists displayed."[25] *Pewani*, the cartoon strip created by Brian Hara, is discussed in the next section.

In spite of the strong western influences indicated above, there is an indigenisation of the new art forms. One of the earliest comments on local art says:

> One European house in my neighbourhood is decorated with a frieze of crude representations of men on foot or on horseback, motor-cars, cycles, birds, animals, snakes, in astonishing variety, done in black or red on white ground by two native artists from Rungwe. Whether the ideas were supplied to them by the white man who owned the house, I cannot tell, but the execution is entirely native ... [26]

Cuthbert Mede's works also:

> are as impressive as they are rooted in Malawian culture. Whether he uses clay, soapstone, wood or serpentine as his medium the works he sculpts are a continuation of his paintings.[27]

> Predominant ... themes are ancestral worship and indigenous values and beliefs, some of which ... cut across the human life-cycles.[28]

---

[24] "Preservation of African Traditions," *Quest*, 2 (Second Quarter 1986), pp. 22, 42.

[25] "Brian Hara Tells Story," *This is Malawi* (April 1981), p. 12.

[26] Mackenzie, *The Spirit-ridden Konde*, pp. 155-156.

[27] "Mede Preserves Malawi's Culture Through Works of Art," *This is Malawi* (March 1976), p. 7.

[28] George Matewere, "Moving with a City on the Move," *Daily Times* (23 October 1985), p. 10.

On viewing his paintings one is struck by a deep-seated link with the traditional past. Done on straw mats and cardboards, his paintings—whether landscapes or something based on mythology—revolve around Malawian tradition. He expresses his strong cultural beliefs in hues that cut across the primary—and secondary—colour spectrum.[29]

Even Vic Kasinja, a graphic artist and the creator of *Joza*, another cartoon strip to be discussed below, admits that his character has "trickster" antecedents.[30]

To conclude this section, the "development of art" in Malawi may be a misleading phrase since, until the opening of this century, there was no discernible "evolution" from an earlier to a later stage to direct influences between different groups. The geometric rock painters did not influence the schematic, although there was considerable overlap between the two. Likewise, schematic rock art has had almost no influence on art in the present century. Instead, the overt and even conscious influences came from western art forms.

In spite of the borrowings from the West, however, what seems to have happened is the indigenisation of those forms (e.g. Cuthbert Mede's *Mona Lisa* on a reed mat). In terms of pictorial representations, the same thing seems to have happened (as seen, earlier rock art was a transfer of wood engravings to the rock surface): *kulembula* (engraving) was replaced by *kujambula* (photography or painting on canvas). The case of murals, sculpture and cartoons is also straightforward indigenisation, comparable to the modern Malawian writer using folkloric elements in verse, drama, fiction, from oral to print and also from the vernacular to the foreign, yet his medium is English.

---

[29] *This is Malawi*, "Mede Preserves Malawi's Culture," p. 6.

[30] "Trickster who is Loved by All," *Malawi News* (14-20 January 1984), p. 5; Vic Kasinja confessed the same thing in a talk on *Joza* at the Forum Series, Departement of Fine and Performing Arts, Chancellor College, Zomba, 27 February 1985.

The Trickster and the Dupe in Scholarship

The Trickster

The trickster in folklore scholarship has been definable by his physical and mental characteristics: a small but clever animal who survives in the world through duplicity. However, he is a rather complex character, as Radin has pointed out:

> [the] Trickster is at one and the same time creator and destroyer, giver and negator, he who dupes others and who is always duped himself. He wills nothing consciously. At all times he is constrained to behave as he does from impulses over which he has no control. He knows neither good nor evil yet he is responsible for both. He possesses no values, moral or social, is at the mercy of his passions and appetites yet through his actions all values come into being.[31]

The trickster, then, is not a one-dimensional character: both positive and negative features co-exist in his personality; motives for action are inexplicable and he is not always triumphant since he can also become the victim of other characters' machinations.

In Malawian folklore, *Kalulu*, the hare, is the commonest trickster figure. Why the hare is singled out for this role is not difficult to decipher: it is small, it is difficult to hunt and catch, and popular belief has it that it sleeps with its large eyes wide open. Furthermore, "*Kalulu*" is in popular parlance, the term for a clever, slick and deceptive person.

The adventures (incidents or plots) which *Kalulu*, the hare, goes through are common in African mythology.[32] The popular ones in Malawi are the following:

---

[31] Paul Radin, *The Trickster: A Study in American Indian Mythology* (New York: Schocken Books, 1972), p. xxiii.

[32] See for example, Finnegan, *Oral Literature in Africa*, or Susan Feldmann, ed., *African Myths and Tales* (New York: Dell Publishing Company, 1963).

a. The hare engages the hippo and the elephant to a tug-of-war in which both the large animals think the hare is the other contestant.

b. The hare, employed as nursemaid to the lion or leopard, eats all the children up and sets the hyena up as the culprit.

c. The hare deceives the hyena into killing his own mother.

d. The hare, after escaping from participating in digging a well during a drought, still enjoys the fruits of the other animals' labours by successively tricking all the guards placed around it.

In some of the stories, however, the hare is depicted as the dupe: e.g. In the race between the tortoise and the hare, the trickster loses.

Kalulu the hare-as-trickster always appears with his foils: *Fisi*, the Hyena; *Mvuu*, the Hippo; *Njobvu*, the Elephant; *Mkango*, the Lion; or *Nyalugwe*, the Leopard, i.e. large animals, slow or dull-witted and, therefore, the dupes. The smaller animals like *Kamba*, the Tortoise, or *Birimankhwe*, the Chameleon, however, feature in most stories when *Kalulu* is evenly matched or out-witted. Whether or not the hare is triumphant the stories reveal the multifaceted nature of this complex figure.

The age-old artist who created *Kalulu* placed him naturally in the rural village context. This was a comprehensible setting in which the narrator, through the medium of animal stories, recreated the everyday events and characters of an African society to reveal its customs and traditions, its social, economic and political fabric, e.g. talking animals getting married, begetting children, dying, settling their cases before the chief or subsisting on the resources of the land. The animal characters dramatised the human strengths and weaknesses, loves and hates, heroism and cowardice, in short, all the themes of a dynamic human society.

Although we may not find direct correspondences between character, plot or action and the contemporary society, most scholars agree that these stories are encapsulations of the history of the society:

> In contexts in which literary expression is neither veiled by being expressed through the written word nor (usually) voiced by

narrators removed from the close-knit village group, comment on human and social affairs can be expressed less rawly, less directly by being enmasked in animal characters ... In a way common to many forms of literature, but doubly removed from reality in being set among animals, the animal tales reflect, mould and interpret the social and literary experience of which they form part.[33]

How the original artist conceived of the original trickster is also worth exploring here. The psychological genesis of the trickster and his relationship to the living society that created him have been discussed by Kerenyi, Jung and Radin. Kerenyi says:

There is much trickery at large in the world, all sorts of sly and cunning tricks among human beings, animals and even plants, which could no more remain hidden from a story-teller whose inner life was as much bound up with the world as his outer one, than they could from an observer at a distance.[34]

After observing the raw external world of man, animal, and plant the original artist recreated the material into the fictional narrative form labelled the trickster circle. But what of the trickster himself as a character, how he begat? Jung offers the following explanation:

He is obviously a "psychologem," an archetypal psychic structure of extreme antiquity. In his clearest manifestations he is a faithful copy of an absolutely undifferentiated human consciousness, corresponding to a psyche that has hardly left the animal level. That this is how the trickster figure originated can hardly be contested if we look at it from the causal and historical angle.[35]

What we have in the trickster, then, is not only an externalisation of the human consciousness but a metaphoric projection of man in society. Radin reiterates a similar point:

---

[33] Finnegan, *Oral Literature in Africa*, pp. 351-352.

[34] Karl Kerenyi, "The Trickster in Relation to Greek Mythology" (translated by R.F.C. Hull) in Radin, *The Trickster*, p. 174.

[35] C.G. Jung, "On the Psychology of the Trickster Figure" (translated by R.F.C. Hull), in Radin, *The Trickster*, p. 200.

In fact, only if we view it as primarily such, as an attempt by man to solve his problems inward and outward, does the figure of Trickster become intelligible and meaningful.[36]

Radin goes further to explain that the animal trickster is only a human in animal form:

> Trickster himself is not infrequently identified with specific animals ... but these animals are only secondarily to be equated with concrete animals. Basically he possesses no well-defined and fixed form ... he is primarily an inchoate being of undetermined proportions, a figure foreshadowing the shape of man.[37]

The traditional artist used the trickster figure to fulfil many functions: didactic (moral), aetiological, edification, entertainment and aesthetic. However multiple the functions, the primary role was the socio-psychological one:

> This figure can be adapted to express the idea of opposition to the normal world or of the distortion of accepted human and social values ... The trickster is being represented as a kind of mirror-image of respectable human society, reflecting the opposite of the normally approved or expected character and behaviour. Again, the trickster can be used to represent traits or personalities which people both recognise and fear ... More than this. Not only does the trickster figure stand for what is feared, his representation in literature also helps to deal with these fears. In the first place, he is represented in animal guise which allows narrator and listener to stand back, as it were, and contemplate the type in tranquillity.[38]

The socio-psychological function of the trickster, thus, played an important role. Release of tension was achieved while at the same time a social therapy was effected, as Horton, quoted by Finnegan, says:

---

[36] Radin, *The Trickster*, p. xxiv.

[37] Radin, *The Trickster*, pp. Xxiii-xxiv.

[38] Finnegan, *Oral Literature in Africa*, pp. 352-353.

the disturbing real-life experience of plausible psychopaths is controlled, confined, and cut down to size.[39]

Finally, in terms of the political role, one scholar states unconditionally:

These tales illustrate the traditional right of the individual to contest irrational authority.[40]

All the above observations reveal society's social, political and psychological need for the trickster. Divorcing the trickster from the society is more or less divorcing the self from the self, since the trickster is one aspect of one's own psychic being: Jung's "psychologem." The individual and the society recognise themselves in the kinds of tricksters they create and the type of adventures they set them.

The Dupe

In scholarship, the dupe has always been defined in relation to the role he plays alongside the trickster figure. Whereas the trickster is small and clever, the dupe is not only big and strong, he is also slow and stupid. The physical and mental characteristics establish a dichotomy of traits, positive for the hero and negative for the victim, almost point by point, quality by disquality.

In Malawian folk literature, *Fisi*, the hyena, is the commonest dupe figure. Why the hyena is singled out for this role is difficult to explain since, apart from his uncouth physiognomy, his association with darkness—he only comes out at night to ravage the villages—and the laughter-producing howl he utters as his signal tune, his anatomy is also associated with potent magical and medicinal properties: medicine men and witches use *Fisi* potions and charms for invisibility and night transport; and thieves for keeping their victims somnolent. *Fisi's* potency also features in girls' initiation ceremonies and in cases of infertile and impotant husbands.

Fisi's ambiguities in folk belief and practice, then, follow the general characteristics of the trickster/dupe paradigm in which in some narratives

---

[39] Finnegan, *Oral Literature in Africa*, p. 353.

[40] Feldmann, *African Myths and Tales*, p. 17.

one is the victor and in others the victim. However, in Malawian folk narratives, *Fisi* has never been depicted triumphant. This important characteristic will be explored when examining *Pewani*, the cartoon figure, since he operated under the same principles governing *Fisi*-the-dupe in folk narratives.

The other dupe figures common in Malawian narratives are *Mvuu*, the hippo; *Njobvu*, the elephant; *Mkango*, the lion; and *Nyalugwe*, the leopard. These animals are given the essential qualities of the trickster's foils: largeness and strength in build, and slowness and stupidity in wit.

The adventures (incidents or plots) in which the dupes are victimised in African mythology have been described by other scholars.[41] The popular plots with *Fisi* as dupe in Malawian folk narratives are the following:

a. *Fisi*, the hyena, is tricked by *Kalulu*, the hare, into killing and eating his own mother.

b. *Fisi*, the hyena, is tricked by *Kalulu*, the hare, into being ridden as a horse and displayed as a beast of burden to his own girlfriend.

c. *Fisi*, the hyena, is tricked out of marriage through his own greed.

d. *Fisi*, the hyena, is accused of stealing castor oil seeds, which everyone knows hyenas do not eat.

e. *Fisi*, the hyena, is punished instead of *Kalulu*, the hare, when *Mkango*, the lion's or *Nyalugwe*, the leopard's children are all eaten up by the nurse.

In some stories, however, other animals are depicted as dupes:

a. *Kalulu*, the hare, loses a race through the trickery of *Kamba*, the tortoise.

---

[41]   See, for example, Finnegan, *Oral Literature in Africa*, or Feldmann, *African Myths and Tales*.

b. *Kalulu*, the hare, is punished for stealing water from a well which he had refused to help dig with the other animals during a period of drought.

c. Baboons or monkeys are killed by Mkango, the lion, through *Kalulu*, the hare's trickery.

d. *Njobvu*, the elephant, and *Mvuu*, the hippopotamus, are tricked by *Kalulu*, the hare, into pitting their strength against each other in a tug-of-war.

As in the trickster narratives examined in the previous section, the original artist placed the dupe with his counterpart in the rural village setting. Through the dupe (and the trickster) and the other animals, the narrator recreated the everyday events and characters of the village society to reveal its weaknesses, hates, gullibility, cowardice, in short, all the negative qualities of human nature.

Even if no direct correspondences could be established between the dupe's encounters in the folk narratives and the society, most scholars agree that the stories are recreations, in fictional or metaphoric form, of the contemporary society's own realities, as we saw with the trickster earlier.[42] Kerenyi summarises the same point: that when we encounter myth "we hear the world telling its own story to itself.[43]

Some scholars have also attempted to explain the origins of the trickster and his dupe, for example, Kerenyi.[44]

As seen earlier too, Jung has explained the psychological origins of the trickster as "a psychologem," an archetypal psychic structure of extreme antiquity.[45] Radin also discussed this figure "as an attempt by man to solve his problems inward and outward."[46] The dupe's origins are similar, if not

---

42 Finnegan, *Oral Literature in Africa*, pp. 351-352.

43 Kerenyi, "The Trickster in Relation to Greek Mythology," p. 175.

44 Kerenyi, "The Trickster in Relation to Greek Mythology," p. 175.

45 Jung, "On the Psychology of the Trickster," p. 200.

46 Radin, *The Trickster*, p. xxiv.

coexistent with, the trickster's since one cannot have his being without the other.

The scholars quoted above have also discussed the functions of the trickster in society. Here we can only quote some of the dupe's functions:

> By portraying him in stories, people can show the trickster as himself outwitted and overreached often by his own wife. Again, by exaggerating and caricaturing him to the point of absurdity, they can in a sense "tame" him.[47]

The social and psychological function is an important apart from the didactic and aesthetic:

> Laughing at a circus demands the capacity to laugh at oneself, to identify with the reversals and risks of identity that take place before our eyes. Wit, laughing at the other, does not work. And this laughing at oneself means accepting the ambivalence of the human condition for which civilisation gives us very little instruction or structured opportunity.[48]

The Trickster and the Media

Joza, the cartoon strip by Vic Kasinja, first appeared on the weekend of 6-12 June, 1981, in the *Malawi News*, a national weekly. *Joza*'s appearance might not have inaugurated a fresh national wave of hero-worship; however, it did foster a heightened awareness of a fascination for or attraction towards the outlaw, the outrageous, or the unpredictable character in the society. The consequences of the phenomenon have wider social implications, which this section examines towards the conclusion. The main aim of this discussion, however, is to argue that *Joza* is, in form and content, not a new but an old manifestation, rooted in folklore and mythology. The medium may have changed, but the function, with some modifications due to the contemporary reality, remains the same as in antiquity.

---

[47] Finnegan, *Oral Literature in Africa*, pp. 352-353.

[48] Stanley Diamond, Introduction to Radin, *The Trickster*, p. xiii.

174

Joza as Trickster

To reply to the objection that *Joza*, a human being, cannot be a trickster, which is normally an animal, we only need to go back to earlier observations that the indeterminate and multifarious manifestations of this character are a composite of man. Furthermore,

> The decisive factor here is not the [trickster's] physical appearance but its trickery ... It should not be forgotten, anyway, that the animal form in mythology is only the phenomenal form, with the real form—glimpsed by the eye of the myth-maker—shining through.[49]

Characters: Naming and Tableaux

a. *Joza*

In common parlance "*Joza*" is a smart, slick or slippery person who survives by his cunning and wits, hence the trickster, *Kalulu*, the hare. *Joza's* foils are also reminiscent of the characters the trickster of folklore interacts with or is at odds with. In fact, some direct correspondences could be established.

b. *Kape*

From the malediction "*chitsilu chofunda kape*" (an incurable fool who would go to the extent of covering himself with a basket-sieve (for beer, etc.) thinking it was a blanket, hence the dupe, Hyena, the stupid slow-thinking animal.

c. *Hippo*

Physical appearance: short, fat, aggressive, in a T-shirt with the name Hippo displayed on it. He is also known, as he is obviously *Mvuu*, the hippo of tug-of war stories.

---

[49] Kerenyi, "The Trickster in Relation to Greek Mythology," pp. 187-188.

d. *Rita*

Young, sleazy, alluring, modern and sophisticated female most of the characters compete for, hence, the female of the suitor stories.

e. *Kadzidzi*

Translated easily into Owl, either "as wise as an owl" or as a bird of ill-omen. Whichever, he out-tricks *Joza*.

f. *The Boss*

Unnamed: powerfully built, ponderous, always exasperated. The Elephant? The Lion? The Chief?

g. *Kwinyani*

Another townster trickster who out-tricks *Joza*.

h. *Koko*

Nephew of *Joza*: innocent, mischievous looking, hence any young inexperienced off-shoot of the trickster family.

i. *Mpondamatiki*

The exploited rich man, hence another dupe.

The summary above reveals the age-old trickster tableaux. Furthermore, *Joza* and his foils exhibit an incapacity to "develop" as characters. In all the strips, analysed either individually or as a tableau, they do not show any signs of moral growth, gaining new insights about themselves or the society in which they live. They remain as incorrigible as they were originally conceived. In this quality they are also obeying the nature of the trickster characters, for there is no

> ... such thing as the "inner development" of the hero. Gods and primitive beings have no inner dimension, and neither have heroes, who inhabit the same sphere.[50]

---

[50] Kerenyi, "The Trickster in Relation to Greek Mythology," p. 184.

Setting

Joza is placed in a recognisable urban context. He can be found at Box 812, Blantyre. His precinct, when not at work or on the road, is Chigumula Bar, Chigumula Supermarket, and Chigumula Football Stadium.

One might object again to the differences in setting between the original folklore trickster's rural village environment and *Joza's* urban contexts. However, folklore has the tendency to move with the times, adapting itself to changing environments.

> All these tricksters, however, are adaptable. They are able to turn any situation, old or new, to their advantage. The tortoise, we are told, now aspires to white collar status in Southern Nigeria and attends adult education classes, while the Spider *Ananse* referees football matches among the Ashanti in Ghana.[51]

Similarly, *Joza*, Esq. aspires to white collar status; his friends call him "Mister J." He is very much part of the newly created or emerging urbanites, living by their wits to survive the realities of domineering bosses, fast women, alcoholism and heartless landlords.

Plot by Type

Joza is not always a trickster, he is sometimes outwitted by his adversaries. Again, he obeys the nature of the trickster tableaux.

> ... not only he ... possesses these traits. So likewise, do the other figures of the plot connected with him; the animals, the various supernatural beings and monsters, and man.[52]

Below are examples of *Joza's* encounters, with their possible ancestry:

    a.   Disguise Motif

         i.   Original Trickster Plots

---

[51]   Finnegan, *Oral Literature in Africa*, p. 345.

[52]   Radin, *The Trickster*, p. xxiii.

The trickster disguises himself with feathers so that he can go to a feast in the bird kingdom. In another plot, he wears horns so that he can feast with antelopes. In both stories he is, of course, unmasked.

ii. *Joza* Versions

Joza disguises himself as a female so that he can enter a night club disco dance free. The ticket-seller recognises him (under the lipstick, woman's comb, bag and skirt) because he has forgotten to remove his trade mark: the inevitable straw in his mouth.

On another occasion he simply removes his striped T-shirt and uses it as a scarf to be admitted free as one of the team's fans at a match.

b. Pretending to be Dead Motif

i. Original Trickster Plots

The original trickster feigns illness or death to escape punishment or to effect duplicity.

ii. *Joza* Versions

Several *Joza* strips depict him feigning illness (bad eye-sight, colds, fainting spells) so he can effect duplicity: to malinger, to get a free bottle of brandy, or to be carried to the first-aid tent in the stadium, past the ticket-seller, of course.

c. Suitor Story

i. Original Trickster Plot

The trickster has to get the female first in order to win her against the rival. The trickster, a slow animal in this case (the chameleon), simply jumps on the tail of the faster rival (the hyena). When the hyena sits down at the girl's place, he is sitting on his rival who apparently arrived earlier.

178

ii. *Joza* Version

> *Kape* buys himself a car and wants to go and show off to *Rita*. The only problem is that the car will not start. *Joza* comes to his aid by climbing behind the wheel and asking *Kape* to push him. When the car starts *Joza* drives off to take *Rita* for a drive, leaving *Kape* flat-footed on the road.

The examples above reveal the central theme of the trickster series: duplicity. However, since the artist placed *Joza* in a contemporary context, it is the same age-old themes dramatised in an urban setting.

Joza in the Real World

Joza had a large following in the country. The strip came second in the "Cartoon of the Year" in 1982. In the same year, Vic Kasinja, the artist/creator was also second in the "Artist of the Year" Competition, according to the Malawi Broadcasting Corporation Listeners' poll.[53] Within a year *Joza* and his creator had moved from twelfth to second place. In the *Malawi News* of 23-29 April, 1983, the following item appeared.

> It's May Fayre time in Blantyre next weekend and the organisers, Blantyre Lions Club, are hoping to find *Malawi News'* popular cartoon characters Joza and his girlfriend Rita among the 10,000 people expected to pack the fairgrounds at Chichiri.
>
> A super look-alike competition based on our page 3 cartoon strip is one of the many attractions planned. And there is a great prize waiting for the couple who, in the judges' opinion, most closely resemble Joza and Rita.[54]

The same item was on the front page of the *Daily Times* of 29 April, 1983. This paper had carried the advert (a picture of *Joza* and *Rita* plus the entry form) in its 28 April, 1983, edition. Since the May Fayre was described as "one of the most popular family fun attractions of the year," the *Joza* enthusiasts had a field day meeting their counterparts: "Meet you at the

---

53 *Malawi News*, 8-14 January 1983, p. 2.

54 *Malawi News*, 23-29 April 1983, p. 1.

May Fayre, Rita," ran the "Look Alike" advertisement. "We will have great fun."

One of the judges was Vic Kasinja, the originator of the *Joza* character.

The Mayor of Blantyre opened the May Fayre. An estimated 15,000 turned up at the Chichiri grounds[55] and K17,500 were collected by the Lions Club.[56] The "Look Alike" winning couple were given "a luxurious week-end at Mzuzu Hotel at Malawi Hotel's, Hertz Car Hire, and Air Malawi's expense."[57] The *Daily Times* carried photos and news of the couple from the winning day to their return trip. Said one of them on landing at Chileka Airport on their return:

> "One of the highlights of the trip was when we were chauffeur-driven to Chintheche Inn, some 50 kilometres in a Hertz Car Hire for a special lunch laid on by the Department of Tourism."[58]

As if this were not enough indication of popularity, the French Cultural Centre organised a month-long exhibition featuring *Joza*. The exhibition was described as "the first of its kind to be held in Malawi." Again, the society was given "the opportunity of seeing their favourite cartoons."[59] The events were covered by both the *Daily Times* and the *Malawi News*, in photos and newsprint. The same sponsorship carried *Joza* to another exhibition held in Lilongwe, the Capital City, in the central region.

It would seem, then, that *Joza* was a national phenomenon. And, if the immense amounts of time and money spent on Joza were seen to be part of the large organisations only, the example below came from an individual who also took *Joza* seriously:

Joza Better than Many
Dear Editor

---

55 *Daily Times*, 2 May 1983, p. 3.
56 *Daily Times*, 2 May 1983, p. 1.
57 *Daily Times*, 2 May 1983, p. 5.
58 *Daily Times*, 19 May 1983, p. 3.
59 *Malawi News*, 11-17 June 1983, p. 1.

I think Joza is one of the best motorists in the country because he observes road signs. (Malawi News, May 7-13). Despite his ignorance about the Zebra crossing, Joza is better than the countless number of drivers who understand what the crossing is meant for but care very little about them. Some drivers even have the temerity to blow their horns for pedestrians who are half-way across the road.

In many places in Blantyre, Zebra crossings are ignored by motorists who don't even slow down.

Don't let Joza beat you in observing road signs.

S_____R_____,

Blantyre.[60]

Tricksters in the Real World

During the same period in which the collection of the *Joza* strip was undertaken, items of trickery, duplicity, victimisation, crime and corruption were also collected. One item of interest because of its wording is the following. (It happened when the *Joza* exhibition had just been announced):

BOGUS MONEY MAKER

A trickster who promised to make money through magic was recently fined K120 by the Limbe Traditional Court in Blantyre. ...

The accused, who had come to visit the complainant's son, insinuated that he could easily make money through magic. "If you give me K70 I will be able to make as much as K1,000 this same night."

Soon after collecting K70, he went to Ndirande, allegedly to look for a certain type of medicine which would be used in making money.

When the accused returned from Ndirande, he demanded extra funds saying: "The man who sells the medicine for making money wanted K120 instead."

However, the complainant admitted she had no money left on her. After some hard negotiations she managed to give him an extra

---

60   *Malawi News*, 21-27 May 1983, p. 8.

K10, a radio, and a pair of shoes. He received the extra goods and never returned.

The matter was referred to the police who later arrested—and charged him with obtaining money by false pretenses.[61]

The plot is a typical trickster one: the money-maker as trickster, the woman the dupe. Not satisfied with tricking her the first time, he comes back for more. Not realising that she's being duped, she supplies more fuel for her exploitation. The forces of equilibrium come in the end to restore order and to see that justice is done.

Although *Joza's* trickery is meant to be light-hearted and humorous, the real world harbours no such intentions. Table 5 below lists some of the local cases of duplicity, crimes, and other malpractices reported in the *Daily Times* and the *Malawi News* during the same period *Joza* rose to prominence.

The Table is not meant to equate the advent of Joza with the rise in crime but to show the real world the artist lives in. In other words, it is not as if Vic Kasinja, the artist, had to go out of his way to create imaginary new plots for *Joza*. As the age-old artist/raconteur, he drew his inspiration from everyday events of contemporary society. As in the old, so in the new artist's vision, duplicity, swindles, embezzlement, rape, murder, treason, robbery with violence, drug and currency smuggling, and child-battering are all around.

Vic Kasinja himself confessed:

> When I get home at night I like to look back on the day and draw the things I've found funny … Out of this has come Joza. I like to think there's something of all of us in his reactions to life.[62]

---

[61] *Daily Times*, 13 May 1983, p. 3.

[62] *Daily Times*, 3 June 1981, p. 7.

TABLE 5: CRIMES, FELONIES, MISDEMEANORS, ETC

No.	Type	Examples	/80 Reports
1	Robbery/Theft	Thuggery, Burglary, Assault, Murder, Impersonation, Forgery Rustling, Poaching, Corruption, Bribery, Overpricing, Treason, Embezzlement, etc.	70
2	(Censored)	(Censored)	
3	Miscellaneous	Arson, Witchcraft/Magic, Marriage Breaches, Drunkenness, Illegal Migrations, etc.	23
4	Drugs/Currency	Smuggling, Trafficking, etc.	12
5	Tax Evasion	Default, Notifications, Convictions, etc.	10

The Dupe in a Modern Context

Most scholars of trickster narratives concentrate on the central figure himself and give scanty attention to the dupe, the hero's victim. Relegation of the victim to a secondary role is perhaps understandable, since the primary interest of the narratives is in how the trickster dupes others. As Kerenyi observed:

> Among plants, animals and man, cunning is brought into the world by those who are stupid enough to get caught. But the mythological theme is cunning first and foremost; it makes stupidity appear as something secondary, including the stupidity of the cunning.[63]

It is important to discuss the dupe as seriously as the trickster hero, not only because the victor could not exist without the victim, but also because the hero is not always triumphant; he, in turn, becomes the dupe

---

[63] Kerenyi, "The Trickster in Relation to Greek Mythology," p. 180.

of other character's machinations. This point was also made by Radin quoted above.

The previous section focused on the trickster figure in Malawian mythology and the modern media.[64] The present concerns the dupe in similar contexts. I have already reviewed the dupe figure in mythology with illustrations from Malawian folk literature. After discussing the common characteristics of the dupe, attention is now drawn to similar traits in *Pewani*, a cartoon strip in the *Malawi News*, in the 1980s. The argument put forward is that the features of dupe-dom in the trickster narratives are capitalised upon by *Pewani*. *Pewani's* primary existence is the dramatisation of settings, situations, events and encounters in which only dupes or idiots find themselves. A third aspect to be examined is the impact *Pewani*, the modern dupe, had on his audience: what uses are made of this figure, and whether or not he is meaningful or relevant to the contemporary society. It will be seen as the discussion proceeds that not only had *Pewani* adopted the age-old dupe-traits of folklore and folk literature, the same message of dupe-dom is continuing to be sent through the cartoon media of modern times.

Pewani as Dupe

On 11 April, 1981, the *Malawi News* intrigued its readers with the following:

> WHAT'S MY NAME?
> The jolly character off to the lands of wonder and dazzling surprises will keep our readers smiling for a few days as he shows everyone how clever he is at getting out of spots. Oh, his name, almost forgot. Now that you have brought it up, that's quite interesting because we thought you might help us get him one—brief—descriptive name which suggests his not-so-bright outlook. What we mean is— uh, he is the sort of fellow who would bonk you with his umbrella on the head just to swat a fly on it.

---

64   Steve Chimombo, "New Contexts for an Old Trickster," unpublished manuscript.

To be truthful, er—give us a name. And you have only a few days. K2.00 prize to the first acceptable name.[65]

The announcement was accompanied by a single-frame cartoon depicting the "jolly figure" with an umbrella on his shoulder and a suitcase in hand, on the road leading to an unspecified destination. In the picture were also what were presumably his family standing behind a closely barricaded wooden fence. Only the heads of these other persons showed, with their hands waving the character off with words of warning: "Watch out on the roads!" "Be on the lookout!" "Remember no more accidents!" and "Come back safely!"

Pewani was born on 17 May, 1981 in the *Malawi News*. The prediction that the readers would be kept smiling by the "dazzling surprises" *Pewani* encountered came true. The prognostication that he would be the "sort of fellow who would bonk you with his umbrella on the head just to swat a fly on it" partially came true. "Bonking" suggests positive action which *Pewani* in the strip is incapable of initiating. The reverse is true: he is always bonked by everything he meets. Only the underlying suggestion of bonking someone with an umbrella just to swat a fly was realised: the low level of the intelligence behind the hand holding the umbrella. *Pewani* as a character lived up to his "not-so-bright outlook."

The physical appearance of *Pewani* was also suggestive: a pear-shaped, hairless head with wide stupefied eyes, air-cooled teeth and protruding ears, underneath which dangled a short squat man in an oversize jacket carrying an umbrella in all weathers and a suitcase at all times and in all places, in and out of doors, at table, in shops and restaurants.

The umbrella and suitcase conveyed the idea of a traveler, someone on the road "off to the lands of wonder and dazzling surprises." *Pewani*, then, was an adventurer discovering the 'wonder' of the world in which he moved: an urban context of machines and man; both are unpredictable and inexplicable. *Pewani* discovered the world is one of dangers, hazards and exquisite pain in which the protagonist always gets the worst of it.

---

[65] *Malawi News*, 11-17 April 1981, p. 16.

In *Pewani*, the stock plots of a dupe are dramatised painfully. He falls into the conventional traps only idiots or fools fall into: touching live wires, hammering his thumb instead of the nail, falling off overloaded trucks, catching his fingers in shutting doors, sitting or stepping barefoot on burning cigarettes, falling off loose walls, gazing into the ends of hoses which are about to be turned on by a prankster, stepping through glass doors, rowing backwards over waterfalls, diving into shallow, rocky or empty pools, being cut by aeroplane propellers, being hit by falling library shelves or coconuts, sleeping on rail tracks in the path of an on-coming train, swallowing flies, or crashing to the ground from the top flour because he thought his umbrella could be used as a parachute.

Pewani also echoes dupes of other nations, for example, the old Nasreddin story of sawing through the branch of a tree one is sitting on. Locally, *Pewani* echoes *Fisi*, the hyena, already established as his ancestor in folklore: *Pewani* never triumphs over his adversary, which, in this case, is the whole urban environment. He is just not equipped to cope with this world of machines and the men behind them.

The parting words *Pewani's* family shouted at his back as he left the security and comfort of home always underlay the strips: Watch out on the roads—*Pewani* did not watch out on the roads, he had the worst road accidents met by a pedestrian. Be on the look out—*Pewani's* sleepy eyes could not warn him of the obvious dangers he would encounter. Remember, no more accidents—he was so accident-prone he was the unlisted candidate for the Guinness Book of Records. Come back safely— it was always doubtful if *Pewani* would return home in one piece.

"*Pewani*" as a name, in fact, means "avoid" or "prevent" accidents, dangers or follies before they actually happen to the victim. Hence, the name was used ironically: *Pewani* met the very dangers he warned others to avoid. The cartoon strip, in all, was a record of all the hazards modern man meets in his day-to-day existence from birth to death. The perpetually perplexed expression on *Pewani's* face summarised economically the "dazzling surprises" that he was caught in, in everything he touched, every step he took, and around every corner he turned.

In the face of all the predictable accidents or inexplicable encounters, *Pewani* was a mute and very solitary being. The two-frame strip emphasised his inarticulacy. The only sounds he uttered were onomatopoeic and ideophonic grunts of pain, anguish and paralyzed surprise:

> DING! when a truck door hit him
> CRASH! when he tripped and fell down
> SNAP! when a rope he was pulling snapped.

Pewani and the Society

Brian Hara, the creator/artist of *Pewani*, was voted the "Artist of the Year" three years running, from 1980 to 1982, according to the Malawi Broadcasting Corporation Listeners' poll. *Pewani* specifically was voted the third most popular cartoon in 1981, and the first in 1982.

As part of the Christmas fun the *Malawi News* of 19-25 December, 1981 ran a "Spot the Difference" competition featuring *Pewani*:

> Our lovable cartoon character Pewani is always getting himself into trouble. Now see how much trouble you have in spotting eight differences between cartoon A and cartoon B. Draw a circle round each area on cartoon B that is different to cartoon A, fill in your name and address in the space provided and you could be in line for a really great gift pack of Cleartone skin products from Nicholas Laboratories. There's skin toning cream, special soap, body lotion, skin softener and complexion capsules in every gift pack.[66]

Pewani enthusiasts entered the competition. Other fans echoed *Pewani's* entry into the world with "letters to the editor."

> Pewani Keeps Us Smiling
> Dear Editor,
> I write to express my admiration over how Pewani has survived a lot of accidents, many of them fatal. I would like to thank his doctor for keeping our funny man alive until 1982. Although belatedly, I

---

[66] *Malawi News*, 19-25 December 1981, p. 11.

declare Pewani "Cartoon of the Year 1981." My special thanks go
to the man who produces this interesting cartoon.

S _____ G _____   ,
Lilongwe.[67]

Other fans noted the silent world in which *Pewani* moved and commented
on it.

> Fan for Pewani
> Dear Editor,
> I am an ardent Pewani fan. I love his "silent language." The
> poor fellow can be understood by the literate and the
> illiterate. Mr. Editor, kindly accept my "pat on the back" for
> the fun we get from Pewani. Send my regards to Mr. Pewani.
> Tell him I really dig him.
> Pewani Fan,
> Blantyre.[68]

The listeners' poll, the competitions, fan mail from the different regions,
all indicate the national interest in the *Pewani* phenomenon. As if the
above were not enough indication of overwhelming popularity, the French
Cultural Centre ran an international art exhibition featuring *Pewani*
between 3 and 23 June, 1983.

Pewani, Joza Face Their Fans

> Pewani and Joza fans have the opportunity of seeing their favourite
> cartoons at the French Cultural Centre in Blantyre and refresh their
> minds to what they have been enjoying in "Malawi News" for the
> past two years ...
> Pewani and Joza have been joined by their brothers from
> overseas. Cartoons and comic strips from France have been
> included in the display ...[69]

---

[67]   *Malawi News*, 9-15 December 1982, p. 7.

[68]   *Malawi News*, 28 November-4 December 1981, p. 7.

[69]   *Malawi News*, 11-17 June 1983, p. 1.

According to reports over 2,000 fans turned up in Blantyre to see the month-long exhibition.[70] And, after the Blantyre success, three months later, to Lilongwe, the Capital City, in the central region.

During the Blantyre exhibition, there was a reception to enable the fans to meet Brian Hara, the creator/artist of *Pewani*. The exhibition, described as "the first of its kind in Malawi," revealed that the audience was clamouring for more:

> Many fans who attended a ceremony at the centre last week insisted that the two cartoons, Pewani and Joza, which are drawn by Brian Hara and Vic Kasinja respectively, should be bound in book forms to enable people [to] turn to the booklets when they want to laugh in [their] homes.[71]

The fascination for the dupe figure has already been discussed: the need for people to laugh at themselves. Another explanation for the popularity was given in another news item:

> But the most interesting thing about Pewani and Joza is that they reflect the local Malawian scene.[72]

The Pewani Syndrome in Real Life

The last quotation above indicates the significance *Pewani* has for the audience. Some buyers of the paper want to read only the *Pewani* strip. For example, the author was once stopped outside a newspaper shop, where he had bought the last copy of the *Malawi News*, with the request:

"I just want to read *Pewani*, please." It was not unusual hear the name shouted at a player in a soccer match who had been out-manoeuvred in play, or at the loser in a karate film. In a night club, a girl was once heard calling a pimp by that name. At another club, the dart board had a sketch with a dart stuck in the eye of *Pewani*, to warn people to keep away from the area. At a recent exhibition of the technical equipment of a recreation

---

[70] *Malawi News*, 2-8 July 1983, p. 5.

[71] *Malawi News*, 2-8 July 1983, p. 5.

[72] *Malawi News*, 7-13 May 1983, p. 1.

centre, one of the officials invited a guest: "Come on, Mr.____, don't be like *Pewani*, leave your umbrella on the table and climb up here." *Pewani*, then, has also come to mean in general parlance a fool, an idiot, or a dupe.

When the author once asked a group of lecturers if they thought that *Pewani* was a national hero, the answer was that he was a "national disaster." A national disaster *Pewani* was indeed. In actual fact the *Malawi News* described him as "the hilarious accident prone '*Pewani*'." The real world of disasters, hazards and fatal accidents, besetting the Malawi scene, however, cannot be described as hilarious. Table 6 catalogues the disasters reported in the local papers during the same period *Pewani* reached his ascendancy.

TABLE 6: ACCIDENTS, DISASTERS, HAZARDS, ETC.

No.	Category	Examples	/80 Reports
1	Road accidents	Hit and run, plunging over bridges, head-on collisions, etc.	29
2	Man vs elements	Lightning, floods, fire, etc.	15
3	Man vs animals	Crocodile, hippo, buffalo, lion, elephant, rabid foxes, dogs, hyenas, jackal, monkey, etc.	14
4	Man vs inanimate	Collapsing walls, swallowing needles, falling paper rolls, falling into latrine, pits, unknown causes.	6
5	Strange births	Four-legged chicken, eight-legged calf, three-legged goat.	5
6	Man vs plants	Falling trees, poisonous mushrooms, etc.	4
7	Man vs birds/insects	Owls, bees, etc.	4
8	Epidemics	Armyworms, cholera, jiggers.	3

From such reports, it is difficult to draw a distinction between *Pewani*, the dupe, and the accidents happening in the real world outside the cartoon strip. It is also difficult to explain, in the final analysis, why *Pewani's* accident-proneness should have gripped the nation so overwhelmingly, the social and psychological reasons given earlier notwithstanding. The final message *Pewani* has for us, then, is that we are really at the mercy of malignant, inexplicable and incomprehensible forces from which we should thank our doctors for saving us, keeping us alive to encounter the next package of disasters.

CHAPTER EIGHT:
TWICE RETOLD TALES

Nancy Schmidt's statements about children's literature are intriguing. In one of her publications she sets out to

> critically examine the authenticity of collections of sub-Saharan African folklore for children which are available in the United States.[1]

In an earlier publication she observes:

> Unless a child recognised the names as being African or read the notes about the author, the African origin of the tales would remain unknown. In such books as these, if the book jacket is removed or if it is never read, the book in essence ceases to be about Africa from the perspective of young readers.[2]

The question that arises in both publications is: Whose children's literature: African, non-African, or both? Even when Nancy Schmidt specifies in later publications, "African Folklore for African Children," and the more impressive *Children's Books on Africa and their Authors*, a closer examination reveals that most of the publications were clearly directed at non-African young readers.[3]

In answering the question "Whose children's literature?" we restrict ourselves to the analysis of texts purporting to be based on Malawian folktales, and more specifically to Geraldine Elliot's four volumes, all of

---

[1] Nancy J. Schmidt, "Collections of African Folklore for Children," *Research in African Literatures*, 2, 2 (Fall 1971), p. 150.

[2] Nancy J. Schmidt, "Children's Literature About Africa: A Reassessment," *African Studies Review*, 13, 3 (1970), p. 472.

[3] Nancy J. Schmidt, "African Folklore for African Children," *Research in African Literatures*, 8, 3 (Winter 1977), pp. 304-326; *Children's Books on Africa and their Authors* (New York: Africana Publishing Co., 1975); and "Children's Literature about Africa," *African Studies Bulletin*, VIII, 3 (1965), pp. 61-70.

which Schmidt annotates briefly in her publications. The volumes are *The Long Grass Whispers*, *Where the Leopard Passes*, *The Hunter's Cave* and *The Singing Chameleon*.[4] All the volumes have been reprinted at least twice, *The Singing Chameleon* three times, suggesting their immense popularity. The purpose for analyzing the volumes is to demonstrate that, although evidently based on Malawian folktales and expressly written for children, the readership was never intended to be black or indigenous Malawian. External and internal evidence will be given to support the contention. External evidence in this case includes authorship, production, distribution and consumption. Internal evidence will come from an analysis of the content and form of selected stories from each volume.

Background

Although serious critical attention to children's literature in Africa starts in the 1960s with bibliographers like Nancy Schmidt, publishing in Malawi dates back to the early Christian missionaries of the Universities' Mission to Central Africa (UMCA) in the 1860s and 1870s. A special problem presents itself here: the bibliographer or critic has to wade through material published for different purposes and readership. The early missionaries were not only learning the vernacular languages and publishing in them, they were also simplifying and translating texts for the newly literate Africans. In this case it is hard to distinguish "children's literature" from literacy materials meant for both youths and adults who were meeting print for the first time in their lives and societies. Even as recently as the 1950s, when the Elliot books were first published, both adults and children attended the classes together. Partly for this reason and also for economic reasons, there was no real distinction in the materials prepared and produced for adults and children. These materials included word lists, dictionaries, grammars, primers and readers in the

---

4   Elliot, *The Long Grass Whispers*; *Where the Leopard Passes*; *The Hunter's Cave*; and *The Singing Chameleon* (London: Routledge and Kegan Paul, 1957).

vernacular, and translations of western literature like Bunyan's *The Pilgrim's Progress* and Aesop's *Fables*.[5]

Before 1980, there is neither a steady gradation of materials nor a discernible development of a body of literature specifically labelled children's or juvenile literature, outside textbooks used in primary or secondary schools. It is only in retrospect, after the rise of three or four generations of literate children, when the concept of literature written for young people was made available to local publishers, that the country is actively encouraging authors to direct their energies towards this market. On the other hand, when Geraldine Elliot was publishing in the 1940s and 1950s there was already a long tradition of children's literature in the West, which she belonged to, grew up in, and was, in turn, contributing to. In fact, all the publications for children written in English before the 1960s were by non-Malawians, well versed in the practice of writing for children.

If we drew up a list of publications of the century ending in 1960, they would fall into one or more categories below. Children's literature written by

a. Malawians, in the vernacular, for Malawian children, e.g. Austin H.C. Mkandawire, *Amhara gha Bana* in Tumbuka.[6]

b. Malawians, in English, for Malawian children, e.g. J.W. Gwengwe, *Sulizo Achieves Greatness*.[7]

c. Non-Malawians, in the vernacular, for Malawian children (it was rare for non-Malawian children to read in the local languages), e.g. White Fathers, *Nkhani za Nyama*.[8]

---

[5]   John Bunyan, *The Pilgrim's Progress*, Fifth Edition (London: S.W. Partridge & Co., n.d.); Aesop, *Fables*, translated by Thomas James and George Tyler Townsend, with the illustrations of Charles H. Bennett (Franklin Center, PA: Franklin Library, 1984).

[6]   Austin H.C. Mkandawire, *Mahara gha Bana* (Lusaka: Publications Bureau of Northern Rhodesia and Nyasaland, 1962).

[7]   J.W. Gwengwe, *Sulizo Achieves Greatness* (London: Evans Brothers, 1968).

[8]   White Fathers, *Nkhani za Nyama* (Likuni: White Fathers' Press, n.d.).

d. Non-Malawians, in English, for non-Malawian children (it was rare for Malawian children to read in English during this period), e.g. Young's series.[9]

The question of whose children Geraldine Elliot is writing for could apparently be answered easily by running through the above list. The answer, however, is not that easy: she belongs to a category of non-Malawian authors living in the country, publishing abroad, but writing in English for non-Malawian children locally and abroad. This is the main thrust of the rest of the discussion.

Historically, then, there are no distinct phases children's literature has gone through in Malawi, only groupings by authorship. First, there were Christian missionary collections and translations. Second followed secular collections and translations. Third, missionary-educated Malawians started contributing to literacy in the country. Fourth, a more recent development, both Malawians and non-Malawians started writing specifically for young audiences in either Chichewa, the national vernacular language, or English, the official language of education, business and government. Geraldine Elliot belongs to the second group which co-exists with all the groups.

External Evidence

To answer the question, "Whose children's literature was Elliot writing?" it is necessary to investigate the circumstances surrounding the publications. The relevant factors are those of authorship, production, distribution and consumption.[10]

---

[9] W.P. Young, *Why Rabbit and Hyena Quarrelled and Other Tales from Northern Nyasaland* (London: The Sheldon Press, 1933); *The Rabbit and the Lion and Other Tales from Northern Nyasaland* (London: The Sheldon Press, 1933); and *The Rabbit and the Baboons and Other Tales from Northern Nyasaland* (London: The Sheldon Press, 1933).

[10] The issue of authorship was already considered to some extent in Chapter Two, Informants, pp. 48 ff.

Authorship

Authorship in this discussion includes the informants, the collector, Geraldine Elliot, and the artist, Sheila Hawkins who illustrated all four volumes. First the informants.

The original informants in all four volumes are anonymous, or only vaguely specified. References to original sources are contained in the subtitles of two volumes "A Book of Stories Based on African Folk-tales" (*The Hunter's Cave*) and "A Book of African Folk Tales" (*Where the Leopard Passes*). The other two volumes have no subtitles. In the foreword, linguistic sources are mentioned briefly. A reviewer quoted in the publisher's blurb reveals the source of *The Long Grass Whispers*: an anonymous informant, "An old Ngoni told these animal adventures to Miss Elliot." *Where the Leopard Passes* has the following in the foreword: "I have still kept to the Chinyanja names." So presumably she took them from the Nyanja. *The Hunter's Cave* has the same reference to "Chinyanja names." *The Singing Chameleon* has its origins in a Nyanja proverb. The conclusion is that the stories are from the Nyanja and Ngoni peoples. However, Nancy Schmidt warns:

> Although these animal tales [in *The Singing Chameleon*] are primarily from the Chinyanja of Nyasaland (Malawi), some of the proper names are Tumbuka or Tonga, while some of the proverbs are from the Tumbuka and Bemba. The sources of the names and proverbs are not indicated in the individual tales.[11]

Although Schmidt's comments refer to *The Singing Chameleon*, we can generalise to the other titles and safely say also that the original tales are largely from Malawians, with a few from non-Malawian Africans.

Geraldine Elliot, the collector, herself lived in Zomba, Malawi (the then Nyasaland) for several years. She was a resident non-Malawian. It has not been established whether or not Sheila Hawkins, the illustrator, was acquainted with Africa. Her illustrations are discussed later.

---

[11]   Schmidt, *Children's Books*, p. 78.

It will be demonstrated below that apart from the anonymity of the original informants, both the texts and the illustrations are non-Malawian in design and intent.

Production and Consumption

The books were published and reprinted in the United Kingdom. They enjoy wide readership in the United States also, where this author bought some of the volumes. Some of the stories have also been televised on children's programmes in the United States. It was the author's children who drew his attention to one such show. (There was no television in Malawi at the time.)

Locally the books are also available in the bookshops where the author recently bought the remaining reprints. The original hardbacks were also available in the bookstores. The author remembers reading *The Long Grass Whispers* in the 1950s. The University Library and some of the branches of the national library also have some of the titles but not all. It has not been established how many primary and secondary school libraries stock which titles. The question of readership will be returned to at the end of the discussion.

Several authorial statements indicate that the books were not intended for local black Malawians and their children. The quotation below (quoted in part in Chapter Two) is from the foreword of *Where the Leopard Passes*:

> Shortly after *The Long Grass Whispers* was published, I met a very charming old lady. "My dear," she said, gently patting my hand, "that book of yours! Dreadful!" My heart sank, but she went on: "It is not the tales—they are delightful and the children love them. It is the names of the animals. Quite unpronounced-able! You ought to have thought of the Grandmothers and Aunts and Uncles who have to read the stories aloud!"
>
> "Oh, dear!" I said. "Are they as difficult as all that?"
>
> "Certainly, they are. Take N-Y-A-L-U-G-W-E. I just have to leave it out and say 'Leopard' but that annoys me!"
>
> I am sorry, and I want to apologise to all the Grandmothers and Aunts and Uncles who hold the same view as my charming old lady, for I have still kept to the Chinyanja names. The stories

197

in this book are all based on genuine African Folktales ... so it seems to me not only right that I should keep to the original names. They are nice names and at least no one will be worried by "Kalulu," the Rabbit, who is the hero of so many African stories.

I do hope the Grandmothers and the Aunts and the Uncles will forgive me! (*Where the Leopard Passes*, p. vii)

This foreword could not have been addressed to the original Malawians. They would hardly have had problems pronouncing the vernacular names for animals. Moreover, at the time of writing (1949), no black Malawian grandmother, aunt or uncle would read aloud to the youth a book of folk stories. They would tell or sing them directly. In any case, as the literacy figures below show, there was no generation of literate grandmothers, aunts or uncles at that time. Furthermore, Miss Elliot would hardly reiterate to the original vernacular sources that her stories were based on "genuine African Folktales." Clearly, the audience is non-Malawian in spite of possibly being in the country with the collector.

The Hunter's Cave has a foreword, too, indicating other readers' discomforts with the Chinyanja names. Miss Elliot retained the names. However, she added a "Postscript, The Unpronounceable Names." The same observations made above apply here.

Not only do authorial statements indicate that the books are for a foreign readership, the publisher's blurb and reviews sustain the same belief:

(1) the ancient tradition of story-telling in Africa, a tradition on which Geraldine Elliot has again based her animal stories.
(2) From her home in Zomba the authoress has sent out to children all over the world a charming Christmas gift.
(3) These tales have the atmosphere of primitive Africa with its unpredictable changes.
(4) The tales are not so much based on actual folk-lore as woven around the proverbs and customs of Central Africa. [12]

---

[12] Elliot, (1) *The Long Grass Whispers*; (2) *Where the Leopard Passes*; (3) *The Hunter's Cave*; (4) *The Singing Chameleon*.

It seems as if the authoress, the publishers and the reviewers agree that the stories are for non-Malawian readers. As the quotes above indicate, the non-Malawians likewise accept that they, indeed, are the intended audience.

Illustrations

Before turning to internal textual evidence, a brief word on the illustrations. The illustrations are mostly of animals with various humorous expressions on their faces. (Most rock paintings or murals, and even recent paintings by Malawians, do not usually depict animals with humorous expressions on them.) There are also drawings of black adults and youths in loin cloths, not specifically Malawian in their features. Some of the drawings are of domestic objects like pots, bowls, barrels, hoes, axes, etc. Most of these are western in design, for example, the axes or spades. Although there may be a Ngoni-like shield, one finds that in some instances there is a western style shop-made bow held by a black boy. All in all, the pictures are not specifically Malawian, they are of a generalised African setting designed obviously by a western artist.

Internal Evidence

After examining the external evidence, we now turn to internal support. Here we are going to examine the content, form and language style.

The tales are of the trickster-and-dupe type. Sometimes the trickster is himself duped, but very often he is triumphant. All the characters are animals and, by name, Malawian animals: *Kalulu*, the Rabbit, *Kamba*, the Tortoise, *Nyalugwe*, the Leopard, etc. The tales are recognisably Malawian.

Perhaps it is in the naming that more evidence accumulates in the intended foreign readership and authorship. A local audience would recognise and get tired of the tautology of repeating the names in both languages. Nor was the author careful in the spelling of some of the vernacular names: *Nadzikambe* instead of *Namdzikambe*, the Chameleon, *Mlungu* instead of *Mulungu*, God, or *Nantusi* for *Nanthesi*, the Toad.

The tales professedly are based not only on African tales but also on "superstitions and customs" (*The Hunter's Cave*, publisher's blurb). However, there is little evidence of specific Malawian beliefs and customs. There is even less proverbial lore, in spite of *The Singing Chameleon* being based on a proverb. The selection of the Chameleon as the key trickster figure in *The Singing Chameleon* is itself significant. Although the Chameleon features as a trickster in some stories in Malawi, these are very few indeed. In other types of stories, the Chameleon features even less. The only stories he features centrally in are the creation myths, in which he is the bringer of the message that man shall die and remain dead forever. For this reason, the Chameleon is really a hated creature: children always kill him on sight by stuffing his mouth with dust or snuff. Why Geraldine Elliot chose a taboo creature and turned him into an artist-poet, singer of tales, may be a function of her being non-Malawian. The other significance of the animal did not escape the publishers' notice:

> With most African peoples the Chameleon is highly unpopular, and he is blamed for the fact that the Bantu are black.

Among the peoples of Malawi, the Chameleon is unpopular because he brought death to mankind, hence his almost ritualistic killing by children everywhere in the country.

The form of Elliot's stories is worth comment, too. Each story has a title before the text proper. The story itself starts, develops and ends without any formulaic patterns. This is different from vernacular oral storytelling techniques (discussed in detail in Chapter Four). The opening formula *Padangotero* (It once happened), the audience responses *Tili tonse* (We are together) and the closing formulae, apart from *basi, mpamene idathera* (that's all, that's where it ended), are all dispensed with. So are the rhythmic, stylised patterns of speech; as are the onomatopoeia and ideophones. All in all, what we have here are texts *written to be read*, not to be told or sung as in the original. All the oral flavour, which was presumably the mode in which they were collected, has been lost, as is the case with the cultural flavour.

In other words, Elliot's style is literary: the written, as opposed to the oral, style predominates, as the examples from some of the texts below demonstrate:

> Golden-red, the full-moon rose; the formless dark took shape. The black still waters of the lake turned slowly to a molten glassy sea; the shadows deepened to a richer violet hue; trees, grasses, flowers and ferns took on a silver sheen and, for a breathless moment, everything seemed hushed and still. Then suddenly a drum began to throb, and another, and another, and another.[13]

Oral dramatic delivery has been replaced by literary language; action by lengthy description.

In another text, the oral raconteur would just have named the plant and the local audience would immediately have grasped the significance which Elliot takes so long to paint here.

> ... there grew a slender dark-leaved shrub whose tiny star-shaped flower—pale as the stars themselves—bloomed almost all the year and, withering turned in time to shiny scarlet berries. These were delicious to eat as a relish, but hot and peppery and, as Nadzikambe [sic] knew, even the smallest taste of them gave one a tremendous thirst.[14]

Furthermore, Elliot goes as far as bestowing talents on the Chameleon which most locals know he does not possess:

> Grey as the ancient rocks around him, Nadzikambe [sic], the Chameleon, sat motionless, listening to the music of the stream. He was by nature a poet, and the sound of falling water always made him feel very poetical, especially if the sun were shining and the birds were gay and full of song. He listened for some time, then started to compose a poem that would do justice to the scene.[15]

The poems the Chameleon composes rhyme. The poems or songs in the Elliot series tend to follow English metre. By contrast, Bantu songs or poems do not rhyme: being tone languages, they have an altogether different way of producing rhythm and euphony.

---

[13] Elliot, *Where the Leopard Passes*, p. 38.

[14] Elliot, *The Hunter's Cave*, p. 116.

[15] Elliot, *The Singing Chameleon*, p. 1.

Finally, the strongest evidence that the stories were not intended for black Malawian children is found in the choice of language: English. Whereas the stories were collected in Chinyanja and Ngoni, Elliot chose not only to translate them but to rewrite them to suit an English reading and speaking audience.

The question of local readership is intriguing. In 1951 when three of the titles (*The Long Grass Whispers*, *Where the Leopard Passes*, and *The Hunter's Cave*) were already published and in circulation, only few local Malawian children (or even adults) could have read them, since the literacy rates were very low:

> It was estimated in 1951 that over half of the children in the Protectorate attended school for short periods between the ages of five and eighteen. It is true that very few pass beyond the lowest classes, and only 339 ... passed the Standard VI examination ... If we take another yardstick, the standard of literacy, we find that for the whole country there are in every thousand people, of all ages, 65 who can read and write [i.e. in the vernacular]. The number of literates per thousand goes up to 72 if we confine ourselves to those between five and eighteen years of age.[16]

In a series of reading interest inventories administered to five Malawian secondary schools in 1975 by the author, none of the respondents reported having read Geraldine Elliot's books.[17]

The problems of writing for children with diverse backgrounds are many, language being only one. Singling out Elliot's books does not mean the situation in Malawi is that bleak. In the same period, vernacular folk stories were also published, including *Nkhani za Nyama* in Nyanja/Chichewa or *Mahara gha Bhana* in Tumbuka. Recently, more titles have been added to the list, *Nthano* and *Tili tonse* being among them.[18] These titles were written by Malawians, specifically for young vernacular readers. Hopefully, Malawian writers in this genre will be more conscious of their audience.

---

[16] Frank Debenham, *Nyasaland: Land of the Lake* (London: HMSO, 1955), p. 171.

[17] Steve Chimombo, "Pupils' Popular Tastes," *ATEM Newsletter*, 2 (1975), pp. 8-20.

[18] Moni Books 2, *Nthano* (Limbe: Popular Publications, 1975); Gumbi, *Tili Tonse*.

CHAPTER NINE:
NEW RIDDLES FOR OLD

When David Livingstone, the missionary-explorer, pleaded in the Senate House in Cambridge on 4th December 1857,

> I go back to Africa to try to make an open path for commerce and Christianity. Do you carry on the work which I have begun. I leave it with you.[1]

little did he realise that whereas his compatriots were busily engaged in commercial and evangelical enterprises, the local folk artist in Central Africa was also constructing, refashioning or recreating riddles inspired by the white man, his culture and his other activities.

This chapter examines the emergence of a number of riddles which seem to have come into existence or been reconstructed or modified from older ones paralleling the advent, settlement and progress of the white man in Malawi. As the discussion reveals, the creations or recreations of the new riddles could not have been independent of the foreign culture, its influence and penetration into not only the indigenous people's lives and fortunes but also the folk artist's imagination. In other words, if riddles are constructed from a people's apprehension of the reality around them, any formulation outside their experience will not find its way into their folklore.

The riddles discussed here cover very specific aspects of Malawi's colonial and post-colonial history. For example, the riddler based some of his artistry on the white man's penchant for renaming the places he explored, visited or settled in. Christian evangelisation also resulted in the renaming of the personal names of converts. The armed forces very often stepped in where peaceful annexation or evangelisation had failed, hence the advent of military riddles. Western education went hand in hand with

---

[1] Frank Winspear, "A Short History of the Universities Mission," *The Nyasaland Journal*, 9, 1 (January 1956), p. 11.

evangelisation under the Christian missionaries before the colonial administration stepped in. Riddles related to literacy and numeracy were constructed. Western trade and industry required an extensive network of roads, rails and waterways where few or none existed before. This network inspired riddles pertaining to transport and communications. The opening up of the country led also to an influx of western commercial artefacts which the riddler incorporated into his repertoire. These historical points need fleshing out briefly before embarking on a discussion of the riddles themselves.

Historical Background

British Central Africa, as Malawi was known in the 1870s, is a landlocked country west of Mozambique, south of Tanzania and east of Zambia. From the 1870s to the 1890s there was no central government, the land being occupied by different ethnic groups like the Chewa in the central, the Yao in the southern or the Tumbuka in the northern regions. Prior to the advent of the white man, the land had been ravaged by the immigrating Ngoni, and was still being depopulated by the slave raiders, the Arabs and the Swahilis. David Livingstone's call for the introduction of legitimate trade arose from this grim state of affairs.

The Universities Mission to Central Africa (UMCA) responded to Livingstone's plea. An advance party arrived in British Central Africa in 1876, followed three years later by the African Lakes Company, the commercial wing of the Christian missions. Other missionary groups, the Dutch Reformed Church and the Catholics, followed. Soon, most of the southern parts of the territory felt the missionary and commercial presence. It was mostly due to missionary pressure that the territory was annexed in 1892 as a British Protectorate with a governor, provincial and district commissioners, the army and police. Administrative centres grew up around such towns as Zomba, the then capital, Blantyre and Lilongwe. It was in these administrative centres that Malawians came into contact with western forms of government.

The Central African Rifles (later, The Kings African Rifles) and the police were used to pacify local protest at the annexation. However, following the suppression of Yao slave traders there was no large-scale armed resistance to the British occupation until 1915, when John Chilembwe and a few of his colleagues staged an uprising. Even this "Chilembwe Uprising" was not countrywide, being confined to Blantyre and Chiradzulu in the southern, and Dedza in the central regions. Another show of resistance was to the Central African Federation in 1953, with Blantyre, Mulanje and Thyolo as the centres of unrest. In these instances, enough military force, arms and tactics were demonstrated to inspire the folk artist. The 1953 resistance ushered in the nationalist ferment of the closing years of the 1950s and the opening years of the 1960s, which saw the renamed Nyasaland a self-governing colony in 1964 and the Republic of Malawi in 1966, under the leadership of Dr. Hastings Kamuzu Banda.

Western education was in the hands of the Christian missionaries from the time of the advent of the UMCA. The colonial administration created a Department of Education only in 1926. The first secondary school was founded in 1940 and the University of Malawi in 1964.

The British system of indirect rule meant that the social life of the indigenous people was left largely untouched. In the villages political authority resided in the headman or chief who acted as the agent for the district commissioner in collecting taxes, recruiting labour and enforcing government policy in return for a fee.

The largely agricultural and pastoral country continued to till and graze under British management. Large tobacco, tea, tung and cotton estates were opened up in the southern and central regions as part of the programme of legitimate trade and industry. New industries were also created in the urban and missionary centres (e.g. printing, carpentry, etc.). It was in the estates and in the new industries that Malawians were also exposed to the western economy and commercial enterprise. On the domestic side, administrators, traders, missionaries and estate owners employed a large number of Malawians as cooks, stewards, and gardeners. Close contact with the white man's culture and wealth ensured another source of inspiration for the folk artist.

All in all, then, Malawians were exposed to the white man on several levels. The colonial government managed their political lives, the missionaries the spiritual, the estates the economic, etc. Labour was exploited, taxes were levied, money was minted and in return the country was governed and protected from further ravages. Should the riddles, then, be seen as a form of resistance to the white man's presence? Yes and No.

Starting with the latter response, from the published sources there does not seem to have been any upsurge of anti-missionary, anti-colonial or anti-white riddles at any given period. The largest collection of riddles dealing with the white man is the most recent. This large number, however, might be due to the fact that the collectors were Malawians themselves, and therefore, the informants were not afraid to contribute riddles that reflected the foreigners and their culture. Taken in isolation, the riddles do not reflect a strong underlying political ideology, nationalism, anti-colonial or anti-white sentiments.

Looked at positively, the riddles came into being as part of an overall reaction to the white man and his culture. If the riddles are taken as complementary to the other folk arts (songs, jokes, narratives, drama) which also responded to the foreign presence, they gain great significance. The riddle as one of the verbal arts has tremendous potential for not only social but also political criticism, explicit and implicit. The riddle becomes a powerful weapon of criticism, warning, ridicule and satire. This is seen in all the areas the riddler directed his attention to: the missionary, the administration, the colonial army and police, transport and communication, literacy, the postal services, or clothes.

When the riddles are seen in this larger colonial and nationalistic light they are no longer static or a children's pastime, but revolutionary verbal weapons for combatting western imperialism, capitalism and colonialism. In this case, the folk artist is an active participant reacting to the historical forces threatening to assimilate, dominate or oppress his society. The riddles are protest manifestoes adapting or modifying the same white man's language, technology or artefacts to his own use. The folk artist has turned his attention to the new living reality that is the white man, his attitudes, perceptions and values, and has made his response. The response also reflects the society's own changing and expanding consciousness as it attempts to understand or come to terms with the new realities.

The idea of the riddler as a revolutionary and the riddle as a nationalistic weapon is quite powerful, seen in this larger context. In its construction and performance, the riddle is most innocuous, subdued but subtle. It is not as visible, it does not advertise itself as loudly and as dramatically, as the protest song, folk story, mask or mime. However, in its very form and provenance it is also the most difficult to suppress: the riddler "throws" riddles to an audience he knows and trusts (strangers are given censored, neutral or watered-down versions). The really powerful riddles are not "thrown" to the very subjects that are being satirised. Hence it is not surprising that Gray, one of the white collectors discussed below, found little evidence of "new" riddles coming into being because of the white man.

Studies in Malawian Riddles

Malawian riddles have been studied from functional (e.g. Gray, Beuchat), grammatico-semantic (e.g. Mapanje), structuralist (e.g. Mvula) and psycholinguistic (e.g. Chimombo) perspectives.[2] The functional approach isolates the uses to which the riddles are put in the society (e.g. education, entertainment, etc.). The grammatico-semantic approach analyses the linguistic structure of the riddle, and makes statements on its meaning and pragmatic reference. The structuralist approach examines the units of the form of the riddle and makes statements about its structure and composition. Finally, the psycholinguistic approach proposes a model of how the human mind constructs and comprehends riddles.

A few of the above studies recognise or examine the effect of culture contact on riddle construction and comprehension. For example, Gray comments on the increased exposure to western culture by the younger generation. However, he states that he saw little evidence in the places he

---

[2]   Gray, "Some Riddles of the Nyanja People," pp. 251-291; P.D. Beuchat, "Riddles in Bantu," in Alan Dundes, ed., *The Study of Folklore* (Englewood Cliffs, NJ: Prentice-Hall, 1965), pp. 182-205; Mapanje, "The Use of Traditional Literary Forms in Modern Malawian Writing"; Mvula, "Introducing Malawian Riddles," pp. 1-63; Steve Chimombo, "A Psycholinguistic Model of Riddle Construction and Comprehension," unpublished manuscript.

had visited (Ntcheu, Dedza, Zomba) for signs of "continued vigorous growth," i.e. new riddles being created, forcing him to conclude:

> The riddles which show signs of having been coined recently do not strike me as being as apt or penetrating as the older ones.[3]

The purpose of this discussion is not to show how apt or penetrating the new riddles are but to demonstrate their powerful presence and their recent recreation which ensure the revitalisation of this genre.

Although her survey of Bantu riddles concentrated on the functional and linguistic aspects, Beuchat also recognised the effect of foreign culture on the data she examined.

> This is seen in the use of foreign words, or when the riddle itself describes some object or custom which is typically European in origin. Images or words of foreign origin are also used in riddles which otherwise seem to me quite old and certainly are typically Bantu in underlying significance.[4]

Beuchat provides us with the basic criteria for distinguishing foreign influences on indigenous riddles: loan words, foreign images, objects or customs. Subsequent discussion is an expansion of these basic features examined under different sub-categories.

The two works reviewed above mention briefly but do not elaborate upon the effects of culture contact on Malawian riddles. This study goes beyond the previous ones by examining exclusively riddles characterised by foreign influences and providing the historical context which made their construction or reconstruction possible. Such a study is vital because it demonstrates the processes whereby the riddler responded to the advent, spread and progress of the white man and his culture in the midst of his own. The study is also essential for comparing how other disciplines (anthropology, sociology, or religion) also recorded the meeting of the two cultures. Within the same field of folklore studies, comparisons can be made with how the other folk literature genres (folk narrative, folk-

---

[3]   Gray, "Some Riddles of the Nyanja People," p. 252.

[4]   Beuchat, "Riddles in Bantu," p. 201.

song or proverb) responded to similar phenomena. Finally, with the recent upsurge of the use of "oral testimony" or "oral history" to fill in the gaps of Malawi's pre-colonial and colonial history, this study bridges two disciplines, literature and history, since what it demonstrates is riddles as history-in-the-making.

Documentation

Sources of the Riddles

The riddles in this discussion are taken from four works published at different periods in the country's history:

1. Edward Steere's *Collections for a Handbook of the Yao Language*. This is the earliest publication containing riddles. The informant was a slave from an unspecified Yao speaking area.

2. R. Sutherland Rattray's *Some Folklore Stories and Songs in Chinyanja*.[5] The second publication with riddles from the Nyanja, Mang'anja, Chewa and Ngoni of Blantyre, Central Angoniland, Dedza.

3. Ernest Gray's "Some Riddles of the Nyanja People." The third collection, from Ntcheu and Zomba Districts, with riddles of the Ngoni, Chewa, Nyanja, Mang'anja, Nguru (Lomwe) and Yao peoples.

4. Enoch Timpunza Mvula's "Introducing Malawian Riddles." The largest collection to date, with data from the widest area too: Dedza, Ntcheu, Likoma Island, Mchinji, Mangochi and Chiradzulu from Ngoni, Chewa, Nyanja, Mang'anja, Yao and Likoma peoples.

Although the publications are from four different periods, the sources are from closely related Bantu-speaking peoples. The Nyanja, Mang'anja and now Chewa officially form one group spanning parts of the southern and central regions. The Ngoni have been enculturated by the other groups to such an extent that there is now no distinct Ngoni language. Although the Yao have been singled out in Steere's collection, no data of significance

---

[5]   R. Sutherland Rattray, *Some Folk-lore Stories and Songs in Chinyanja* (1907) (New York: Negro Universities Press, 1969).

have been used in this discussion. Gray's Yao riddles are in Nyanja translation. Likoma has not been taken as a separate ethnic group, only dialectal differences (as those existing between Nyanja, Mang'anja and Chewa) being recognised. Thus, the data for this collection have some homogeneity from a seemingly heterogeneous group covering several hundreds of square miles in the districts most widely exposed to western culture during the period under discussion, 1860-1980.

A comparison of the published corpus from the four periods is the most convenient method so far for judging whether or not there was any influence on the riddle's form and content. Any original or foreign forms can be compared with others from the previous or subsequent collections. Furthermore, the same riddle's development can be seen, analysed and described.

Technical Issues of Documentation

1. The numbering codes found in the original publications have been preserved for ease of reference. The collector's last initial (i.e. first letter of surname) precedes each riddle for cross references. Thus, the following obtains:

    SR = Steere + Riddle + Number, e.g. SR 1

    RR = Rattray + Riddle + Number, e.g. RR 19

    GR = Gray + Riddle + Number, e.g. GR 37

    MR = Mvula + Riddle + Number, e.g. MR 102

    CR = Chimombo+ Riddle + Number, e.g. CR 1[6]

2. All the English translations are also taken from the original sources. No attempt has been made to change them in any way.

3. The vernacular wording and spelling found in the original has been preserved. No attempt has been made to update the orthography or to change dialectal differences from standard practice.

---

[6] The author's personal collection of riddles.

Primary Sources

Wherever primary sources are given, e.g. Gray, they are indicated. Unfortunately, this is not possible for the other collections, where no information is given even on informants, e.g. Rattray. Mvula acknowledges different collectors' sources by district only (as does Gray). The issue of informants and other documentation is discussed at great length in Chapter Two, with reference to oral literature in general.

It is a pity that the original informants were not given names, ages, sexes, and especially professions and statuses, so that not only their identities but also their social class (chief, headman or elder) could be ascertained. In the absence of such documentary evidence, it can only be speculated that the riddles were originally constructed by artists who, of course, had some contact with the white man and his culture. In this case, the riddlers probably included western-educated Malawian clerks, soldiers and pastors, apart from school children.

It is also a problem that accurate dating for historical purposes is impossible in a study where exact times and places are important. The lack of specific dates is reflected in this study, which cannot pretend to discuss the riddles in relation to the distinct historical stages the country went through: UMCA, colonial (pre-federation, federation, post-federation), self-government, post-independence and republic. The best we can do is use the specific events, objects, or items for establishing the period referred to. The alternative adopted here was to group the riddles thematically, as will be seen below.

Other related problems are the contexts, the occasions for performances and the performances themselves. The sources do not indicate the original settings and purposes for the riddle-throwing. Important aspects of the performances are whether or not the riddles were part of verbal acts (narratives, singing, sayings, instruction), as they usually are; whether or not they came before, during or after such acts. The audience, a crucial factor in the verbal arts, is lacking also: what was the composition? Were they relatives only, or visitors or strangers (black or white?) who could have helped, especially in the riddles of the white man?

Finally, although the riddles are taken from the Chewa-speaking peoples, and geographically the southern and central regions of the country are covered, it should not be forgotten that the original riddle was in each case constructed by an individual, it was presented initially to close relatives or friends in the home or village setting, before becoming propagated orally, and before being frozen in the printed form on which our discussion is based. However, the fact that the riddle has taken these routes is a reflection of its acceptance by the larger community. Its continued existence suggests that the riddle encapsulates the society's beliefs, values, perceptions, or ideas. Another proof of acceptance is not only its reappearance in different publications but also the accumulation of variants in the same community or in different dialects or languages in the country.

The problems sketched above, however, do not nullify the genuineness and legitimacy of the data. The advantages of the sources used here are stability of the medium and the "new" date of publication of the printed riddles.

Classification of the Riddles

Under Gray and others, "the white man's culture" is a category on its own. What follows is a reclassification of this major category according to what use is made of the white man's culture, based on the criteria suggested by Beuchat. Here we depart again from previous practice by using both the question and answer parts as valid elements or units of analysis since both can reveal foreign influences. A lot of useful information would have been missed had the classification used only one element.

Seven broad categories have been identified: (1) Place names; (2) Personal names; (3) Christian teachings; (4) Military and police activities; (5) Literacy and numeracy; (6) Transport and communications; (7) Commercial and other artefacts. The discussion follows this order, since the first category covers the advent and settlement of the white man, followed by the pacification through the word of God, and, if that failed, through armed force and education. Expansion through wider transport and communication made possible the propagation of commercial items and other artefacts. Although most of the processes were simultaneous, it is only through the imposition of some order that they can be discussed systematically and clearly.

Place Names

When Gasper Bocarro passed through Central Africa in 1616, he found a network of trade between the Lake and the East Coast. Even though he might have been the first white man to be seen by inland Africans, the traders may have had contacts with white men earlier than this date. In any case, parts of Central Africa were known to Europeans by the end of the 17th century, and began to appear on European maps from the early 18th century.[7] For present purposes, however, we need not go as far back as the 17th century. It is doubtful whether any fruitful riddle invention related to the white man took place then.

Neither the early nor the later journeys of Dr. David Livingstone are fruitful, when we examine the published data. The germination of ideas may have been there, but it is our contention that sustained contact on a day-to-day basis was needed to influence large scale creativity. Thus, it is only when the first group of missionaries arrived in the country that we start finding references to the white presence in riddles.

A number of riddles soon came into being based on the white man's penchant for renaming places after his own towns. Henry Henderson and his group of UMCA founded Blantyre on 23rd October 1876, to give rise to a transformation of an older riddle.[8]

GR 11:   *Njobvu yafera ku Blantyre, kuno mafupa okha gobede.*
          The elephant has died at Blantyre, here the bones only (fall) with a hollow sound.

A: *Nkhungulupsya.*
          Burnt-grass particles (blown about by the wind after a bush fire.)

---

[7]   R.A. Hamilton, "The Route of Gaspar Bocarro from Tete to Kilwa in 1616," *The Nyasaland Journal*, 7, 2 (July 1954), p. 7.

[8]   W.H.J. Rangeley, "Early Blantyre," *The Nyasaland Journal*, 7, 1 (January 1954), p. 37.

It is a transformation of an older one since, apart from the onomatopoeic *gobede*, only the place name is different from the following:

MR 80:   *Njobvu yafera ku Dowa, koma kuno mafupa okha-okha.*
                An elephant has died in Dowa, here only the bones fall.

A: *Nkhungulupsya.*
                Burnt grass particles blown about by the wind.

Substitution has occurred only where the place name is slotted in. The same statements could not be made about the next riddle, where genuine creativity is demonstrated.

MR 166:   *Kumubulabula kumtaya.*

A: *Ku Blantyre.*
                (No translation given)

The riddle is a sophisticated scrambling of the syllables contained in the English/Scottish "Blantyre." The riddle could not have been possible before the advent of the UMCA 1876, when Kabula, the original place whose name was taken from a nearby stream, was rechristened by Henry Henderson. In the riddle, the usual devices for disguising the question have been dispensed with, leaving only the onomatopoeic *bulabula* and at the same time making it almost impossible to decipher it without prior knowledge of the new riddle's answer itself.

The map of British Central Africa was rewritten with new English names in a similar fashion. Blantyre was a mission station in the south, named after David Livingstone's birth place in Scotland. Other mission stations sprang up in the central and northern regions. Livingstonia, named after Livingstone himself, is the most famous example. The colonial administration contributed also, with some towns renamed, like Port Herald, Cape Maclear; local hills had English epithets, (e.g. Mount Mulanje, Vipya Plateau), if not complete English names like Kirk Range; local streets were named after famous administrators or company officials like Henderson and Buchanan in Blantyre and Limbe. That it was a truly British colony was reflected also in the obvious street names like Victoria Avenue, Jubilee Road or Kings Road.[9]

The penchant for renaming had its corollary: the distortion or defacing or mutilation of local names. David Livingstone initiated the first howler: the big lake was renamed Lake Nyasa, a tautology since the vernacular *Nyasa* also means "Lake" (i.e. the lake became Lake Lake). The land became Nyasaland, the land of the lake, mixing the elements! The other lakes were more fortunate in that the local names were retained (e.g. Lake Chilwa). Dedza, a district in the central region, was a misunderstanding and mispronunciation of Kamtedza, by Livingstone again.[10] Another later corruption was Kotakota, a district in the northern part of the central region, whose name is now restored to the original Nkhotakota.

Personal Names

Apart from places being renamed, some clan or ancestral names were christened after saints and other western figures. (To this day, some candidates are denied baptism if they do not adopt a Christian or western name.) The following is a simple illustration.

MR 209: *Make Mariya madzi ndikatunga kuti?*
Mary's mother, where can I draw water?

A: *Chiswe.*
Ants – never run out of saliva.

Mary here could be Christ's mother or Mary Magdalene. The riddle, however, is neutral: it could be a recent creation or a reconstruction from an older one using a local name. However, the published works do not give a variant to compare it with. A better illustration is the one below:

MR 64: *Alusiya bvoko.*
Miss Lucy is noisy.

---

9   W.H.J. Rangeley, "The Origins of the Principal Street Names of Blantyre and Limbe," *The Nyasaland Journal*, 11, 2 (July 1958), p. 49.

10   W.E. Lewis, "Place-Names," *The Nyasaland Journal*, 9, 1 (January 1956), p. 71.

A: *Ndege.*
            An aeroplane.

Both Lucy and aeroplanes are, of course, western inventions. The riddle can, therefore, be dated to post-1933, when the first aeroplane flew into the country. Compare MR 216, under *Transport and Communication*, below.[11]

Another riddle belonging to this category, which demonstrates a more sophisticated construction, is the one below:

MR 474:   *Kuluka aluka a Lukaku sindingakuthe.*
            The weaving that Mr. Weaver weaves beats me.

A: *Dzungu.*
            Pumpkin.

Strictly translated, "Mr. Weaver" should be "Mr. Luka," giving us not only the Christian name but the clever interweaving of vernacular syllables to produce a truly original riddle tongue-twister. It is a reconstruction, since a variant goes like this:

MR 204:   *Kuluka achita kuziluka sindingakuthe.*
            Plaiting they do but I can't.

A: *Njuchi.*
            Bees.

Another variant elaborates on the reconstructed riddle, to produce

MR 208:   *Kuluka aluka a Lukasiku sindingakuthe.*
            The way Mr. Lukasi plaits; I can't manage.

A: *Njuchi.*
            Bees.

In MR 204, the play upon sounds is made possible by the grammatical necessity of the infinitive as subject and its re-use as a verb in the same

---

[11] C.D. Twynam, "Nyasaland Mails and Stamps," *The Nyasaland Journal*, 1, 1 (January 1948), p. 18.

sentence *kuluka … kuziluka*. In MR 208, the elaborateness is developed from the same grammatical possibilities. Furthermore, note that the addition of the western name Lucas and the extension of the syllable *-si* and the particle *-ku* in turn serve to link the negative and the particle in the last word *sindingakuthe*.

Personal names in the larger context deserve a separate study on their own. Some Christian names were appropriated by the *nyau* secret society, new masks created and named after Christian figures. *Maliya* (Mary), *Yosefe* (Joseph), *Simoni Petulo* (Simon Peter), were new masks and mimes. The colonial administrator was not spared, starting with the D.C. mask for the District Commissioner and his *Galimoto* the motorcar as his mode of transport. Outside the secret society most common names became the first names of even non-converts.

The acquisition of western names reached ridiculous heights when household goods, food and utensils were acquired as personal names, especially by the Yao, who became famous for being the white man's house servants. Yao women's clan names could be *Abiti Selempani*, *selempani* being a corruption and vernacularisation of "frying pan," or *Anasiketi* from "skirt," or *Wadi Sofiti* from "soft." Yao men could have names like *Handiwochi* from "hand" or "wrist watch," or *Wimini* from "women," *Supuni* from "spoon." Food-stuffs also were a source of the new naming: *Shuga* from "sugar," *Kabichi* from "cabbage" This tendency reached such extremes that even names of diseases or chemicals were adopted indiscriminately. The most common ones are *Asima* from "asthma" and *Asidi* from "acid." The current nicknames of "Joe Frazier" and "Tar Baby Bazooka" or "Hitman" for local boxers stem from the same impulses.

Christian Teachings

In spite of the widespread Christianisation of the society it is surprising that only a few riddles (as distinct from other folklore genres) are specifically about Christianity or Christian teachings. It is also sometimes difficult to establish whether or not the riddles in this category are new or reconstructed. Most riddles in this group, however, mention specific aspects of Christianity, making them easy to identify. For example,

MR 56:   *Akulu a mpingo anyamula ndi tchalitchi komwe.*
           The church elder has carried the church on his back.

A: *Nkhono.*
           A snail.

In traditional Malawian religion, there is no such label as *akulu a mpingo* (church elder), designating a rung in the hierarchy; in any case, *mpingo* refers only to any Christian denomination, apart from the general term descriptive of a group of people (e.g. *mpingo wa anthu* or *mpingo thu, thu, thu.*)

One of the central teachings Christians propagate is the concept of original sin, which can be expiated only through conversion and baptism. Subsequent relapses into sin can also be forgiven through confession or repentance. The three riddles below utilise these concepts.

MR 56:   *Abatizeni akome ambuye.*
           Baptise him and he will be nice.

A: *Mchere ku ndiwo*
           Salt to meat.

The idea of making a substance more acceptable or presentable through seasoning is captured in the metaphor of baptism. In spite of baptism, however, man is still prone to sin and the riddler has this to say:

CR 1:   *Belo analetsa koma abvalira-bvalira.*
           The bell was banned but he still wears it.

A: Machimo.
           Sins.

Reference is to bell-bottom trousers, which were banned in the 1970s. The government act is likened to the Ten Commandments. So, to help the sinner on the straight and narrow path, the word of God needs to be drummed constantly into his ears:

MR 430:   *Momwe anayambira uwocherera njinga yanga.*
           It's a long time since he started welding my bicycle.

A: *Mau oyera.*
            The gospel.

That is, the work of the preacher is never completed.

If there are only a few riddles on Christian missionaries, the other folk genres are not lacking in their repertoire. The creation of new masks by the *nyau* secret society has already been mentioned above, under personal names. It could be observed further here that the masks are mimes or small plays enacting not only the parts of the names behind the masks but other missionary behaviour or characteristics. Below is a comment on *Simoni Petulo*:

> As the name implies, this is a recent *Cinyau* named after the apostle Simon Peter ... as a result of members of *nyau* attending Christian schools and churches and of Christians becoming members of *nyau*.[12]

The other masks in this group had similar sources of inspiration. *Maliya* (Mary) and *Yosefe* (Joseph) characteristically dance or appear together.

> *Maliya* with baby is a very special request item called by the *mwini maliro*. *Maliya* is generally accompanied by *Yosefe*. Being a request item, *Maliya* is generally very expensive and the *mwini maliro* may have to pay up to £3 for *Maliya* and baby. *Yosefe* looks after the baby while *Maliya* dances ... Those biblical *nyau* are not fierce and do not assault people.[13]

The joke genre also has numerous examples of the white missionary figure, especially the cassocked Catholic father and the Presbyterian church elder, as the butt. The jokes range from comments on missionaries, mispronunciations, or misrepresentations of the vernacular language to the hypocritical practices of some of them. This is another rich area deserving a separate study.[14]

---

[12]   Rangeley, "'Nyau' in Kotakota District, Part 2," p. 29.

[13]   Rangeley, "'Nyau' in Kotakota District, Part 2," p. 30.

[14]   Jessie Sagawa, "Some Malawian Jokes."

Military and Police Activities

Dr. David Livingstone's appeal for the occupation of Central Africa was taken up not only peacefully through evangelisation but also by force. The suppression of the slave trade and the colonisation of the country were violent historical facts. The Central African Rifles were engaged in local and overseas campaigns by the 1890s. It is hardly surprising, then, that a number of riddles draw attention to the colonial army, for

> It was through its military forces as much as its missions that European culture was brought to the indigenous inhabitants.[15]

The riddle below has several variants all centred on the behaviour of soldiers guarding a white man.

MR 48: *Asirikali ndandanda! mzungu pakati.*
Soldiers standing, a whiteman at the centre.

A: *Mafuwa ndi moto.*
Hearth stones and the fire.
(See also MR 305, MR 402, MR 407)

This riddle could be compared with a variant from an earlier publication.

GR 103: *Anthu azungulira, ndi mfumu yao ali m'kati.*
The people are round about, and their chief is in the middle.

A: *Mafuwa.*
The cooking stones.

The concept of soldiers is quite rich in that, in the variants, it not only generates guarding, marching towards and surrounding in military formation in the question. It also, in the answer, presents homely or domestic images of the fireplace, or eating habits. All these devices are possible to the riddler.

There was a close relationship between the army and the police in the early history of the country. (Both were known as *asirikali* before *polisi*

---

[15] George Shepperson, "The Military History of British Central Africa: A Review Article," *The Rhodes-Livingstone Journal*, 26 (December 1959), p. 26.

was loaned for the police.) Operations could be conducted by either, if not both, in some instances. This fact was captured by the riddler in:

MR 170: *Mapolisi a ku Dedza kuponya nkhondo chogadama.*
Dedza policemen battling against their foes while resting on their backs.

A: *Minga.*
Thorns.

This riddle refers not only to military training but also to skill or powers.

Now compare how the same answer produces a reverse riddle for the same institution.

MR 169: *Kanthu kang'onong'ono kuimitsa mapolisi.*
A very little thing halting policemen.

A: *Munga.*
A thorn.

Here the mighty police force is incapacitated by a tiny thorn.

The strong army presence in the colonial period is also reflected in the renaming of places of military importance. Some places were named after white military officers, e.g. Fort Manning or Fort Jameson. These, like Fort Hill, were strategic military posts. Other places were named after colonial administrators like Fort Johnston. Sharpeville was named after a military officer who later became a governor.[16]

Some of the historic exploits of the army were captured in song:

Panamveka mbiri	News was heard
Pa Karonga po:	From Karonga:
Tengani ziwaya asilikari	Take your irons, soldiers,
Gwadani pansi nkhondo yafika.	Kneel down, war has come.

---

[16] See, for example, T. Cullen Young, "Place-Names in Nyasaland," *The Nyasaland Journal*, 6, 2 (July 1953), pp. 35-36; T.D. Thomson, "Place-Names in Nyasaland," *The Nyasaland Journal*, 6, 1 (January 1953), pp. 64-66.

Oh! walephera! Walephera!	Oh, he has failed! He has failed!
Walephera Jeremani!	He has failed, the German!

The song refers to the King's African Rifles campaigns in Karonga, in the north of the country, bordering on Tanzania, which used to be German East Africa. The defeat of the Germans in the Second World War is neatly summed up in this simple song.

The foregoing group of riddles deals with subjugation of the people through military force while the next group covers subjugation through the power of the word.

Literacy and Numeracy

A century or two before the advent of western man, Central Africans were exposed to the Arabic script and some Yao chiefs were even corresponding with the coastal Arabs using either Arabic or Swahili as the medium. Although the Arabic script was in the country much earlier than the Roman, there are no riddles specific to the Muslim religion or culture, only Swahili loan words. Reference to literacy and numeracy seems to depend on western education since, perhaps, it was more widespread and aggressive, and went hand in hand with evangelisation (which the Muslims were not interested in at this early stage). Some riddles seem to be devoted to the act of writing itself, or numeracy. For example,

MR 86: *Popita kubusa ng'ombe yanga inali yonenepa, koma pobwera kumudzi ndafika nayo yoonda.*
My cow was fat when going to the pasture; but when I returned home it was thin.

A: *Sopo/Pensulo.*
Soap/a pencil.

MR 226: *Ziwiri tayimusi izo azungu alephera kupeza.*
Two times that Europeans can't find the answer.

A: *Mchenga.*
Sand.

222

The irony here is that the white man, who brought Arithmetic or more specifically the multiplication table, fails to calculate how many grains of sand there are.

Other riddles are variations on numeracy. The following riddle, although using onomatopoeia, depends on numeracy:

MR 325:   *Gujuguju 19 bifolo.*
          (Untranslated).

A: *Nkhono.*
          A snail.

It has the figure "nineteen" as a distractor. A more elaborate counting system is used in the next example:

MR 375:   *Ndachoka pano kupita ku Mbamba ndi tambala wanga mthumba. Panjira ndatola atambala asanu ndi anayi. Kufika ku Mbamba, mjomba andipatcha atambala asanu ndi awiri. Ndafika ku bawa ya a Kamwanja, a Kamwanja andipatcha atambala asanu. Ndi chiyani?*
          I left this place for Mbamba with one tambala in my pocket. On the way, I picked nine tambala. When I reached Mbamba, my uncle gave me seven tambala. I went to Mr. Kamwanja's bar and he gave me five tambala. What is it?

A: *Chaka cha 1975.*
          The year 1975.

The riddle takes the counting system as a scrambling device. Furthermore, the time scheme, 1975, is a western way of reckoning time. This puts the riddle into the category of a truly new creation, since there is no way a date like 1975 could have been computed among a calendarless people that depended on the moon, the seasons, and historical events or catastrophes for reckoning time.

Western education was, and still is, in great demand. Candidates used to trek hundreds of miles to the centres of education like Livingstonia, Blantyre or Domasi (Zomba). The first classes admitted both children and their parents; functional literacy classes were also mounted periodically;[17] illiteracy was indeed a stigma.[18] Jokes and skits were created about illiterates and their problems of communication and economic survival in the new society. For example, the dishonest delivery boy who appropriated one of his master's items, not knowing that the accompanying note mentioned the specific number being sent. He "fought" the note later for telling on him.

Some songs also were composed deriding the pretentiousness of illiterates. For example:

Anthu osaphunzira	The uneducated people
Eeh kunyada	Eeh, they are proud:
Atenga pensulo	They take a pencil
Aika pa mutu.	Put it on their heads.
Eeh zachisoni!	Eeh, how sad!
Eeh taona!	Eeh, just look!
Eeh Anzako!	Eeh, at your fellows!
Eeh Kunyada!	Eeh, how proud they are!

The illiterate people pretend they are educated by showing off the tools of western education. The song shows them up by being sung by the children who are proud to be educated themselves.

Transport and Communication

As mentioned in the previous section, candidates seeking education trekked hundreds of miles to the centres of learning. It should be mentioned here that the same applied to job-seekers, since there were only a few towns, especially in the South, like Blantyre and Limbe, the industrial capital, and Zomba, the political capital, where employment in the new cash economy could be found. Outside the country, people trekked for weeks to the mines of Zambia or South Africa and the farms of

---

[17] J.L. Pretorius, "A Short Report of the Literature Situation in Nyasaland," *Books for Africa*, 18, 3 (July 1948), pp. 37-38.

[18] Nyasaland Protectorate, *Annual Report of the Department of Education for the Year Ended September, 1931* (Zomba: The Government Printer, 1932), p. 11.

Zimbabwe. Apart from the slave caravan routes the territory was undeveloped at the close of the 19th century and in the first quarter of the 20th. The first wagon road was completed from Katunga to Blantyre in 1892.[19] Interestingly enough, this road took roughly the same route David Livingstone had taken when he came to the country. It is the same road, now much improved, that goes south from Blantyre to Chikwawa. Transport was by *Mtengatenga*, a group of pedestrian load carriers, between the administrative and commercial centres of the country.

In spite of the advent of eastern and western man in Central Africa prior to the 1860s, there were no postal services until 1891. The early postal services were characterised by considerable delays. For example, in 1892 the internal mail took "about 17 actual days en route from Blantyre to Karonga, plus a wait of anything up to four weeks" before reaching its destination, and even in 1922 the weekly overland service by mail runners took nineteen days.[20] The local riddler summed up the experience with

MR 357:   *Ndidaponya kalata yanga kalekale ku Nkhotakota koma mpaka pan yankho silidabwere.*
I posted my letter to Nkhotakota a long time ago, but up to now the reply has not come.

A: *Tsamba.*
A leaf.

This riddle could have been constructed at any stage of the country's postal services, from 1891 to the present. We prefer to think that the local artist did not have Nkhotakota specifically in mind, since it did not have a post office until recently. Furthermore, in the vernacular it is not clear whether the letter was posted in or to Nkhotakota, since either is possible. In any case, mail by rail was only possible from 1908, and only from Chiromo to Blantyre; mail by motor from 1922, only between Zomba and Fort Jameson (now Mchinji); and by air from 1933, between Blantyre

---

19   Rangeley, "The Origins of the Principal Street Names," p. 48.
20   Twynam, "Nyasaland Mails and Stamps," p. 20.

(Chileka) and Lilongwe.[21] Outside those direct routes, the situation was bleak, forcing the local riddler to desperation, if not disgust.

MR 477:   *Kalata yanga ndaponya opanda tsalani.*
           I send my letter without saying goodbye to it.

A: *Chimbudzi.*
           Stool.

The riddle registers total despair of ever hearing from the recipient!

As indicated above, rail transport was introduced in the country in 1908. A riddle that uses the image of the train is:

MR 243:   *Sitima ipaza ndi dondo.*
           A train that travels along forests.

A: *Bongololo.*
           Millipede.

Incidentally the vernacularisation of the word "steamer" can refer to the surface rail as well as the lake steamer services. The impact of the steamer has been mentioned in the context of naming also:

> The use of "Stima" or "Sitima" (steamer) as a British Central African Christian name, however, indicates the fascination which the new European modes of transport held for Africans: one heroic Corporal Stima is noted by Colonel Moyse-Bartlett.[22]

The next development was the air services of 1933, which in turn brought into being their own riddles.

MR 216:   *A Manesi bvoko.*
           Miss Manesi is very noisy.

A: *Ndege.*
           An aeroplane.
           (See also MR 64)

---

[21] C.D. Twynam, "Incidents in the Posts of Nyasaland," *The Nyasaland Journal*, 7, 1 (January 1954), pp. 46-50.

[22] Shepperson, "The Military History of British Central Africa," p. 29.

This riddle notes the noise only, whereas the next riddle focuses on the capacity to fly as well as the noise.

MR 65:   *Mphamba wanga wolira m'mwamba mokha.*
             My eagle crows *[sic]* only in the sky.

A: *Ndege.*
             An aeroplane.

Some of the folk songs dealing with transport and communication describe the awesome intelligence that produced the underlying technology. For example,

Azungu nzeru	The white man is intelligent
Kupanga ndege	He made the aeroplane
Sikanthu kena	It is nothing
Koma ndi khama	But determination

Commercial and Other Artefacts

All the other items or objects which on their own do not make substantial history, or cannot be ascribed to any one particular epoch, but to the general advent or presence of the white man, have been grouped under this general heading. Some of the riddles come under this category either simply by the use of a loan word or by the description of the concept mentioned.

John and Fred Moir of the African Lakes Company, who came in the wake of the UMCA in 1889, contributed greatly to the introduction of western commerce and cultural items. The riddler did not forget them.

GR 107:   *Ng'ombe za mandala zoyera mpuno.*
             The cattle of Mr. Moir have white noses.

A: *Minsi.*
             Pestles.
             (See also MR 7)

Source. Angoni. Gowa School, Ntcheu District

The accompanying note explains:

Mandala was the Native name of Mr. John Moir, one of the two brothers Moir, the founders of African Lakes Corporation, Nyasaland's leading trading firm. He was called *Mandala* because of the reflection caused by the spectacles he wore. The white floury ends of pounding sticks are likened to the white noses of cattle (presumably imported first by Mr. Moir).

The riddle, however, seems to be independent of the referent since there is a variant:

MR 82:   *Mbuzi za atate anga zoyera mipuno.*
         My father's goats have white noses.

A: *Minsi.*
         Pestles.

A group of riddles refer to the white man's clothes in a situation where only bark loin cloths were used. The trousers riddle below is descriptive:

MR 79:   *Ndimayenda, koma nditafika pa mphambano nifunsa anthu njira ya kumsika adandiuza kuti nditsate ziwiri.*
         As I was walking down a road, I reached a road junction and asked people to show me the way to the market; and they instructed me to follow both roads.

A: *Buluku.*
         A pair of trousers.

The riddle describes the shape of the trousers. Other riddles describe the manner in which the garment is worn.

MR 131: *Mayi atiyitana kuti tilowe m'nyumba anzanga onse alowa; koma ine sindinalowe.*
         Our mother has asked us to enter the house; my brothers have entered the house, but I haven't.

A: *Jakete silipisiridwa.*
         A jacket is never tacked [sic] inside a pair of trousers.

Other clothes items are mentioned in MR 442 (suit), MR 469 (shoes), and GR 42 (Khaki material).

228

Apart from being simply descriptive, some riddles draw correspondences with local phenomena.

MR 203:   *Mwana wa amfumu wabadwira mjakete.*
               The chief's son is born with a jacket on.

A: *Chimanga*
               A maize cob.

With western clothing came also western ways of sewing, e.g. with a sewing needle: MR 156, MR 189, MR 190, MR 258, MR 284, MR 372. A representative of the sewing needle group is:

MR 415:   *Kamwana kang'onong'ono chithewera umo!*
               A tiny baby in a large napkin.

A: *Singano.*
               A sewing needle.

Other miscellaneous riddles mentioning western cultural items, too numerous or unrelated to quote here, are: bottle (MR 50), box or suitcase (MR 180, MR 256, MR 376), spoon (MR 436), matches (MR 198, MR 292), lighter (MR 197), teapot (MR 384), sieve (MR 311), tickey (MR 228), wheelbarrow (MR 371), window (MR 191, MR 382), grinding mill (MR 298, MR 414, MR 449).

There were instances in which the local cloth manufacturers tried to sew western style suits from the local bark cloth with great but temporary success due to the material.

The manner of wearing western clothes is also captured in some proverbs. The commonest is *China ndi china jekete sabvitikira* (literally: "You cannot tuck in a jacket"). The proverb developed from earlier ones like *China ndi china mutu wa kamba sudibwa* (literally: "the head of a tortoise is never eaten") and *China ndi china nkhwani saotchera* (literally: "Pumpkin leaves are never roasted for food"). This is a parallel example of how other art forms were also evolving alongside the riddles under discussion.

Some songs were used to draw attention to certain deprivations felt by the composers. Two examples will suffice:

Pumbwa alira ndi usiwa	*Pumbwa* weeps because of poverty
Mugule nsaru	Buy a cloth
Pumbwa alira ndi usiwa	*Pumbwa* weeps because of poverty
Mupatse pumbwa	To give *pumbwa*
Pumbwa aura ndi usiwa	*Pumbwa* weeps because of poverty
Atotinyasa	He's offending our sight
Pumbwa alira ndi usiwa	*Pumbwa* weeps because of poverty

The new style clothing and cloth are too expensive for the poverty-stricken. The *pumbwa* bird is being used to convey the nanny's plight to her masters so that they can help her clothe herself.

The second song deals with an equally serious theme:

Amuna anga	My husband
Mundigulire wailesi	You should buy me a wireless [radio]
Ndidziyesa mwana	So I can pretend it is a child
Mkachoka	When you are away.

The song is about a sterile husband: the childless wife is urging, if not deriding, the man to at least have a substitute voice in the house when there are no children's voices around.

Riddle Creation or Reconstruction?

The foregoing has demonstrated that the vernacular riddle has undergone great transformation due to the influence of western man and his culture, not only at the superficial levels of word, phrase or image but also at the more significant levels of form or structure, content and meaning. This section discusses the crucial questions of creativity or re-creativity, since these were only mentioned in passing above.

It is significant to note that riddle collections before 1930 (i.e. those collected by Steere and Rattray) do not exhibit any foreign influence, in form or content. After 1930 (Gray, Mvula) there are some noticeable changes.

Structural Changes

It is easy to notice structural changes. For example, in 1907 Rattray recorded

RR 21: *Kantu kokalemekeza, kolira kukagwira ndi manja awiri.*
A little thing of such importance that, when you wish it, you go and take it with both hands.

A: *Ntedza.*
A groundnut.

By 1939 what Gray found was:

GR 47: *Ngakhale Mzungu mkukalemekeza.*
Even the European respects it (or gives it honour).

A: *Ntedza. (Timagwira ndi manja awiri.)*
A peanut. (We always grip it with both hands.)

Source. Ngoni. Ntcheu District.

Both riddles, presumably from the same ethnic group, refer to the polite Malawian practice of receiving or holding objects with both hands as a sign of respect, veneration or honour. The earlier riddle makes no reference to the white man and his customs. The recent riddle has undergone structural changes. Here it is not simply a matter of inserting *Mzungu* (a white man) at the convenient point. The change includes references to the white man's penchant for disregarding other people's customs (i.e. receiving objects with one hand): in the presence of a peanut, at least, even the European shows respect!

Meaning

Some of the changes in the riddles occur at the level of meaning, as the examples below demonstrate:

GR 18:   *Cija ndici*
            That's this.

A: *Citunzitunzi.*
            A photo.

Source. Nyanja. Zomba District.

In a note to the above Gray explains that the usual form of the riddle is

GR 18b: *Ako! aka!*
            That! This!

Ab: *Citunzitunzi.*
            A shadow.

In this case, the answer is the *shadow* of a person: it is longer in the morning and short at noon. The coming of photography forced the riddle to change not only in form but in meaning too. This was in spite of the fact that the vernacular term for both "shadow" and "photo" or "picture" is *chithunzithunzi* or, simply, *chithunzi*.

It is after analyzing the different ways in which the riddles have been created, re-used, re-constructed, that we find surprising Gray's comments (quoted earlier) that he saw little evidence of "continued vigorous growth." And, as the examples in the discussion have demonstrated, these riddles are as "apt or penetrating as the older ones." Furthermore, as the quantity of the new riddles in the recent collections shows, more exposure to the west ensures a perpetually increasing repertoire.

We now turn to the values, attitudes, beliefs and ideas the riddles encapsulated. It will be seen that the several kinds of riddles in the discussion reveal ambivalent, neutral and sometimes contradictory attitudes towards the white man and his culture.

232

Attitudes

Some of the conflicting attitudes towards the white man can be illustrated by comparing the "aeroplane" song mentioned under Transport and Communications with "Europeans are Little Children" in Chakanza's "Nyasa Folksongs."[23] There is admiration in the former and ridicule in the latter. The numerous jokes about illiteracy demonstrate the acceptance of western education. The changes over time can also be illustrated by the way even folk dance and music blended with some western forms. Some of the *nyau* dance steps easily adopted or were easily adapted to rock-and-roll. The breakdance craze among the youth in the 1980s has its local counterpart in *Beni* dancing. The riddles themselves reflect these contradictions.

The riddles on place names tend to accept the naming as such and use the new names in a strikingly new way. The scrambling of "Blantyre" (MR 166) is a case in point. However, it could also be taken as a satirical twist poking fun at the white man's inability to pronounce vernacular place names correctly, as in Livingstone's distortion of "Kamtedza" to "Dedza." Had the other riddle (GR 11), on the elephant dying in Blantyre and only the bones spreading so widely, been a new creation, it would have had additional significance. Blantyre, being the industrial capital of the country, controls most of the economy of even the remote villager. However, this point is negated in the next riddle (MR 80), where Blantyre is substitutable with Dowa, a small, insignificant district in the central region. What is interesting is the reaction to English or British place names. in the independence period. In the nationalist ferment, most place names were Malawianised. For example, Nyasaland became Malawi (and Lake Nyasa, Lake Malawi), Port Herald became Nsanje, Fort Jameson became Mchinji. Some street names were changed; some of the local politicians were immortalised: for example, Dunduza Chisiza and John Chilembwe. The first Malawian president's middle name, Kamuzu, graces streets in Blantyre, Limbe, and Lilongwe, the capital city since 1975, with names like Kamuzu Highway, or Kamuzu Procession Road. Other institutions are similarly named: Kamuzu International Airport, Kamuzu Central Hospital or Kamuzu

---

23   E.T. Chakanza, "Nyasa Folk Songs," *African Affairs*, 49, 195 (April 1950), pp. 160-161.

Academy. However, some place names retained the British Christening: Blantyre, Cape Maclear, Kirk Range; some street names still persist: Victoria Avenue, Henderson Street, etc.; some institutional names stuck: Queen Elizabeth Central Hospital, Henry Henderson Institute. These retentions reflect the same ambivalence noted earlier.

A similar phenomenon is noticed in the personal names. Although some Christian denominations insisted on a saint's name for the first name of their converts, an uneasy compromise was struck by accepting two first names: a Malawian and a Christian name; for example, the Catholic church accepted on baptism Napolo Alexander, or Christopher Zangaphee (both sons of the author). In most cases, it is not the pure Christian name that is adopted, sometimes it is the vernacularised name that is heard, distorted beyond recognition (*Mariya* or *Maliya* for Mary (MR 209), *Lusiya* for Lucy (MR 64), *Luka* for Luke (MR 474) or *Lukasi* for Lucas (MR 208). The *nyau* sect's *Simoni Petulo* for Simon Peter and *Yosefe* for Joseph have been seen already. One cannot discern the "frying pan" in *Abiti Selempani*. Perhaps the originals can be recognised in *Anasiketi* for skirt," *Kabichi* for "Cabbage" or *Supuni* for "spoon." As in the place names, however, the post-independence period brought an atavistic wave. Old Malawian names like *Nyangu* (rain priestess), historical names like *Chilembwe*, and those of politicians like *Dunduza* have been adopted; old clan names like *Banda, Phiri, Nkhoma*, have been appended to surnames. Very often the Christian name is suppressed by using only the initials, the rest being Malawian.

Christianity pervades the whole society. Official holidays include Christmas and Easter. Independence Day is opened by interdenominational Christian (Catholic, Anglican and Presbyterian) services. The riddles quoted here select very revealing areas for comment. Although MR 56 ("The church elder has carried the church on his back" for "A snail") seems to be a plain statement in translation, it is actually ridiculing the enormity of performing such a feat. The common riddle is laughing at the religious fanaticism observed in some church elders. MR 439 ("Baptise him and he will be nice" for "Salt") is another indication of ironic resignation to conversion: in a society with its own indigenous religion, baptism ensures that the convert can go and see his "new" lord after death. The next two riddles, CR 1 ("The bell was banned but he still wears it" for "Sins") and MR 430 ("It's a long

234

time since he started welding my bicycle" for "The gospel"), comment also on the futility of some of the religious observances: man is so prone to sin that repeated injunctions do not seem to work. The latter verges on irritation and frustration by the recipient: Why is the work of the church still incomplete? so that he can do something else (like riding his bicycle for example).

The riddles on Christian teachings should be taken together with the satirical jokes on some of the members' hypocrisy or pharisaical activities in the society. The joke about the white priest preaching that the congregation's hearts should be as pure as his white handkerchief which he pulls out of his pocket only to discover that they are knickers makes its own point.[24] Another joke on the church elder's troublesome "soft organ" which leads most people into sin is heard or read in two ways: the tongue and other erectiles. The *nyau* sect's creation of *Yosefe* (Joseph) is a further case in point: much as he represents the Catholic priests he is also a satirical figure for the priests' and other people's impotence or sterility.

Turning now to the armed forces, similar conflicting attitudes and perceptions appear. Much as the society appreciated (and still appreciates) the role of the army and the police in suppressing the slave trade and internecine wars, and maintaining law and order, they are regarded with terror. They were created for the government or the administration and not the common man, who was always the victim. In "War came from the Boma,"[25] a case study was made of the local man's perceptions of the army and the police as being there to wage war or at least bring war to his doorstep. MR 48 ("Soldiers standing, a whiteman at the centre" for "Hearth stones and the fire" [see also GR 103]) is purely descriptive. However, metaphorically the destructiveness of the fire and the white man is implied. Ironically, too, there is the juxtaposition of war (soldiers) with the domestic setting of the hearth. MR 170 ("Dedza police fight their wars while resting on their backs" for "Thorns") is also

---

24 Sagawa, "Some Malawian Jokes."

25 Sean Morrow, "'War Came from the Boma', Military and Police Disturbances in Blantyre, 1902," paper presented to the Central African History Conference, Lusaka, Zambia, 4-5 April 1986.

descriptive. MR 160 ("A very little thing halting policemen" for "A thorn") is an ironic commentary on this powerful institution.

The attitudes towards the armed forces were brought dramatically to the surface during the nationalist ferment of the 1950 and early 1960s. During the resistance to federation and the fight for independence the black officers were in a dilemma: to quell the protestors or to join them. The folk-song composer summed it up with:

Chisoni mapolisi	Pity the police
Manyaziwo.[26]	Shame on them

They were seen to be turning upon their own people, and antagonistic towards their own people's aspirations for self-government.

The subjugation of the people through the written word (literacy and numeracy) is also fraught with conflicting attitudes. Mention was made of the composition of satirical songs laughing at the illiterate on one hand while within the same society the affected manners of the educated were frowned upon. Much as western education was the desired thing, the society also saw the huge gaps being created between the educated and uneducated. Some riddles on literacy are purely descriptive (e.g. MR 86, MR 168, MR 325, and MR 375 in the text). Even then, they demonstrate what uses have been made of literacy and numeracy. On the other hand, MR 226 ("Two times that Europeans can't find the answer" for "Sand") can be understood in two ways: the perception that nothing can fail the white man, but in this case, he has reached his wits' end.

It is interesting that in the nationalist ferment during colonial days, even in the "Chilembwe Uprising," western education was seen as the key to liberation. In the post-independence period, too, in spite of Africanisation and the return to the roots and traditional ways, the western educational system has not been scrapped or changed. In actual fact, it has been augmented with the introduction of tertiary education (the University of Malawi) and an Eton-type grammar school, Kamuzu Academy. The centre of the educational system (curricula and syllabi) is not Chichewa, as the

---

[26] W.N. Dzimphonje, "Letters to the Editor," *Tikambe* Supplement to *Malawi News* (17 July 1976), p. 2.

official vernacular language, but English. English continues to be not only the medium of instruction in secondary and tertiary education but also the language of government (including parliament) and commerce.

Although the pervasiveness of English deserves separate discussion, it is remarkable that the majority of the riddles discussed here use English loan words in some form or other. All the aspects discussed: naming, Christianity, armed forces, transport and communications or commercial artefacts, have English loan words. However, riddles using English per se are rare in the data. An example follows:

MR 95: *Ndaponda mzungu. Wati, "Yes."*
        I have trodden on a whiteman; he has said, "Yes".

A: *Tsamba likapondedwa limati "Tswaa!"*
        A fallen dry leaf.

Enough has been discussed already under Transport and Communications to indicate the riddler's frustration at the considerable delays in the postal systems (MR 357), resulting in total despair (MR 477). The resignation of MR 477 ("I sent my letter without saying goodbye to it" for a "stool") used the excremental vision of the satirist to make its point. There are few riddles which use this technique. That it is used here for this institution is symptomatic of the bleakness of the situation which was also felt under general transport: "Letters to the Editor" are still published in the local papers drawing attention to some of the frustrations experienced. On the other hand, the vehicles used seemed to have fascinated some so much that they adopted them as their own personal names. *Sitima* was mentioned earlier. Another one is *Basikolo* bicycle. It was also mentioned earlier that respect and awe went to the makers of the new technology, in spite of this attitude being undercut in the verbal arts too. A riddle like MR 216 ("Miss Manesi is very noisy" for "Aeroplane") makes its statement on two levels. It selects "Miss Manesi," i.e. a white female, as representing all talkativeness and noise-producing objects. It is not only the noise of the aeroplane which is the object here. The word "^{n}bvoko" carries other implications of unnecessary, showy stubbornness or mule-headedness. The observation applies not only to the object mentioned but also to its makers.

Conclusion

The riddles discussed in this chapter span more than a hundred years of Malawian history vis-à-vis its encounters with the white man. The riddles note, describe, comment, analyse the new culture in all its aspects. The riddles adopt certain attitudes: acceptance, ridicule, satire, depending upon the object and the riddler's perceptions, beliefs and motives. The reconstruction of reality is not a simple matter of appropriating the new culture, some of it was adapted or modified to suit the aesthetics of form and content.

The riddles should be seen against the broad canvas of what the other verbal arts were undergoing in responding to the foreign culture. Apart from formal or structural and semantic changes, the riddle was also a weapon utilised to find meaning or come to terms with the white presence. As part of the anti-colonial and nationalist consciousness of the people, the riddle form has contributed greatly in the manner discussed here. The ambivalence shown in some of the riddles is not unique; other verbal arts, genres, and observable historical, sociological, psychological responses reveal similar characteristics.

Perhaps there was not much mobilisation of the riddle to serve anti-colonial nationalistic feelings as had been done in the fight for independence.[27] Perhaps there was not much mobilisation of this genre in the post-independence period to consolidate the regime of Dr. Banda as was being done by the *Mbumba* or the Malawi Women's League and Malawi Young Pioneers or Youth League. Perhaps the riddle has not been incorporated as much as theatre and drama (Theatre for Development) into national development programmes. However, all signs are there of its continued growth in form and content in the same manner as in the past.

---

[27] George T. Nurse, "Popular Songs and National Identity in Malawi," *African Music*, III, 3 (1964), pp. 101-106.

CHAPTER TEN:
DREAMS AND THE NEW DISPENSATION

> "What was it that first led you to think of Christ and Christianity?" I have asked my young candidates for entrance into the catechumenate. I have had various answers. "It was a dream," some said.[1]

If Nthondo in Ntara's *Man of Africa* had been asked a similar question, the response would have been the same: dreams.[2] Nthondo's road to Christian conversion is strewn by dreams so integrated with the narrative that it is largely through them that Ntara not only provides commentary but also seeks to arouse in his character "the voice of conscience hitherto dormant but waiting the call of Christ to awake to life."[3] The purpose of this chapter, then, is twofold; an examination of the nature of Nthondo's dreams before and after exposure to Christian influences, and how Ntara manipulated the content of the dreams to achieve his aim of converting the character.

Man of Africa is a fictional biography set in Chewa society during the latter half of the 19th century. Nthondo, the central character, is born and grows up in traditional rural Chewa society. Through contact and the coming of Christian missionaries to this society, however, Nthondo is, before his death, converted to Christianity. Thematically, then, the novel dramatises an African's spiritual journey from traditional Chewa to western Christian values.

Since the novel dramatises the birth, growth and death of Nthondo, the movement from traditional rural society to urban, and the transition from pre-Christian to Christian Chewa society, it is easy to distinguish dreams

---

[1]   Alexander Hetherwick, *The Gospel and the African: The Impact of the Gospel on a Central African People* (Edinburgh: T. and T. Clark, 1932), p. 117.

[2]   Samuel Yosia Ntara, *Man of Africa*, translated by T. Cullen Young (London: Religious Tract Society, 1934). All page references are to this edition.

[3]   Hetherwick, *The Gospel and the African*, p. 117.

typical and atypical of a Malawian. It is also easy to separate Nthondo's (or Chewa) pre-Christian and Christian concepts of sin, guilt, conscience and punishment. As the discussion progresses, it is discernible, however, that the dreams provide a powerful instrument for implanting in Nthondo the Christian notions of evil, good and salvation which eventually lead to his complete conversion.

Since Nthondo in his pre-Christian state had no access to Christian concepts of sin, guilt, conscience, grace and salvation, it could be argued that Ntara's own Christian foreknowledge influences, interferes with or distorts the content of some of the dreams placed at certain points in the narrative as the character progresses towards his conversion. The reader of *Man of Africa*, therefore, seems to be exposed to two texts. First, what Nthondo as a non-Christian is not supposed to know before exposure to Christianity and second, what only Ntara as a Christian writer could know. These parallel texts affect the reader's responses in the ways discussed below.

Since Ntara's Christian sensibilities so affected his rendering of the dreams, the narrative, character and theme, it will be necessary to briefly summarise his own biography. Pachai writes: "If any institution can lay any claim at all to having encouraged Ntara, it is the Dutch Reformed Church Mission at Mvera and at Nkhoma."[4] Ntara's father, a teacher, is believed to have been one of the first pupils of the mission. Ntara, born in 1905, was educated at Mvera, from where he left school after the third year to do private study until he obtained a South African Junior Certificate. He taught in various primary schools in the central (Chewa) region, including Nkhoma and Kongwe. He was on the Board of Censorship and was also "a much respected and valued Elder of the Church of Central Africa Presbyterian, having served on many important committees of the C.C.A.P."[5]

Man of Africa was first published by the Nkhoma Mission Press in 1933 and translated for publication by Reverend Cullen Young for the Religious

---

[4]   B. Pachai, "Samuel Josiah Ntara: Writer and Historian," *The Society of Malawi Journal*, 21, 2 (July 1968), p. 60.

[5]   Pachai, "Samuel Josiah Ntara," p. 65.

Tract Society in 1934. Ntara also wrote other biographies, both fictional and non-fictional. *Namon Katengeza* is a biography on the first Malawian to be ordained a minister by the Dutch Reformed Church, *Headman's Enterprise* is a biography of a historical person, and *Nchowa* is a fictional biography. That Ntara was also closely familiar with his Chewa people is witnessed by his other books, *Mbiri Ya Achewa* (A History of the Chewa) and *Mau Okuluwika m'Cinyanja* (Idiomatic Expressions in Chichewa).[6]

Dreams and Conversion in Africa

Although the approach adopted here is purely literary and is based on fictional work, it is important to see the dreams in *Man of Africa* as part of "dreams and conversion" studies done in the history of the Christian church in Africa. Sundkler surveys reports of African clergy who answered God's call initiated by a dream or a vision. Bishop Akinyele, a Nigerian given the choice between being a private secretary to the Governor of Lagos and the church, chose the latter because of a dream. Pastor Wembo Nyama, a Congolese, decided on his calling through a dream. An unnamed South African pastor was also called in a dream. The authority of dreams to play a decisive part in the Africans' conversions is never questioned. Another East African principal of a theological seminary "insisted that most of his candidates had been called through dreams."[7]

Sundkler classifies conversion dreams into three: (a) being called to the ministry by a luminous figure; (b) climbing a mountain or struggling out of a pit to reach a theological college; and (c) the struggle between dark powers and the power of the white Christ. As Table 7, below, shows, the dreams in *Man of Africa* are relatable to Sundkler's categories (a) and (c). The dominant religious symbol in Nthondo's third dream is the luminous figure (and the shining staff). Nthondo's last and major dream is a lengthy one describing the struggle between Christ and the devil for the dreamer's soul. The second category is not represented, presumably because after

---

6   Ntara, *Namon Katengeza*; *Headman's Enterprise*, translated and edited by T. Cullen Young (London: Lutterworth Press, 1949); *Nchowa* (Nairobi: Longmans, Green and Co., 1949); *Mbiri ya Achewa* (Nkhoma: CCAP, 1944); *Mau Okuluwika m'Cinyanja*.

7   B. Sundkler, *Christian Ministry in Africa* (London: SCM Press Ltd., 1962), p. 22.

conversion Nthondo did not go all the way to join the Christian hierarchy: he died as chief of his people.

TABLE 7: NTHONDO'S DREAMS (*MAN OF AFRICA*)

Type	Theme	Instrument		Setting	
Secular	The Chase	1	Dead Friend	1	Land of Darkness
		2	Lions	2	A Hunt, unspecified
		4	Dead Father	4	Unspecified
Religious	Guilt and Punishment	3	Luminous Person	3	Unspecified
		5	Heaven (white figure) Hell (Horned & Tailed Figure)	5	Strange Country

Ntara's Presbyterian Church does not depend so much on dreams, dream narration and interpretation as, say, Zionist or Pentecostal sects; however, dreams and conversion feature highly in some of the published accounts of elders, pastors or deacons. Msyamboza's conversion in *Headman's Enterprise*, Ntara's historical biography of a Chewa chief, is activated by a dream. Two aNgoni, Daniel Mtusu Nhlane and Andrew Mkochi in Fraser's *Winning a Primitive People*, have dreams and visions even after conversion. The opening quotation of this chapter, from Hetherwick's *The Gospel and the African*, is taken from Yao converts. The dreams in *Man of Africa*, then, are not purely fictional constructs, the creation of Ntara's imagination. They belong to the experiential process of some Africans who are undergoing a spiritual or psychic crisis in their lives.

One or two dreams in a novel may not be significant; however, five or six suggest the great importance Ntara attached to them. In this too, Ntara was working within the tradition of dreams and conversion:

> In cases where an individual shows greater resistance to the call, the dreams may be experienced over a long period of time.[8]

---

[8]   Sundkler, *Christian Ministry*, p. 24.

That the dreams in *Man of Africa* are part of the "dreams and conversion" convention can be further demonstrated by comparing the novel with two others. After the publication of *Man of Africa,* the author was asked by his sponsors to write a similar fictional biography centred on a female character. *Nchowa* was the result. In spite of the parallels of birth, growth, and death, Nchowa, the female counterpart to Nthondo, never has a single dream in the whole narrative. In spite of contact with the white man, Nchowa, furthermore, has no religious crises of the kind Nthondo has, since western Christianity is not even mentioned in the story. Nchowa is a perfectly integrated Chewa woman operating in her own traditional society, and Ntara did not find it necessary to plague her with perplexing dreams.

TABLE 8: GWENEMBE'S DREAMS (*SIKUSINJA NDI GWENEMBE*)

Type	Theme	Instrument		Setting	
Secular	The Chase	1	Lions	1	Bush
		2	Dead Brother, Arrow	2	Unspecified
		3	Armed Men Dismemberment	3	Unspecified
Religious	None	None		None	

Another contrasting text is Gwengwe's *Sikusinja ndi Gwenembe,* a modernised Chewa folk narrative on fratricide, guilt and punishment.[9] In the original folk story, guilt is personified by the blood of the dead brother turning into a bird and publicising the crime. Gwengwe retains the bird but goes further by giving the murderer a set of dreams after the perpetration of the crime. Table 8, below, tabulates these dreams. Since Nthondo's life before Christianity is crime-ridden, including attempted manslaughter, and, since both authors are working within Chewa folklore and beliefs, we should expect some similarity in the kinds of dreams the characters have. As Table 8 shows, however, Gwengwe's folktale has only secular dreams

---

9   Gwengwe, *Sikusinja ndi Gwenembe.*

of the same chase theme as *Man of Africa*, with lions, the dead brother and persons as the instruments for making the character conscious of guilt. *Man of Africa*, on the other hand, has two religious dreams on the same theme, with a luminous person, Christ, and the devil, as the ultimate judges (see Table 7). In other words, the folktale resolves the conflict within Chewa tradition and the novel in the new Christian dispensation. The dreams in the folktale dramatise events in the life of the dreamer (even the first one in which he climbs a tree to run away from lions is based on reality: Gwenembe is sleeping up in a tree). The two religious dreams in the novel are outside the experience of the dreamer: at this stage Nthondo had no access to the Christian symbolism, especially of the last dream. As Curley put it, in conversions,

> The dream which contains religious images demonstrates that the narrator has been in touch with God, whereas a dream which is devoid of religious content is regarded as a message. The latter type of dream, when properly interpreted, may offer a clue which will help to solve some past or present problem.[10]

In this case, Nthondo's dream belongs to both, whereas the dreams in the folktale are messages to the murderer to prod his non-Christian conscience. Whereas the dreams in the folktale are "revelations of what had happened, and what generally should not have," interestingly enough the religious dreams in *Man of Africa* foretell what will happen in future: the last one even projects events after the dreamer's death.[11]

Dreams in Malawi

Dreams are believed to be an important mode of communication in which the spirit world imparts knowledge, advises, warns, instructs or even reveals itself to the living. Dreams link spirit and ordinary man. Cullen Young and Hetherwick enquired about the origins of dreams as understood by the Malawians with whom they worked. Both Christian

---

[10] Richard T. Curley, "Dreams of Power: Social Process in a West African Religious Movement," *Africa*, 53, 3 (1983), p. 26.

[11] S.R. Charsley, "Dreams in an Independent African Church," *Africa*, 43 (1973), pp. 244-257.

missionaries were informed that in significant dreams it is the spirit of a dead ancestor which comes to the dreamer with a message or warning, or just to make his/her presence known to the descendant.[12]

Hodgson investigated the reasons why people dream in Yao, Ngoni, Nyanja and Chewa society in Dowa District, where Ntara, the author of the novel, lived and worked. The ten Malawian village headmen interviewed all concurred; people dream because they have a spirit which survived them after death.[13]

On the question of what to do with dreams, both Malawians and scholars confirm the need for interpretation either by the dreamers or, if this is beyond them, someone else. Cullen Young states that the publication of a dream is a "public duty that is never evaded."[14] Hodgson's interviewees also reiterate the need for referrals (an older man or woman) when one is unable to interpret one's own dream.[15] That the dreams themselves are interpretable is evidenced not only by the investigations carried out in the field by the above but also other published works by Malawians themselves on the interpretation of Malawian dreams.[16] Most of them would agree, however, that the interpretation depends not only on the dreamer and his context but also on the dream and content. Furthermore, the interpretation would depend on a scale with the known, common or familiar persons, objects and events at one end and the unknown, uncommon or unfamiliar at the other.

In analyzing the dreams, it will be convenient to have this scale in mind, although shorter ones have been suggested:

> There are two kinds of dreams: first, dreams about things and conditions of which the dreamer has prior knowledge; secondly,

---

[12] T. Cullen Young, *African Ways and Wisdom* (London: The United Society for Christian Literature, 1937), p. 46; Hetherwick, *The Gospel and the African*, p. 55.

[13] A.G.O. Hodgson, "Dreams in Central Africa," *Man*, 39 (April 1926), pp. 66-68.

[14] Cullen Young, *African Ways and Wisdom*, p. 46.

[15] Hodgson, "Dreams in Central Africa," p. 67.

[16] Gwengwe, *Kukula ndi Mwambo*; J.D. Msonthi, *Kali Kokha N'Kanyama* (Lilongwe: Likuni Press, 1969).

exceptional dreams about things and conditions of which he has no such knowledge. The latter are inspired by God.[17]

Were Nthondo's religious dreams, then, inspired by God, even prior to his exposure to Christianity? The thrust of the argument is that they were inspired by the author. Another possible framework is Seligman's. He placed all dreams in Central Africa into three categories which avoid the simple and misleading dichotomy of "secular" or "religious" (which religion?)

1. Those that are both sensible and intelligible, telling a connected story of the everyday world, the meaning of which is obvious … In these dreams the mental processes resemble those of waking life. …

2. Dreams which tell or enact a connected story and have an evident meaning, but their contents, in whole or in part, strike us as unnatural, and we cannot fit them into the fabric of our waking life …

3. Dreams of which the content is bizarre, confused and nonsensical; such dreams often have a peculiar quality of unreality and can scarcely, if at all be related to waking thought … Much of the strangeness of these dreams is due to the symbolism used to express the dream thoughts. …[18]

It will be found that the dreams in *Man of Africa* can each be slotted conveniently into one of the three categories, depending on their content. It will be demonstrated further that Nthondo's dreams prior to exposure to Christianity belong to the first two categories; thereafter, contact effected, his dreams take on the unnatural, bizarre and symbolic quality mentioned in the last group. When interpreting the dreams also, Seligman's framework will be found extremely useful, since in the first category are placed dreams in which "the mental processes resemble those of waking life." These dreams belong to the world of "simple wish fulfilments." The second and third categories are more problematic, since

---

[17]   Sundkler, *Christian Ministry*, p. 24.

[18]   C.G. Seligman, "Note on Dreams," *Man*, 120 (December 1923), pp. 186-187.

> In dreams in which symbolism occurs it is important to ascertain whether the symbols are peculiar to the dreamer or generally recognised by the tribe or group as having a constant meaning. If the latter, then a particular dream or symbol becomes an omen and so influences the life of larger (or smaller) groups.[19]

In trying to establish whether the dreams in the novel are peculiar to the dreamer or the tribe or foreign to both, we shall refer to some of the works above which have local interpretations relevant to similar dreams dreamt by the characters.

The work on dreams in Malawi reviewed above has revealed some common features: the presence of a spirit (the dreamer's or a dead ancestor's); the belief that dreams have some accepted meaning within the society of the dreamer; and the practice of publication. *Man of Africa* demonstrates similar features: when Nthondo dreams he is told, "that is the work of the ancestor-spirits" (p. 24), when his father dreams, his friends immediately recognise it as part of their system of beliefs: "That is a good dream ..." (p. 24), yet there is need for further interpretation from an elder: "I would like to go where I could get some sort of idea of what explanation that dream has" (p. 24). Before going on to discuss the nature and function of the dreams in the novel, however, it will be necessary to explore the crucial notions of evil, sin, guilt and punishment which make Nthondo's Christian conversion possible in this context.

Traditional Codes and Christian Concepts

To understand fully why Nthondo and the other characters are made to behave in the way they do, it is important to compare (and contrast) the two sometimes irreconcilable systems under which the author is operating.

Ntara deliberately makes Nthondo's growth from childhood to maturity one strewn with senseless, irrational and incorrigible criminal deeds. The life of crime starts in the "lad's sleeping place," where his companions teach him how to steal. The life of a herdsboy, Ntara suggests, also teaches

---

[19] Seligman, "Note on Dreams," p. 188.

Nthondo to cheat, lie, fight and be insolent towards his elders. Ntara, then, sees the lad's sleeping place as the breeding place of evil, immoral behaviour and lawlessness.[20] Ntara makes Nthondo grow from bad to worse: he breaks away completely from his mother, his uncle cannot stand him; he is forced to leave the village and live with his "name relations," and does not come to his mother's funeral, earning him the epithet "child of a hardened heart." Ntara seems to subscribe to Hetherwick's Christian missionary view of traditional Malawian society:

> the African youth grew up—with no moral discipline save his own superstitious fears, no teaching of self-restraint or high ideals of life. The boy especially was free as the air to follow the whims, desires, and promptings of his own sweet will. ... Chastisement of either sex was rarely given, except it were out of loss of temper on the parents' part.[21]

Yet traditional Chewa society does have its own system of ethics, laws and regulations embodied in the *gule wamkulu* or *nyau* society. Initiation into *nyau* society is mandatory for youth, since it is not only a central Chewa religious rite but also it ensures acceptance into adult society. Ntara, however, does not permit Nthondo in the story to get initiated into the *nyau* society, which would have ensured that he observed the Chewa traditional code of conduct, morality and ethics. This alone in the pre-Christian Nthondo would have effected a conversion within the Chewa's own system of beliefs.

Ntara does not explain in the story how Nthondo, a true Chewa youth, could not have been initiated in the *nyau* society, thereby creating strange inconsistencies like, for example, having Nthondo admitted into the men's talking place, attending and judging court cases, being married in the traditional manner, and finally being elected chief (who is also the titular head of *nyau* society). A Chewa society would not have appointed an uninitiated or untutored person as its chief in the pre-Christian stages of the story. Worse still, the uninitiated person is not considered to be a man at all: he is less than a child. The only conclusion to be drawn from this

---

[20] For a corrective to this view, see Msonthi, *Kali Kokha N'Kanyama*, pp. 31-32.

[21] Hetherwick, *The Gospel and the African*, pp. 18-19.

oversight is that Ntara either did not want an integrated Chewa character or, since Christianity had yet to come to this society, he wanted Nthondo's conversion to be effected only in the Christian context.

It is plausible that Ntara should want such a conversion to be effected this way, since he sets up an elaborate programme of creating Christian notions of guilt, sin and conscience where presumably none existed in Nthondo before. There are several passages in the story prior to the advent of Christianity in which Nthondo cannot articulate or verbalise, or lacks the vocabulary to explain, his criminality. On the road to Halale (now Harare), Nthondo and his companions run out of provisions and are reduced to eating wild fruit. In the face of hunger, Nthondo's kleptomania gets the better of him. He is caught stealing sorghum:

> "Why did you steal?" they said, and he replied, "Because I was hungry." "But if that were so," they asked, "why did you not ask?" "Because," said Nthondo "I was blind with hunger." (pp. 93-94)

He can only explain stealing either in terms of fulfilling basic human needs or in terms of sorcery. When he is let out of Halale prison, he seeks help from a medicine man, explaining

> "I am constantly in trouble and am sure that sorcerers (*afiti*) are dancing their witchcraft against me." (p. 100)

In his pre-Christian state, Nthondo cannot explore within himself to find reasons for his evil conduct. Similarly, the story does not explore the notions of guilt and consciousness of wrongdoing. In this again, Ntara seems to subscribe to Hetherwick's views on the natives:

> We find no way of approach through any sense of guilt or consciousness of sin. When any question of moral conduct is present, conscience at no time enters as a deciding factor in native life. The main determining factor in such matters is the fear of consequence which alone deters the Native from any course of moral misconduct, and keeps him in the right path ... It is not surprising that we can find no conception of sin as a moral lapse or

failure ... In the native tongue, there is, therefore, no word for "sin" and none corresponding to our idea of conscience.[22]

It is interesting to compare Hetherwick's views with the Chewa system of dealing with an incorrigible person. We find Nthondo's uncle reminding his now adult but criminal nephew of his duties not only to himself but to his people:

> "A man who thieves has no love for people, and will not be loved. Furthermore, such a one dies before his time because all people complain about him, they whom he has thieved from; and they quickly bring such a one to death. Consider how you were more than once near death at Halale, as a result of your thieving. Do not think that I am judging and condemning you or trying you: that is not it at all. You know the proverb that says, 'An old man's words are beautiful: you may rest upon them.' These words of mine, therefore, do you carry in memory in the days ahead. There was a time when you were a fine child, with no thought of such a thing as that you could be a thief; but now! Have you lost your reason? Be careful and wise now. In these days the country is full of medicine and poisons. Have nothing to do with stealing, or you will find yourself with a twisted mouth." (pp. 108-109)

Nthondo's uncle appeals to his nephew's sense of clanship: a good leader holds the clan together; people only follow a leader who in turn exhibits a strong moral fibre. Love and clanship go together: if you steal from the people you lead, do not expect them to love and follow you. He also appeals to Nthondo's life: how in Halale he came near to death and how death would dog him if he persisted in wrongdoing. He next appeals to age: the uncle's words have worldly experience behind them and it is better for the nephew to heed his advice. He gives examples of the times that Nthondo was once a fine person. Lastly, he appeals to Nthondo's fear again: people will bewitch him as a consequence of his crimes. The admonitions do not contain any Christian sentiments, language or allusions. Questions of Christian sin, guilt and conscience do not emerge at this stage, since Christianity has as yet to appear. In making Nthondo's

---

[22] Hetherwick, *The Gospel and the African*, pp. 110, 112.

uncle speak from the Chewa's code of conduct, and in making Nthondo fail to reveal concepts of guilt and conscience prior to Christianity, Ntara was also working within the Christian missionary views on the native.

In the translation of the Bible into Chinyanja (now Chichewa)

> The translators had to build up a term for "conscience" in which the primary idea was that of "digging," or "rousing memory" in the heart. In the latter case, the word "heart" is used to express the idea most akin in the native mind to that of moral conscience … Gradually this word has been Christianised, and is now understood in its new application as standing for "conscience." In the same way, "evil" in the native mind signifies something that is "hurtful" and "damaging" —ugly", "distasteful", or "displeasing." There is no ethical significance in the word. Murder is "bad," because it is injurious to human life, which may always be appraised at a value. Murder, like other "crime," may be compensated by money payments. Breaches of the moral law as "lying," "stealing," or even "adultery," are recognised as "evil," only because damaging to property. As in the case of "conscience," the translators of Scripture had to take a word in the native tongue, it may be with sinister associations, and baptise it into Christian usage. For the expression of the idea of "sin," they took a term which meant only to "err," or to "make a mistake," and adapted it to ethical usage. [23]

Put briefly the native is a beast with no conscience; therefore, it is the duty of the Christian evangelist to create consciousness of guilt in the African.

Ntara also saw it as his Christian duty to create the uncreated conscience of his character. The instrument he used was a large dosage of troublesome and perplexing dreams in Nthondo.

Dreams in Man of Africa

Before going into Nthondo's dreams proper, it might help to start with Nthondo's father's dream. The father's dream will also serve as a point of

---

[23]   Hetherwick, *The Gospel and the African*, pp. 112-114.

comparison with his son's dreams, for, although the father dreams but once, the context and subsequent events throw a great deal of light on the pattern that we see emerging in the analysis of Nthondo's own dreams.

Father's Dream

> "I dreamed, and I had cut my trap for the edible-ants on the ant-hill. I finished it and the ants swarmed and filled it. I told my daughter to call her mother to bring something to take away the ants in, but though she came I never could finish them all. I went cold with fright ..." (p. 24)

Background

Nthondo's father was seized by a policeman, and taken from his village to the Government Station, where he and some men seized from other villages in the same way were forced to build a bridge for the colonial government's road network into the village. At the camp, they were not given any food or shelter. At the time of seizure, Nthondo's father had been making a *dewere* (female garment), and his wife was pregnant. Before he had the dream, he complained to himself about the treatment the labour gang were receiving at the hands of the agents of the government:

> "Look at that! Did I leave misfortune behind at home? People do not mind being reduced to husks of maize if they still have their freedom! But to come to this! However, it doesn't matter." (p. 23)

Form and Content

It is obvious that the father's immediate situation had nothing to do with the content of the dream. The time was the dry season: "the grass was dry at that season" (pp. 23-24), i.e. since flying ants appear only in the wet season, the dry season also has nothing to do with the content of the dream. As expected, his immediate desire is to communicate the dream to his fellows and ask for its interpretation. He ends his telling with "I would like to go where I could get some sort of idea of what explanation that dream has" (p. 24). He has already some idea what it means, though, because the preceding remark was, "Do you fancy that is some sort of lie?"

i.e. he wishes someone to contradict what he feels is the standard interpretation of the dream. His friend tells him "That is a good dream" (p. 24).

Interpretation

The interpretation, of necessity, must come from the character's own way of interpreting dreams, or be revealed or abstracted from subsequent events. Therefore, the dream refers to the birth of his son. Hitherto he has had only girls. ("Do you fancy that is some sort of a lie?" may refer to his having an intimation of the sex of his child.) The abundance of the flying ants may refer to the society's expectancy of male children's roles. "Male children are wealth, ... If he lives he will supply you with blankets" (p. 17). Later, when the dreamer tells his mother-in-law that he was "troubled with dreams," he is told emphatically: it was "just the birth of this child," to which the father owns. "Certainly; that may be true" (p. 26). (The "cold with fright" refers to his inability to contain the flying ants, i.e. the subsequent children and grandchildren in the male line. Later Nthondo has twins who probably will have more twins indefinitely.)

The dream is very local (belonging to Seligman's first category); it paints a normal Chewa scene: during the rainy season men dig ant-hills and place containers for the edible flying ants to fall in. Part of the interpretation of the dream is also supported outside the story by scholars on dreams. Hodgson says:

> If one dreams of an ant-heap, one's wife is pregnant by another man, the likeness being due to the fact that an ant-heap is always slowly increasing is size. [24]

Gwengwe states:

> *Munthu akalota alikupha inswa pachulu adziwe kuti apeza mwai posachedwa pa moyo wache.*[25]

---

[24] Hodgson, "Dreams in Central Africa," p. 68.

[25] Gwengwe, *Kukula ndi Mwambo*, p. 112.

> If a person dreams that he is killing flying-ants at an ant-hill he
> should know that he will soon be lucky.

Dreams, then, have immediate or distant application and reference. Another point to be made here is that dreams are always omens. Some dreams portend luck, others evil consequences. Hodgson's informants confirm this observation:

> It is unlucky if one of the objects of the dream is confused or
> grotesque, as, for example, if a person or animal has some of the
> characteristics of another. The spirit of the dreamer is troubled and
> must be appeased by the dreamer washing his person in medicine
> made from the roots of the *mtsizi* tree and by a beer dance.[26]

These observations are pertinent to Nthondo's dreams, as we shall see. Hodgson's "troubled" mind of the dreamer has the notions of appeasement include not only the spirit of the dreamer but that of the dead also who are supposed to bring the dreams.

Nthondo's First Dream

> One night he dreamed, and the dream was that he entered a land
> of darkness where his eyes could hardly see. And the young fellow
> who was fatally wounded that night in the food-fields long ago
> began to chase him. He was not clearly visible but Nthondo could
> see his teeth which had become very long. Nthondo tried to escape,
> but that companion of the old days never actually came near
> enough to catch him. Then he awoke, shivering and trembling with
> fear. (p. 96)

Background

Nthondo is in prison in Halale (Southern Rhodesia now Zimbabwe). He had been caught stealing pumpkins from his white employer's garden. He was bound hand and foot in chains, tied to a horse and taken to the police station where he was sentenced to three weeks imprisonment. In prison, his work consisted of digging pits, cutting wood, pulling carts, etc. This is

---

[26]   Hodgson, "Dreams in Central Africa," p. 68.

not the first crime he commits: he has had a long record of petty thefts perpetrated at home, and the villages he travelled through on his trip to Halale. In Halale he continued his life of crime. However, this is the first time he has been put in prison (his own society never had this institution).

This is also the first time Nthondo dreams. Hitherto no dream was mentioned by the author (except his father's, which was never repeated); henceforth his life is punctuated if not dominated by dreams. It is worth mentioning here that all the dreams occur when the characters are under the colonial government's agents, white employers or evangelists of the Christian missionaries, never under the Chewa village hierarchy prior to exposure to foreign influences.[27]

Form and Content

The young fellow in the dream was an accomplice in one of Nthondo's escapades. The two went at night to steal green maize from a garden whose owner had publicly declared he would shoot anyone or anything he saw trespassing in his garden. Nthondo had enticed his friend to go and steal with him. When his friend was shot Nthondo ran away from the scene. It was only later that he told the elders that his friend had been killed. That earlier crime was committed in a garden; a garden also is the scene where Nthondo's present crime was committed. The two crimes appear to be responsible for the present dream.

Interpretation

The dream is in an unspecified setting. It is useful to note from the outset that Nthondo's dreams are always in unrealised regions unlike his father's dream or dreams by other characters in other works to be discussed later. The "land of darkness" could be either a physical place like Halale which, to Nthondo, 'as a strange and new place to come to and work in, or the prison itself, which was his first experience, although the cell is an enclosed

---

[27] It could be argued that Nthondo may have been exposed to Christian teachings in Harare; however, the text does not indicate this. The presence of the police, prisons and, therefore, a colonial settlement before Nthondo's birth is also free of Christian underpinnings. These are some of the difficulties with the text on one hand and Ntara's intentions on the other, where Christianity does not feature at all until the last dream.

place whereas the dream suggests an open place; The "land of darkness" could also be the spiritual state of the dreamer in which "his eyes could hardly see" and in this state the "truth" was not "clearly visible." All Nthondo could discern in this eerie darkness was an object of torture or persecution: elongated teeth. There is no direct infliction of pain: only the suggestion that it is there, hence creating more acute mental torment. The dreamer wakes up "shivering and trembling with fear."

When Nthondo is let out of prison (after sickness due to bad prison food and being given four lashes), he goes to seek work from his former white employer, who sets his dogs on him. Nthondo gets a mauling from the dogs and a beating from his white employer. He ascribes all these actions to someone informing on him to the ex-employer. His friends in town remark that he "seemed as if he were under some power that made him always be stealing" (p. 97). These events and the remarks made by his friends are pertinent to the next two dreams, where they will be discussed more fully.

Nthondo's Second Dream

> He had gone hunting with other people and two lions chased him, and caught him, and devoured him. (p. 99)

Background

Nthondo is serving his second sentence in prison. Leading an ox cart, Nthondo had been hit accidentally with a whip by the driver. The two fought and the driver was beaten unconscious. Nthondo was sentenced to six months' imprisonment.

Form and Content

Like his first dream, this one contains the chase again, with Nthondo fleeing for his life. Unlike the first dream, however, this time Nthondo is "devoured."

Interpretation

The following interpretation of a similar dream occurs in Hodgson:

> A dream of frequent occurrence is one of being chased downhill by a lion, the common symbol for chieftainship. If the dreamer escapes, he himself will become a chief or otherwise rise to importance: but if he is seized by the lion, it means that a chief is plotting against him.[28]

In the story, Nthondo is the chief's nephew and, therefore, the rightful heir. The audience understood or accepted it as the natural course of events. The ill-feeling of the uncle against his nephew, however, arose out of Nthondo's kleptomania, not out of the future ascendancy to the chieftainship. Furthermore, as it turns out, Nthondo does rise to the chieftaincy without any conflict and with active exhortation. Since the dream is contrary to Hodgson's and, therefore, Chewa interpretation, we shall put it under the author's programme of creating a conscience in Nthondo.

Nthondo's Third Dream

> He dreamed again and saw a man brightly dressed, holding a shining staff, who pointed at him with the staff and said, "I shall punish you if you do not cease your wrongdoing." (p. 99)

Background

This is another dream in prison after the fight with the driver of the ox-cart. The dream immediately follows the second one after Nthondo goes back to sleep the same night.

Hitherto the dreams have taken the form of a chase. The first chase had no outcome because the pursuit had no end to it, except that the dreamer woke up and the sequence was broken. The second chase resulted in the annihilation of the dreamer. We have already rejected the idea of interpreting the second dream in the context of Chewa dreams and

---

[28] Hodgson, "Dreams in Central Africa," p. 67.

257

interpretation. The dream seems to belong to the Christian programme discussed above in which Ntara first showed the criminal the consequences of his evildoing. After establishing that annihilation would follow criminal pursuits, Ntara adopts the strategy of making the criminal conscious of his guilt first, then indicating what the consequences would be if he did not mend his ways. Such a strategy in Hetherwick's and Ntara's world makes sense: the sinner should never be annihilated without realising and admitting that he was living in sin.

Form and Content

The setting is unspecified but the unnamed man is concrete. He is "brightly dressed, holding a shining staff." Whereas the first dream contained a grotesque human being, luminous teeth pursuing Nthondo in earie darkness, and the second dream had fearsome lions devouring the dreamer, the third dream has a bright quality to it. However, threatening the staff might be, the man's brightness is attractive. The attractiveness was also absent in the previous dreams.

Interpretation

Nthondo in his pre-Christian state still interprets the third dream as engineered by malevolent external forces. These forces are consulted by the only method he knows: after being released he goes to a medicine man. In Ntara's programme, however, the brightly dressed man can only be either an angel or a prophet.

Nthondo's Fourth Dream

> ... he dreamed that his father who had died so long ago had made a catch of fish and that he, Nthondo, begged some. But in the dream his father refused saying, "You are not my child now because of the shame you brought by that thieving habit of yours." Whereupon Nthondo secretly stole one of the fish and his father began to chase him. Try as he would to run and even to leap through the air Nthondo found himself helpless so that his father took him, caught him by the neck and moaned upon him. (p. 124)

Background

Nthondo and his companions are at Kapata, where they have just been employed by a white man as load-carriers to Kabula. They sleep at Kapata and prepare to leave the following morning.

Form and Content

The fourth dream is still in the nature of a chase. In it, and for the first time, Nthondo re-enacts the act of thieving. His father, it should be noted with Hetherwick's observations in mind, does not chastise him after capture but "moaned upon him." It should be noted further that fish do not occur anywhere in the story except in this dream. Nthondo's folk, we are told, lived in the hill region to the west of Lake Nyasa and Nthondo's father by profession is a *dewere* cloth maker (his other occupation was mat-making).

Interpretation

The dream belongs to Seligman's first category, and the closest it gets to Hodgson's Chewa dreams is the following:

> If one dreams that one is catching fish, the dreamer will find a bag of money; but if the fish are of a slippery variety, like mudfish, the dreamer will not be able to keep the money, which will soon be lost or stolen.[29]

Gwengwe is not helpful either in the interpretation. He only says dreaming of fish signifies luck.[30] Other scholars are silent on fish.

However, Nthondo does not catch the fish, he steals it from his father who made the catch. The question of finding a bag of money does not arise in the wilds of the country between Kapata and Kabula. The petty payment they get after the load-carrying would not be considered a bag of money either. In any case, Nthondo and his companions do not come easily upon

---

29   Hodgson, "Dreams in Central Africa," p. 68.
30   Gwengwe, *Kukula ndi Mwambo*, p. 112.

money: they have to sweat for it, carrying the heavy loads on their heads, trekking across half the country.

The dream, then, is part of the series that Ntara has set up in his own scheme of things. In contrast to Nthondo's father's resourcefulness (in the first dream he was catching flying ants), Nthondo is characterised by living on his wits: begging is met with refusal; he has brought shame to the family through his "thieving habit"; and, rather than changing, Nthondo responds characteristically. Furthermore, the father rejects his son: this act of abandonment should have jerked Nthondo back to his senses. When he wakes up after the dream, he makes significant observations to his companions:

> "These dreams are troubling me always. I cannot find peace. And it
> is not as if that which I have laid before you is the only one. There
> are many others." (p. 124)

He also interprets the father's moaning as "he tried to kill me." We are told he is afraid to go back to sleep afterwards and talks until the following morning.

This is the second time a dead person is sent to "awaken" or train Nthondo's conscience. When Nthondo asks his friends to "explain" the dream for him, they impress upon Nthondo the gravity of the dream:

> "When one dreams of the dead that is the work of the ancestor-
> spirits. It is therefore laid upon you that you bathe with the
> medicine of ancestor-visitation, lest you go mad … Go and dig the
> roots of a *mathilisa* tree, the tree that some call *cibvumulo*. That is
> the medicine." (p. 124)

The companions' advice is in keeping with Chewa practice, as earlier observations confirm. Furthermore, the prescription is typically Chewa. The contradiction, then, lies in the nature and purpose of the dream in the story. For it could be argued that Ntara, knowing Chewa customs so thoroughly, would have known that in the matrilineal society he has so carefully described, the father has no claim over the son. The son's upbringing is the sole concern of the uncle on the mother's side (i.e. after he has left the mother's hearth). Furthermore, Nthondo's father dies when the son is still a child. Whether or not the child still remembers the father

260

in manhood is only speculation. The only resolution here is to see Nthondo's uncle (if not Ntara, Nthondo's author) as the father-figure in the dream. The dream, then, echoes the scene between uncle and nephew mentioned earlier. The constant battles, verbal and physical, waged between uncle and nephew find their resolution in the dream. At the same time the dream forms part of the series Ntara set up for Nthondo's education into Christianity.

The dreams Ntara gives Nthondo have prepared the ground for the awakening of his conscience. Two pages after the fourth dream, Nthondo and his companions, for the first time in the story, come into contact with Christian teachings. Nthondo has his fifth and last dream immediately after.

Nthondo's Fifth Dream

> ... Nthondo dreamed a dream that he had come into a country that was strange to him and in which he found some people tormented by fire that burned out their eyes, while there were others singing many songs and these the very songs that he had heard that day. Each section had its master. Those in the fire had as master a terrible figure of a man with a pair of horns and a tail at the tip of which fire burned. But the other section had as master one very tall and all clothed in white. On noticing the arrival of Nthondo these two leaders began to strive with each other. The terrible one clutched Nthondo round the middle and tried to pull him to the fire while the attractive-looking one took him by the hand. "Let this man alone!" shouted the terrible one, "so that I may take him away. He is bad." But the other said, "He is mine; I paid for him." As they struggled thus, Nthondo awoke. (pp. 132-133)

Background

Nthondo and his companions are on their way from Kapata to Kabula as load carriers. They stop in an unspecified village for the night. The following morning, they are invited by the villagers to a Christian Sunday service. The night following the service, Nthondo has the dream.

Form and Content

Nthondo comes into a strange country where people sing the songs "he had heard that day," i.e. Christian songs. That some people were "tormented by fire that burned out their eyes" is not within Nthondo's experience before and after the visit to that village. The "terrible figure of a man with a pair of horns and a tail at the tip of which fire burned" is also not within Nthondo's experience before and after the visit to the village. The man "clothed in white" could be a residue of his contact with white men in Halale or Kapata. The striving for Nthondo is inexplicable in the context of the story. Why the terrible one should pull Nthondo to the fire because he was "bad" and why the man clothed in white should state "He is mine; I paid for him" are also beyond the experiences of the dreamer.

Interpretation

Hodgson's informants have this to say about fire:

> If one dreams of a fire burning, the dreamer will be involved in a serious misfortune, generally in a lawsuit. If the fire goes out, the dreamer will emerge from his suit satisfactorily, the rise and decline of the fire symbolising the outbreak and subsidence of the case. To dream of a great bush fire augurs the advent of war, but if ashes and smoke only, without flame, are observed, the war will come to a speedy and satisfactory conclusion.[31]

Salaun only has a house burning but the interpretation is similar: If the dreamer's house were burning, he will be sick or have some *mlandu* (lawsuit).[32]

The suggestions from Hodgson's and Salaun's interpretations of fire agree on the profundity of the dream verging on "serious misfortune," "sickness" or lawsuit. What Nthondo's dream indicates in the story, however, is a great spiritual crisis in the life of the dreamer: the awakening of conscience. The dream belongs to Seligman's third category and it is

---

[31]   Hodgson, "Dreams in Central Africa," p. 67.

[32]   Salaun, "Initiation to Malawi."

significant that this is the first time Nthondo's dreams fall into this category. It is significant also that this is the last time Nthondo dreams.

It is important, in order to understand this dream, to examine what occurred before and after the dream in the story. The visitors on waking up in the morning hear a bell and ask what it means. They are told:

> "We of the village ... all of us here, are accustomed on this day which we call *Sabata* [Sabbath], to give honour to *Mulungu* [God] who made all people, both black and white and all other kinds that are on earth. Our reason is that. in the old days our ancestors erred in the sight of *Mulungu* and he had it in his mind to punish all people, but his child *Yesu* [Jesus] spoke up and said, My Father, I will go and die for them; even I. And so it came about. He died and then He arose again and is now up above there. It is His desire now that we should show love to Him through our making requests, and if we do not enter into this relationship of love with Him, He cannot love us where He is. Thus it is that those who thieve, or kill, or are adulterers, or bear hatred, do not receive Him; only those of good and open heart." (p. 127)

Part of Nthondo's dream is explained by this passage: when the "terrible figure of a man" says Nthondo is "bad," it must have been a crystallisation of "our ancestors erred" and *Mulungu's* decision to "punish all people." And when the man clothed in white says to Nthondo in the dream: "I paid for him" it is an echo of "I will go and die for them." Part of Nthondo's dream is also explained by the sermon he attended:

> When the prayer ended, the teacher took up a large black book and read from it these words:
>
> *"Do you not know that the unrighteous do not receive the Kingdom of God? Do not be led astray; the vain-glorious, or those who worship images, and those who commit adultery, or those who are weakened by evil-living, or sodomites, or thieves, or the covetous, or the drunken, or those who bear ill-will to others, or brigands, cannot get in to God's Kingdom. And there are some of you who were like that but you have been cleansed and purified and counted as righteous folk in the name of our Lord Jesus and by the Spirit of our God."*

and he added also these words:

"*Evil people have no peace, says my God!*"

Then the teacher forced home the words as follows:-

"The person who does not learn from Jesus and follow after Him cannot receive freedom in the sight of God. God hates wrongdoing of the kinds that have been mentioned. Even though we of these present days do not find God coming and visiting us as He did to the ancestors of yore, we yet believe that God does come to us in visitation. Sometimes it may be as we read His Word. Sometimes He visits us in our dreams. Can one who says that he belongs to God dream dreams of being chased by someone? Or of a wild beast that strives to seize him so that he wakes with shuddering and terror! Are there not such dreams? But can one who belongs to God experience such? Don't deceive yourselves; one who belongs to Jesus finds good things even here in this world. Many are harassed with load-carrying work. Sometimes they have decisions given against them in the courts. Sometimes they get lost in the bush. But there is no other reason except that they have not received Jesus in their hearts. *Evil men have no peace, says my God!*" (pp. 129-131)

Considering that it was the travellers' first and last visit to the village, the teacher was very skillful in relating his sermon to the audience, particularly the visitors. Too skillful, in fact, for it is only Ntara, the author, Nthondo, the dreamer, and his companions who have access to Nthondo's previous dreams about being chased by someone or by wild beasts.

We suspect that Ntara, the author, not the teacher, is preaching to his own character: explaining why he had terrifying dreams. exhorting him to mend his ways if he is to have any peace of mind and directing him how to seek salvation. Ntara's description of the reception confirms these suspicions:

> The travellers listened to all that was said and though they itched as they sat, they did not scratch lest they should not hear well, because the speaker seemed as if he was simply laying bare their very faults and failings. Particularly was this so with Nthondo. (p. 131)

When Nthondo reveals his thoughts to his companions later in the evening, the "awakening of conscience" is complete:

"My heart is dark … at what I have heard this day. At the very beginning, as they sang, I said to myself, Now what can these things be? And those words broke my strength when he said, The evil-doing person cannot be accepted by God. That filled me with shame and sorrow, because I am the very worst of thieves and boasters and killers. That is what finished my strength. … Even though I return home I give up all thieving and these other things now." (pp. 131-132)

As if echoing Hetherwick's ideas, Nthondo locates the emotions in the region of his "heart." However, not acquainted with Hetherwick's works, Nthondo still lacks the vocabulary to articulate exactly what it is he feels. He can only articulate on the level of the physical world, "broke my strength," and commonest feelings, "shame and sorrow." As Hetherwick would put it: he lacks words for expressing guilt, sin and conscience. Nthondo's preacher/teacher does not help him either, because the reading and the sermon for that day did not include these notions.

Nthondo tries again to explain the state he feels he is in and clothes it in language he and his friends understand.

"What about a foul cloth that we put in the sun after we have been drenched with rain; is it not possible for it to become clean?" (p. 132)

The following morning after the service and his dream Nthondo looked "unhappy" (p. 133).

Nthondo's dreams cease when they have performed their function in the story and in the dreamer. Henceforth, Nthondo's bad habits cease: he is a changed man when he returns home. People ask his companions what has come over him. They think it has something to do with his trip, because the Nthondo they knew is not there anymore. He takes an interest in civic affairs of the village and takes his rightful place at his uncle's side.

Soon the question of marriage comes up: his uncle provides him with a girl, she's too young, and Nthondo exercises his independence of mind: he rejects her and looks for his own woman from another village. At his wife's village again, he is very progressive and industrious.

Although the temptation to steal comes again from a friend, Nthondo's answer is: "I couldn't do it even though someone commanded me to do it; it is not right" (p. 142). Earlier on, another friend reminded him of the sermon and the two held a discussion on "evil" and "wrong." Nthondo, after a single exposure to a Christian service, now has the language of Christians. He has internalised the voice of conscience.

He also becomes successful in everything he does. In domestic and public life, he is always thinking of new projects to work on. However industrious, progressive and successful Nthondo becomes, thought, he is not a happy man. He looks about him and he finds something lacking in his village: the Christian School. Twice his friends ask him about his moodiness (pp. 140, 142); his answer is the same: school. When a white missionary eventually comes to ask the village headman's permission to build a school in the village, Nthondo votes for it against all the rest.

After convincing the elders of the youth's desire for school, a school and a resident teacher are established. All attend school, young and old, male or female. Soon Nthondo "never missed a single day because he loved this reading and hymn-singing" (p. 171). But still he was not satisfied. He visits the teacher privately: "I am going to lay before you what is in my heart" (p. 172). He then tells the teacher about his dreams, and asks "what ought a person to do who wishes to live well?" (p. 172) The teacher reiterates what the other teacher had preached in his sermon:

> "Those dreams were sent by *Mulungu* for reason of the ill things which we people do on this earth down here; things that *Mulungu* takes no pleasure in, and indeed he made it clear long ago that he would deal in judgement with anyone who did such, things. If, therefore, you desire peace and a quiet mind you have to believe Jesus and trust Him; that done, you are secured. (pp. 172-173)

It doesn't take Nthondo long to be "secured." Soon Nthondo and "certain others" are baptised and become Christian. Nthondo remains a Christian to his death.

Conclusion

We have seen how Ntara "awakened the voice of conscience hitherto dormant but waiting the call of Christ to awake to life" in Nthondo. This process is achieved largely through dreams coming to Nthondo when he is under the influence of "civilisation" and the agents of the "civilising missions." The dreams are instruments to prod a dormant conscience into full consciousness of its evil or fallen state. Even after a realisation of its state, the owner cannot save himself except through the teachings of institutionalised Christian religion. Hence the establishment of church and school.

The first movement was to take the pre-Christian Nthondo from his village to Halale, ostensibly to seek work but on Ntara's part to seek "grace."[33] In Halale there is no room for the search for salvation: man is too busy making money or exploiting man. Halale, then, is only another "evil." The second movement took Nthondo to Kapata and Kabula via the village of the Christians. It is here that the first contact is made with the agents of salvation. The third movement is the advent of Christianity in Nthondo's village and Nthondo's subsequent road to a state of "grace."

This study has been largely literary: the dreams were taken and interpreted as narrative structures. Anthropological or sociological aspects were touched upon, in so far as the text itself referred to them or as were required for a proper contextual interpretation. Western psychoanalytical approaches (e.g. Freud) were excluded, since it was felt necessary to interpret the material in their African context to avoid distortions or misrepresentations. A follow-up study, however, could examine the relationship between the author and his character as the narrative and the dreams unfold.

Although the figures Nthondo sees in his dreams take different shapes: dead companion, lions, brightly dressed man, father, Christ, through them we can see Ntara, the author, battling with the pre-Christian soul of

---

[33] The author is ignoring two earlier movements. The first is Nthondo's 'exile' to his "name relations" and the second is his temporary sojourn at Mnjondu, his wife's village. These two movements are part of the larger movements in which they occur, and are, therefore, complimentary to Nthondo's 'education'.

Nthondo; struggling to create the uncreated conscience in Nthondo; salvaging the broken pieces and, having accomplished that, hurriedly killing him in the last chapter, which is the shortest, most summarily written chapter of the story. While the interpretation of the earlier dreams can be done within a traditional framework, that of the final one, as of the series as a whole, requires the context of Christian conversion and even a specific mood of missionary Christianity.

CHAPTER ELEVEN:
THE PERCEPTION OF ARTISTIC SKILL

As indicated in Chapter Three, work on indigenous aesthetics is in its infancy. It is also growing slowly, since only a few artists and scholars are addressing themselves directly to the issue. In this chapter, we confront the issue of artistic skill squarely by examining tests rendered by artists-in-the-making: students and young children. The previous chapters analysed fully-fledged texts produced by mature artists who are presumed to be well-versed in the performance of their respective arts. What about apprentices, children? How should we rate their skill? Again, *Ulimbaso* comes in as a very useful framework.

The first section of this chapter uses the audience's or reader's response to fledgling narratives. The comments are based on *ulimbaso* intuitions. The second, and last, section analyses children's songs to demonstrate that even at this level the products can be as complex and satisfying as those rendered by adults. By focussing on these two important manifestations of the verbal arts: narrative and song, *ulimbaso* is more clearly demonstrated to be a working instrument.

The Perception of Narrative Skill

There are several variants of "The Hare and the Well," the oral performance of which was discussed in Chapter Four. However, two unpublished versions have been selected for discussion, since they are quite similar to the one discussed earlier, making it possible to make comparisons and gauge various degrees of creativity or originality, given the same basic plot, character, setting and theme. Selected are Variant 2, "Kalulu the Hare in Time of Hunger"[1] and Variant 3, "The Well of Water and Troubles."[2] Both variants were written by first year students at

---

[1]   Beslem T. Nthambi, "Kalulu the Hare in Time of Hunger," unpublished manuscript.
[2]   Gilbert K.K. Ng'ona, "The Well of Water and Troubles," unpublished manuscript.

Chancellor College, University of Malawi, in the early-1980s, as part of the students' English Writing programme assignment. The class assignment was "Write a folk story you know from your own village." Although there were several samples of trickster stories, these were the only "Hare and the Well" variants.

Variant 2: Kalulu the Hare in Time of Hunger

Once upon a time, there was a great famine in the whole world. All the great lakes, rivers, streams, and small springs had completely dried. The king of the animals, Lion, called all the animals to come at his home for an emergency meeting. When the day had come, all the animals gathered in front of King Lion's house except for Kalulu the Hare, who had lazily stayed at his home. King Lion then said "Listen friends, countrymen and oh! you honourable people. I am the one who called you to this meeting. You all see that many of our friends are dying of hunger and thirst and in no time this effect will face us. Would you also like to die this way?" All the animals roared, "No. No." The Lion continued on. "Then my friends I have thought it wise, that with the effort of you all at that big swamp which is no more a swamp, we could surely dig a pool of water. So would you all gather tomorrow morning at the big swamp." All the animals agreed to this and then left for their homes.

On the promised morning, all the animals except Kalulu the Hare and Tortoise did not turn up [sic]. The Lion commanded the smaller animals to start. These small animals included the monkeys, goats, sheep, antelopes and many others. The small animals jumped all about the swamp but not a trace of water was seen. When the smaller animals were completely exhausted the bigger animals were to take over. First the Buffalo jumped into the swamp and started jumping up and down trying to squeeze water out from the dry swamp with his heavy hooves but in vain. Then the other bigger animals, rhinoceros, giraffe, and elephant took over, but still nothing

270

came out. When all the animals were exhausted and sitted [sic] resting they saw Kalulu the Hare and Tortoise coming. The animals were furious over the late comers and wanted to beat them to pulp, but Kalulu's sweet tongue calmed them down. Tortoise then asked the Lion if he could get the permission to dig for water. All the animals laughed, but Tortoise pressed on his request. The Lion then gave him permission to do his wish. Tortoise jumped into the swamp, in no time they all saw water coming up and Tortoise scampering away from the swamp. The animals all cheered for Tortoise's success.

King Lion roared and all the animals kept quiet. He then spoke to the animals that all the animals were free to drink the water except for Kalulu the Hare who had missed the previous meeting and hadn't taken any part in digging for water. Kalulu the Hare laughed loudly and said they would see and ran off to his hiding place. All the animals rejoiced drinking and washing in the water. Hyena was chosen to be guard over the water during the night. Then all the animals parted to their various homes.

At night Kalulu the Hare came back to the swamp to drink some water. Kalulu to his surprise saw that the water had been put under guard. When he saw it was the Hyena on guard, he thought of a trick to play on him. Kalulu the Hare saluted the Hyena by saying. "Oh, honourable Hyena I wanted to bring you something at your home but since you were not present I had to give up the idea." Hyena asked, "What is it my son?" Kalulu the Hare giggled and said, "Should I go and get it?" "Sure," remarked Hyena. Kalulu ran straight to a nearby village and stole a goat skin which had been left lying outside the house. He then ran back to the swamp and gave the skin to Hyena. Hyena thanked Kalulu the Hare and immediately started eating the skin forgetting his task. Kalulu the Hare stole off to the water he drank and enjoyed himself in swimming. He then urinated and defecated besides the pool and ran off happily home.

271

The following day, when the animals came to drink some water they saw Kalulu the Hare's feaces [sic] and that's right away knew Kalulu the Hare had come to drink the water, so Hyena was proved irresponsible. Lion then chose the Bear to be guard overnight. At night Kalulu appeared, when the Bear saw Kalulu he wanted to catch Kalulu but Kalulu dodged. He then spoke sweetly to the Bear, that he had brought him a present. Bear asked to see the present. Kalulu gave him a tin of honey. Bear thanked Kalulu and forgot about the water to be guarded against animals like Kalulu the Hare. Kalulu took this opportunity to drink, wash and defaecate by the water and ran off well to his home. Animal after animal tried to catch Kalulu the Hare but none succeeded to withstand his tricks.

One day Tortoise volunteered to guard the water. He told other animals to cover him with mud and be left by the pool. During the night Kalulu the Hare came to the pool. Seeing no one on guard he went to drink, wash and defeacate [sic] by the water. When going he went towards Tortoise as he took him to be a mound of soil. When he saw very close to Tortoise, Tortoise quickly caught Kalulu. The next day all animals were called at King Lion's home to see Kalulu killed. Kalulu told the Lion that if they threw him hard on a rock he wouldn't die, but if thrown lightly on a heap of ash he would surely die. So Lion ordered the Elephant to throw Kalulu the Hare lightly on ash. To their surprise Kalulu the Hare immediately after falling, woke up and ran straight to the deep forest and thus fooled all the animals.

Variant 3: The Well of Water and Troubles

If you looked at the sky on that day you could think that there had never been clouds since the creation of the world. It was a very hot day perhaps so hot that the countryside seemed to be in a pot that had been placed on fire. There had been no rain for two successive years and all the rivers had been

272

reduced to mere stretches of sand. Near a huge baobab tree by the river Chankhalamu all the animals were holding a meeting to discuss on how they could get water. Nwafu the elephant who was the king of the beasts was the only animal moving his lips seriously announcing what was to be done.

"Silence." shouted Nwafu the elephant, "I haven't finished speaking." His speech had been interrupted by a scream from a bush baby who appeared to [be] the most thirsty among the animals.

"Now," continued Nwafu, "seeing that some of you are careless and that some of our fellow animals haven't turned up, there will be rules as regards to the use of the well after it has been dug." He paused and scratched his forehead with his muscular tusk.

"The first rule," he continued, "is that no one will be allowed to draw water from the well if he has not taken part in digging. The second is that no one is allowed to bathe in the well. Anyone found doing so, will be liable to death sentence."

There was a big applause from the crowd. There was a large number of animals at this meeting. All the animals were there save for the birds which did not have to participate in the digging because they could fly to far off lands to look for water. Despite the king's decree that all the animals had to come, Kalulu the Hare did not come. He was only good at cheating and he hated work like death. The other animals did not know that Kalulu the Hare was absent.

The work began in the middle of the day and because the ground was stone-dry they worked until very late in the afternoon. When the sun touched the horizon, the animals were rejoicing at the top of their voices having found water. The well was not very deep but large. And when dusk came, the animals dispersed to their various homes. News reached Kalulu the Hare that the well was dug. On hearing this, Kalulu was glad.

"Well," Kalulu said, opening his mouth with pride as if it were a cut in the side of a pumpkin, "If that is true that a well has been dug I will see what I can do with it." And he added, "I hope I am warmly welcome to it."

On the morning of the first day following the digging of the well all the animals went to their various work where they returned until late in the afternoon [sic]. They did this for many days and each time the animals returned to the well, it was dirty. During their absence, Kalulu went to the well to draw water and to bathe in such a way that he left the well black with mud.

One day Nsofu [sic] the elephant decided to put a guard at the well, Kolwe the monkey was the man on duty during the first week. Kalulu came to the well and before he drew water, Kolwe came out from his hiding place and caught Kalulu before he could escape. Kolwe said that he would never let Kalulu free until all the animals saw him.

"My friend," Kalulu began, "I have something very sweet to give to you only if you could let me free." "Nothing is sweeter than the praise and the honour I will get from our king for capturing you," answered Kolwe. He was mistaken, Kalulu had honey in his gourd which on offering some to Kolwe to taste, Kolwe forgot everything and let Kalulu free. In the evening Kolwe gave all sorts of lame excuses for failing to catch Kalulu. This happened several times and in the end of his watch days Kolwe even went to the extent of saying that their enemy possessed magical powers which put him to sleep each time Kalulu came to the well.

Fulwe the tortoise suggested to other animals that if they made a large stool with a hole in the centre of the seat he knew how he could catch the enemy. Many of the animals looked at Fulwe's suggestion as fantasies and mere ambition. Nevertheless, some of them did as Fulwe had said. After the stool had been made it was placed beside the well with Fulwe under it. Kalulu came again with his gourds only to find no

Kolwe or any other animal at the well this day. Perhaps the animals had given up the idea of catching him Kalulu thought. But no, he was mistaken. His doom had come. As usual, he drew water, bathed and before he could go he saw a stool which he sat on without thinking why it was there. Kamba the tortoise under the stool got hold of Kalulu by the tail through the hole. Kalulu tried to take off the stool, but could not succeed. He was tightly held to it and the stool was too heavy that even if he wanted to go with it, it was impossible for his strength. He pleaded and pleaded, mentioning and even pointing to his honey, but Fulwe never answered him back. Before long, the other animals came for it was already late in the afternoon. On seeing Kalulu all the other animals except Kolwe who already knew Kalulu, were very surprised and angry for being troubled by Kalulu a small chap. Fulwe was praised for his success in spite of his small size. Kalulu was then handed to the king, Nsofu the elephant to be punished.

Kalulu had done two mistakes, first he had not come to dig the well and second, he bathed in the well, a law whose punishment was death.

Near to where Nsofu stood were a large stone and a heap of grass. Nsofu while holding Kalulu in his tusk asked the other animals which was better to smash Kalulu, on, the rock or heap of grass. Some of the animals wisely chose the rock. When Kalulu heard the rock mentioned being of great cunning whispered to himself but clearly enough for others to hear.

"Yah! my life."

"You see," some of the animals said, "if you smash him to a rock he won't die." Because Kalulu said "Yah! my life," they thought perhaps Hares don't die when hit to rocks. They thought Kalulu would escape.

"No!" cried a greater number of animals in a thunderous voice, "just throw him on the grass."

"Eh! what a terrible death," Kalulu whispered again when he heard them mention grass because he knew he would not die on grass. There was a great contradiction for a long time. Some of the animals were beginning to lose their temper and they would have ended up in fighting.

Nsofu the elephant also turned to be a fool. He sided with those that had suggested grass as a better place to throw Kalulu on. When Kalulu heard Nsofu's final decision he pretended to be very sorry uttering the phrase, "my death," several times. Nsofu was their king, seeing that the king was siding [with] the wrong ones, all the other animals agreed that they should kill Kalulu by throwing him on the heap of grass. Nsofu raised his tusk as high as it could go. He threw him with all his force on the heap of grass.

Did Kalulu die? Oh! no. There he was on all his four [sic], running for his life at the speed of lightning. All the animals including those who were pretty sure they could do nothing but joined in chasing Kalulu. It was in vain. Kalulu was gone and they were left in confusion to deal with themselves for quarrelling.

Plot

Both stories have the same basic plot: a time of drought, a meeting of the animals to dig a well, the hare's non-participation, and deception of each of the guards at the well, the hare's capture and the attempts to punish him. Some of the details, however, differ.

In Variant 2 the order of digging the well is from the smallest to the largest creatures. When all the animals fail, the tortoise, who had been hitherto absent appears and succeeds in providing the water. The hare appears on the scene with the tortoise, but, because he does not take part in digging, is told directly that he is barred from using the well. When guards are placed, the hare dupes both in turn by enticing them with their favourite foods: the hyena, a goatskin and the bear, honey. Several other animals, not mentioned by name, are also deceived, although the manner of the deception is not indicated. Each time the hare uses the well, he drinks, urinates and defaecates on it afterwards. In the end, the tortoise, camouflaged as "a mound of soil," manages to capture the hare. The mode of death is to be banged against "a rock" or "thrown lightly on a heap of ash."

In Variant 3, the rules forbidding the hare from drawing water are formulated *before* the well is even dug. In spite of the regulations, the animals do not even place a guard at the well for some days. It is only after the hare has left signs of his presence, leaving the water "black with mud," that they put the monkey on guard for a week. Each time the hare visits the well, he manages to deceive the monkey with honey. In the end, the tortoise volunteers to stand guard. The tortoise hides under a stool with a hole in the middle and grabs the hare by the tail when he sits on it. The mode of death is being struck against either a "stone" or "a heap of grass."

There were several possibilities for extending the stories on the plot level alone. The simplest one is suggested by the different rules being used to deceive several guards in turn. The stories only have one (Variant 3) or two (Variant 2) guards before the tortoise comes in. The other possibility was to extend the chase after the hare escapes punishment in the end. A variant also exists in which this happens up to the banks of a wide river. One of the animals throws a hoe handle (or a log) inside which the hare was hiding across the river, thereby inadvertently helping the trickster effect his final escape. The stories above, however, did not go beyond the initial escape. The third possibility was to work within the confines of the story. In Variant 2, for example, each successive group of animals has the potential of being sub-divided for suspense before the tortoise comes in. Both the mound of soil (Variant 2) and stool (Variant 3) are motifs used in another version in which glue is applied to the tortoise's shell. When the hare gets stuck on it, the tortoise simply carries the trickster to the rest of the other animals. More possibilities than the above belong to the realms of individual creativity and not to ready-made motifs.

Characters

The characters in the stories are different animals, although they perform similar functions. In Variant 2, the leader is "King Lion" and the guards are successively hyena, bear and tortoise. Other animals are mentioned by groups: the small animals: monkeys, goats, sheep, antelopes; the big animals: buffalo, rhinoceros, giraffe and elephant. In Variant 3, Nwafu or Nsofu the elephant presides over the rest of the animals. The guards are the monkey and the tortoise. Naming also occurs: Kolwe the monkey, Fulwe or Kamba the tortoise. This version also mentions why the birds did not participate: "they could fly to far off lands to look for water." In both, the protagonist is the hare.

Although characterisation is by stereotype: the trickster and his dupes, a certain amount of individuation is possible. In Variant 2, the hare's laziness and sweet tongue are brought out. The lion's concern for the animals dying in the drought is also indicated. In Variant 3, the monkey's initial response to the hare's sweet tongue is an alternative: "Nothing is sweeter than the praise and honour I will get from our king for capturing you." However, he succumbs in the end.

Setting

The setting in folk stories is not so elaborate. However, the two versions have slightly different settings in time and space. Variant 2 has on a certain "day" for the meeting and on the "promised morning" for digging the well. Towards the end of the same day, the water is found. The hare comes out at night to perform his duplicity, which fact the animals discover the "following day," until "one day" when the tortoise captures him (at night) and delivers him to the rest of the animals the next day. Time in this version is unspecified, although in place it moves from the lion's home, to the swamp (and well), to the village and back.

Variant 3 has the meeting on an unspecified day, and presumably on the same day the well is dug and water found: "The work began in the middle of the day ... until very late in the afternoon." More specific time is mentioned thereafter: "on the morning of the first day ... late in the afternoon" for several days before a guard is placed at the well. The first guard is placed for a week, towards the end of which the tortoise takes over. The hare is captured "late in the afternoon." The basic setting in this version is also the place of the meeting and the well.

The differences in how the setting was treated is shown in how the two versions open. Variant 2 begins:

> Once upon a time, there was a great famine in the whole world. All the great lakes, rivers, streams, and small springs had completely dried ... the animals gathered in front of King Lion's house ...

Places in this version are merely mentioned without details added. Variant 3 is more elaborate:

> If you looked at the sky on that day you could think that there had never been clouds since the creation of the world. It was a very hot day perhaps so hot that the countryside seemed to be in a pot that had been placed on fire. There had been no rain for two successive years and all the rivers had been reduced to mere stretches of sand. Near a huge baobab tree by the river Chankhalamu ...

There is enough detail for the reader to appreciate the setting. Similar vividness occurs in the body of the story: "the ground was stone-dry ... when the sun touched the horizon ... the well was not deep but large. And when dusk came ..."

Theme

Duplicity as the theme has already been mentioned under characters. However, there are other sub-themes which could have been exploited. Variant 2 has the leader's concern over the plight of his subjects. There is also the idea of small animals succeeding where big ones have failed.

Variant 3 brings out the leader's authority so strongly, initially, that his foolishness in the end is also very dramatic. The monkey's initial heroic response to temptation has also been remarked upon, followed by his successive victimization, to the extent of inventing lies to cover his weakness. The tortoise's incorruptibility stands out in the face of the monkey's surrenders.

Language

The style of both versions is effectively prose that was written to be read. It was also possible to write prose as if it was going to be spoken or was taken from spoken sources, as Variant 1, translated earlier. Both these variants are nearer to written prose. The styles, however, are distinctive.

Variant 2 is content to give a straightforward, unadorned rendition. In some places, adjectives, adverbs or expressions of degree are given: "great famine," "completely dried," "lazily stayed," "The animals were furious over the late comers and wanted to beat them to pulp, but Kalulu's sweet tongue calmed them." Expressions of this kind, however, are kept to a minimum. Dialogue also occurs only twice, the rest of the story being in reported speech.

Variant 3 extends description to details: "moving his lips seriously"; "he paused and scratched his forehead with his muscular tusk." There are also some similes and metaphors "he hated work like death," "opening his mouth wide with pride as if it were a cut in the side of a pumpkin."

Authorial commentary and asides also abound in Variant 3: "they thought that perhaps ...; but no, he was mistaken. His doom had come." This extends to attempts to portray what went through a character's mind: "Perhaps the animals had given up the idea of catching him Kalulu thought."

Variant 3 also has the greater amount of dialogue occurring at each major development of the story. Dialogue adds to the vividness and immediacy of the on-going activities.

In addition, the writer of Variant 3 tries to involve the reader. The story ends with:

> Did Kalulu die? Oh! no. There he was on all his four, running for his
> life at the speed of lightning.

Perhaps the language of Variant 3 is studied in its literariness. There are cliches like "he hated work like death." The image of the mouth opening like a pumpkin could have been borrowed from pictures. Borrowing is also found in Variant 2, where the Shakespearian echoes of "friends, countrymen and oh! you honourable people" are too obvious to pass without remark. It is clear, then, that exposure to literary sources can also influence the style of a folk narrator (or folk story writer).

The Evaluation of Narrative Performance

It is unfair to compare Variant 1, analysed in Chapter Four, with Variants 2 and 3 in this chapter. The contexts were different: a fireside oral performance with a live audience composed of relatives and friends of different ages and sexes, and a classroom exercise written for a lecturer. The students did not provide a vernacular text on one hand, on the other they were not translating either: they wrote straight into English, hence the English version is also not comparable with the author's translation of Variant 1 in the manner done here. Furthermore, the students' experiences in folk narrative were not the same as those of the oral narrator of Variant 1 (the students were in their twenties, the oral narrator in his late forties). Finally, the students were writing for a grade whereas the oral narrator was entertaining friends and relatives, although he had been forewarned that the tapes would be used for classes in oral literature at the University of Malawi.

In spite of the overwhelming unfairness mentioned above, a few appreciative remarks could be made. In Variant 1, the plot borrows freely from other folk narratives: the motif of taking off the skin to effect duplicity is found in several trickster stories. Variant 1 uses song (or choral responses) as an integral structural device. There are descriptions of the hare's family feigning illness, at play, and being accomplices to duplicity. Several events in different settings are orchestrated simultaneously in the first version. All these possible extensions of the original story are almost completely absent in the students' written versions.

Control of Form

This section, which analyses the form of children's songs, is simply a further demonstration of how much skill goes into what on the surface could be taken as simple texts.

It will be observed that most of the songs are characterised by their brevity: *Chelule gona!* has two words. The song can be extended simply by sheer repetition, which puts the bird to sleep. Another example, *Kazitere bwenzi zikoma*, has three words extended using the same technique. At beer parties, the three words can extend to fifteen minutes or more in performance. The repetition of the same words over and over is not the only device of this nature. Anadiplosis can be employed skillfully, and with more sophistication, as a formal controlling device in some of the songs. At its simplest, the device employs a word found in the previous line to start the next, as in the example below:

Modzi, wiri, ndawerenga,	One, two, I have counted;
Ndawerenganji? Mapira	Have I counted what? Millet
Mapira si anga nga Fulukute	Millet is not mine, it's Fulukute's
Fulukute si wanga, nga, nga, nga	Fulukute is not mine, mine, mine

This children's counting song is sustained to four lines by anadiplosis. However, there are other unifying devices at the phonological and morphological levels, too. Consider, for example, the euphony of *nda* and *nga* found in different contexts. At the syntactic level, there are combinations of positive and negative declarative sentences with the interrogative in the middle acting as a fulcrum to propel the song for the next few lines. Beyond the fourth line, however, continuation would be a burden unless other devices were utilised.

The counting song above is in reality a nonsense song. (It is even a pseudo-counting song since it cannot count beyond two.) It makes no sense beyond the joy of playing around with syllables and words. The pounding song below, however, using the same devices, makes more sense:

Alamu ndipatseni kaufa	In-law give me a little flour
Kaufa ndiphikire alendo	A little flour to cook for guests
Alendo abwera kunyumba	Guests have come home
Kunyumba, eh, Kunyumba, eh	Home, eh. Home, eh.

As in the children's counting song above, four lines is all the pounding song can take using this device. It is possible, however, to sustain longer lines than the examples above. The Yao *jando* initiation song below extends the possibilities:

Azichanga lero	Zichanga today
Azichanga atawire ndalaja jao	Zichanga today built his shack
Ndalaja jao atite ja mwinani	His shack he said would be an
Ja mwinani ngwele ngaponde	upstairs one
Ngwele ngaponde ni	An upstairs one he said he would
wakolopweche	climb up

Ni wakolopweche ni kuichila	He would climb up and he fell down
pasi mwaulaya	And he fell down reaching the
Mwaulaya sichile pasi	ground scandalously
kuchanga	Scandalously reaching the ground
Pasi kuchanga Azichanga lero	The ground Zichanga today
Azichanga lero lero tulepere[3]	Zichanga today, we are baffled

Using the interrogative to extend a text beyond its normal confines was remarked upon in the children's counting rhyme. Some chants or song actually use it as the only formal syntactic controlling device. The children's nonsense verse below is a good starting point:

Wadyanji?	Ndadya umba
Umbanji?	Umbakazi
Kazinji?	Kazitola
Tolanji?	Tolanyoka
Nyokonji?	Nyokoyako.[4]

The chant is untranslatable because it uses nonsense syllables and words. Using amadiplosis at the syllable level it again sustains itself at the syntactic level by changing declaratives into interrogatives. This can be extended also as the Yao *chitagu* below:

Itagu

Nda	Ndakulume
Kulume	Kulume Mbali
Mbali	Mbali katete
Katete	Katete mbukwa
Mbukwa	Mbukwa akongwe
Kongwe	Kongola imanga
Imanga	Imanga nyumba
Nyumba	Nyumba lenga

---

3   Nyenje, Samuel Makoka Village.

4   Gwengwe, *Kukula ndi Mwambo*, p. 61, has a different version.

Lenga   Lenga m'ngonji
M'ngonji   M'ngonji ngonjipe[5]

Meaningful statements or questions can be made also using the same
interrogative device, as the *Chule* frog song below illustrates:

Chule, Chule, Nanthesi

Chule, chule, chule,		Frog, frog, frog,	
	Nanthesi		Frog
Ndikutuma chani?		What did I send you for?	
	Nanthesi		Frog
Ndakutuma madzi		I sent you to fetch water	
	Nanthesi		Frog
Wandipatsa chani?		What did you bring me?	
	Nanthesi		Frog
Wandipatsa dothi		You brought me mud	
	Nanthesi		Frog
Kwa, kwa, kwa		*Kwa, kwa, kwa*	
	Nanthesi		Frog

As can be seen the songs are highly organised and complex texts however
brief they are. The performance of the songs brings in the missing
elements of the verbal arts: the songs were composed to be performed:
they live in the performance: one has to watch them in action to
appreciate them fully.

Conclusion

It will be seen from the foregoing chapters that *Ulimbaso* is indeed a
dynamic concept. Underlying all the arts, it manifests itself in the ways
demonstrated here and in other forms too. We have only examined
narratives, songs, riddles, dreams, and the visual arts. Other forms not
considered here in any detail are proverbs and jokes. It was felt that

---

[5] This is a fuller version, collected from Samuel Makoka Village, than the one given in
Macdonald, *Africana*, Vol. 1, p. 50.

proverbs are condensed narratives already, and, as such, are considered in the appropriate chapter. Jokes are also narratives in their own right, but the analysis of jokes could not be included in this volume for reasons beyond the author's control.

It will be seen also that the general movement of the discussion has been from the traditional rural setting to the modern urban context. This movement does not affect or upset *Ulimbaso* in any way, since it is a dynamic and flexible instrument that not only embraces changes in the indigenous arts themselves but also incorporates non-indigenous forms. *Ulimbaso* dynamises both the old and the new.

BIBLIOGRAPHY

Aesop. *Fables*. Trans. by Thomas James & George Tyler Townsend, illustr. by Charles H. Bennett. Franklin Center, PA: Franklin Library, 1984.

Beuchat, P.D. "Riddles in Bantu." In Alan Dundes, ed., *The Study of Folklore*, pp. 182-205. Englewood Cliffs, NJ: Prentice-Hall, 1965.

Blackmun, Barbara & Schoffeleers, Matthew. "Masks of Malawi." *African Arts*, V, 4 (1972).

Bunyan, John. *The Pilgrim's Progress*. Fifth Edition. London: S.W. Partridge & Co., n.d.

Chadza, E.J. *Nchito ya Pakamwa*. (1963). Lusaka: The Zambia Publications Bureau, 1967.

Chadza, E.J. *Tiphunzire Chichewa*. Blantyre: CLAIM, n.d.

Chafulumira, E.W. *Banja Lathu*. (1942). Lusaka: NECZAM, 1972.

Chakanza, E.T. "Nyasa Folk Songs." *African Affairs*, 49, 195 (April 1950).

Charsley, S.R. "Dreams in an Independent African Church." *Africa*, 43 (1973).

Chimombo, Steve. "A Psycholinguistic Model of Riddle Construction and Comprehension." Unpublished manuscript.

Chimombo, Steve. "Folk Story Analysis: Basic Approaches." *Kalulu*, 1, 1 (1976).

Chimombo, Steve. "Functional Aspects of Children's Songs." *Kalulu*, 2 (June 1977).

Chimombo, Steve. "New Contexts for an Old Trickster." Unpublished manuscript.

Chimombo, Steve. "Pupils' Popular Tastes." *ATEM Newsletter*, 2 (1975).

Chimombo, Steve. "The Dramatic Experience in Malawian Folklore." *Outlook*, 2 (1975).

Chimombo, Steve. "The Dupe in a Modern Context." *Baraza*, 3 (April 1986).

Chimombo, Steve. "The Trickster and the Media." *Baraza*, 2 (June 1984).

Chipinga, C.C.J. *Atambwali Sametana*. Blantyre: Malawi Book Service, 1972.

Clark, J. Desmond. "Prehistory in Nyasaland." *The Nyasaland Journal*, 9, 1 (January 1956).

Cullen Young, T. *African Ways and Wisdom.* London: The United Society for Christian Literature, 1937.

Cullen Young, T. *Notes on the Customs and Folklore of the Tumbuka-Nkamanga Peoples.* Livingstonia: The Mission Press, 1931.

Cullen Young, T. "Place-Names in Nyasaland." *The Nyasaland Journal*, 6, 2 (July 1953).

Cullen Young, T. "Some Proverbs of the Tumbuka-Nkamanga Peoples of the Northern Province of Nyasaland." *Africa*, 10, 3 (July 1931).

Culler, Jonathan. *Structuralist Poetics.* London: Routledge and Kegan Paul, 1975.

Curley, Richard T. "Dreams of Power: Social Process in a West African Religious Movement." *Africa*, 53, 3 (1983).

Debenham, Frank. *Nyasaland: Land of the Lake.* London: HMSO, 1955.

Duff, Hector. *Nyasaland Under the Foreign Office.* (1903). New York: Negro Universities Press, 1969.

Dundes, Alan. "The Making and Breaking of Friendship as a Structural Frame in African Folk Tales." In Pierre Maranda & Ellie Kongas Maranda, eds., *Structural Analysis of Oral Tradition.* Philadelphia: University of Pennsylvania Press, 1971.

Dzimphonje, W.N. "Letters to the Editor." *Tikambe* Supplement to *Malawi News* (17 July 1976).

Elliot, Geraldine. *The Hunter's Cave.* London: Routledge and Kegan Paul, 1951.

Elliot, Geraldine. *The Long Grass Whispers.* London: Routledge and Kegan Paul, 1949.

Elliot, Geraldine. *The Singing Chameleon.* London: Routledge and Kegan Paul, 1957.

Elliot, Geraldine. *Where the Leopard Passes.* London: Routledge and Kegan Paul, 1949.

Feldmann, Susan, ed. *African Myths and Tales.* New York: Dell Publishing Company, 1963.

Finnegan, Ruth. *Oral Literature in Africa.* Nairobi: Oxford University Press, 1976.

Gayle, Addison Jr., ed., *The Black Aesthetic.* Garden City, NY: Doubleday, 1971.

Gray, B. *The Phenomenon of Literature.* The Hague: Mouton, 1975.

Gray, Ernest. "Some Proverbs of the Nyanja People." *African Studies*, 3 (September 1944).

Gray, Ernest. "Some Riddles of the Nyanja People." *Bantu Studies*, 13 (December 1939).

Gumbi, E.M.S. *Tili Tonse*. Limbe: Popular Publications, 1984.

Gurr, Andrew & Zirimu, Pio, eds. *Black Aesthetics, Papers from a Colloquium held at the University of Nairobi, June 1971*. Nairobi: East African Literature Bureau, 1973.

Gwengwe, J.W. *Chimangirizo ndi Chifupikitso*. (1968). Nairobi: Oxford University Press, 1970.

Gwengwe, John W. *Kathyali Psyipsyiti*. Blantyre: Malawi Publications and Literature Bureau, 1968.

Gwengwe, John W. *Kukula ndi Mwambo*. (1965). Limbe: Malawi Publications and Literature Bureau, 1970.

Gwengwe, J.W. *Ndakatulo*. Nairobi: Oxford University Press, 1976.

Gwengwe, J.W. *Sikusinja ndi Gwenembe*. (1965). Limbe: Malawi Publications and Literature Bureau, 1969.

Gwengwe, J.W. *Sulizo Achieves Greatness*. London: Evans Brothers, 1968.

Hallowell, A. Irving. "Two Folktales from Nyasaland." *Journal of American Folklore*, XXXV (July-September 1922).

Haring, Lee. "A Characteristic African Folktale Pattern." In Richard M. Dorson, ed., *African Folklore*. New York: Anchor Books, 1972.

Hetherwick, Alexander. *The Gospel and the African: The Impact of the Gospel on a Central African People*. Edinburgh: T. & T. Clark, 1932.

Hodgson, A.G.O. "Dreams in Central Africa," *Man*, 39 (April 1926).

Holland, Madeleine. "Folklore of the Banyanja." *Folklore*, XXVII (1916).

Johnson, Lemuel A. *Toward Defining the African Aesthetic, Annual Selected Papers of the African Literature Association*. Washington, D.C.: Three Continents Press, 1982.

Jung, C.G. "On the Psychology of the Trickster Figure." Trans. by R.F.C. Hull. In Radin, ed., *The Trickster*.

Kalindawalo, A. *M'thengo Mdalaka Njoka.* Lilongwe: Longman (Malawi) Ltd., 1974.

Kamende, Z.P. *Chakudza.* Limbe: Malawi Publications and Literature Bureau, 1967.

Kerenyi, Karl. "The Trickster in Relation to Greek Mythology." Trans. by R.F.C. Hull. In Radin, ed., *The Trickster.*

Koma-koma, W.P. *Mganda Kapena Malipenga.* Limbe: Malawi Publications and Literature Bureau, 1965.

Kumakanga, S. *Nzeru za Kale.* Lilongwe: Longman, 1931.

Lewis, W.E. "Place-Names." *The Nyasaland Journal*, 9, 1 (January 1956).

Linden, I. "Chewa Initiation Rites and Nyau Societies: The Use of Religious Institutions in Local Politics at Mua." In T.O. Ranger & J. Weller, eds., *Christian History of Central Africa.* London: Heinemann, 1975.

Lindgren, N.E. & Schoffeleers, J.M. *Rock Art and Nyau Symbolism in Malawi.* Malawi Government: Department of Antiquities Publication No. 18, 1978.

Loga, John. *Muni wa Chichewa: Ulalo 3.* Blantyre: Blantyre Print and Packaging, 1972.

Macdonald, Duff. *Africana or the Heart of Heathen Africa, Vol. I.* (1882). London: Dawsons, 1969.

Macdonald, Duff. "Yao and Nyanja Tales." *Bantu Studies*, 12, 4 (1938).

Macdonald, James. "East Central African Customs." *Man*, 22 (1982).

Mackenzie, D.R. *The Spirit-ridden Konde.* London: Seeley Service and Co. Ltd., 1925.

Makumbi, Archibald. *Maliro ndi Miyambo ya Achewa.* (1955). London: Longman Group Ltd., 1970.

Malawi Government. *Malamulo a Pamseu.* Zomba: The Government Printer, 1962.

Malawi News. "Trickster who is Loved by All." (14-20 January 1984).

Mapanje, J.A.C. "The Use of Traditional Literary Forms in Modern Malawian Writing." Unpublished M. Phil. Thesis, University of London, 1975.

Matewere, George. "Moving with a City on the Move." *Daily Times* (23 October 1985).

Mchombo, S.A. "Cryptic Meaning in Chichewa Poetry." *Kalulu*, 1, 1 (June 1976).

Mchombo, S.A. *Mapande: A Study of Chichewa Metrics.* London: n.p., 1977.

Mchombo, S.A. "Msinja Tapes." Unpublished materials, n.d.

Melville, J. & Herskovits, Frances S. *Dahomean Narrative: A Cross-Cultural Analysis.* Evanston: Northwestern University Press, 1958.

Metcalfe, Margaret. "Some Rock Paintings in Nyasaland." *The Nyasaland Journal*, 9, 1 (January 1956).

Mgawi, K.J. *Gwira. Pali Moyo.* Blantyre: CLAIM, 1985.

Mkandawire, Austin H.C. *Mahara gha Bana.* Lusaka: Publications Bureau of Northern Rhodesia and Nyasaland, 1962.

Morrow, Sean. "'War Came from the Boma', Military and Police Disturbances in Blantyre, 1902." Paper presented to the Central African History Conference, Lusaka, Zambia, 4-5 April 1986.

Mphonda, A.H. *Miyambi Yatsopano.* (1965). Limbe: Malawi Publications and Literature Bureau, 1975.

Msosa, Watson J. "On Devising an African Poetics." Unpublished manuscript. Zomba: Department of English, Chancellor College, n.d.

Mvula, E.T. *Akoma Akagonera.* Limbe: Popular Publications, 1981.

Mvula, Enoch Timpunza. "Chewa Folk Narrative Performance." *Kalulu*, 3 (May 1982).

Mvula, Enoch Timpunza. "Introducing Malawian Riddles." Supplement to Kalulu, 1, 1 (June 1976).

Nankwenya, I.A.J. *Zofunika Mgramara wa Chichewa.* Lilongwe: Longman (Malawi) Ltd., 1974.

Nazombe, Anthony. "African and Afro-American Approaches to a Black Aesthetic." Paper presented to the Third Symposium of American Studies in Africa, University of Botswana, Gaborone, 4-7 September 1986.

Ng'ona, Gilbert K.K. "The Well of Water and Troubles." Unpublished manuscript.

Ntaba, Jolly Max. *Mwana wa Mnzako.* Limbe: Popular Publications, 1982.

Ntaba, Jolly Max. *Mtima Sukhuta.* Limbe: Popular Publications, 1985.

Ntaba, Jolly Max. *Ikakuona Litsiro Sikata.* Blantyre: Dzuka Publishing Co., 1986.

Ntara, Samuel Yosia. *Headman's Enterprise*. Trans. & ed. T. Cullen Young. London: Lutterworth Press, 1949.

Ntara, Samuel Yosia. *Man of Africa*. Trans. T. Cullen Young. London: Religious Tract Society, 1934.

Ntara, Samuel Yosia. *Mbiri ya Achewa*. Nkhoma: CCAP, 1944.

Ntara, Samuel Yosia. *Nchowa*. Nairobi: Longmans, Green and Co., 1949.

Ntara, S.Y. *Mau Okuluwika m'Cinyanja*. (1964). Lusaka: NECZAM, 1972.

Ntara, S.Y. *Msyamboza*. Nkhoma: CCAP, 1965.

Ntara, S.Y. *Namon Katengeza*. Nkhoma: CCAP, 1964.

Ntara, S.Y. *Nthondo*. (1936). Nkhoma: CCAP, 1966.

Nthambi, Beslem T. "Kalulu the Hare in Time of Hunger." Unpublished manuscript.

Nurse, George T. "Popular Songs and National Identity in Malawi." *African Music*, III, 3 (1964).

Nyasaland Protectorate. *Annual Report of the Department of Education for the Year Ended September, 1931*. Zomba: The Government Printer, 1932.

Pachai, B. "Samuel Josiah Ntara: Writer and Historian." *The Society of Malawi Journal*, 21, 2 (July 1968).

Paliani, Sylvester. *1930 Kunadza Mchape*. Lilongwe: Likuni Press and Publishing House, 1971.

Paliani, Sylvester. *Sewero la Mlandu wa Nkhanga*. (1952). London: Macmillan, 1982.

Phiri, Paladio G. *Nsembe ndi Miyambi ya Achewa*. Kachebere Major Seminary, n.d.

Pretorius, J.L. "A Short Report of the Literature Situation in Nyasaland." *Books for Africa*, 18, 3 (July 1948).

Quest. "Preservation of African Traditions." 2 (Second Quarter 1986).

Radin, Paul, ed. *The Trickster: A Study in American Indian Mythology*. New York: Schocken Books, 1972.

Rangeley, W.H.J. "Mbona The Rainmaker." *The Nyasaland Journal*, 6, 1 (January 1953).

Rangeley, W.H.J. "'Nyau' in Kotakota District." *The Nyasaland Journal*, 2, 2 (July 1949).

Rangeley, W.H.J. "'Nyau' in Kotakota District, Part 2." *The Nyasaland Journal*, 3, 2 (July 1950).

Rangeley, W.H.J. "The Origins of the Principal Street Names of Blantyre and Limbe." *The Nyasaland Journal*, 11, 2 (July 1958).

Rangeley, W.H.J. "Two Nyasaland Rain Shrines." *The Nyasaland Journal*, 5, 2 (July 1952).

Read, Margaret. *Children of their Fathers.* London: Methuen and Co. Ltd., 1959.

Rothenberg, J. *Technicians of the Sacred.* New York: Doubleday, 1986.

Sagawa, Jessie. "Some Malawian Jokes." Unpublished manuscript, 1983.

Salaun. "Initiation to Malawi." Unpaginated manuscript, n.d.

Sanderson, G.M. "Inyago, The Picture Models of the Yao Initiation Ceremonies." *The Nyasaland Journal*, 8, 2 (July 1955).

Sanderson, G.M. "Tumbuka Proverbs." *The Nyasaland Journal*, 5, 1 (January 1952).

Savory, Phyllis. *Fireside Tales of the Hare and His Friends.* Cape Town: Howard Timms, 1965.

Savory, Phyllis. *Tales from Africa.* Cape Town: Howard Timms, 1968.

Schmidt, Nancy J. "African Folklore for African Children." *Research in African Literatures*, 8, 3 (Winter 1977).

Schmidt, Nancy J. *Children's Books on Africa and their Authors.* New York: Africana Publishing Co., 1975.

Schmidt, Nancy J. "Children's Literature about Africa." *African Studies Bulletin*, VIII, 3 (1965).

Schmidt, Nancy J. "Children's Literature about Africa: A Reassessment." *African Studies Review*, 13, 3 (1970).

Schmidt, Nancy J. "Collections of African Folklore for Children." *Research in African Literatures*, 2, 2 (Fall 1971).

Schoffeleers, J.M. *M'bona the Guardian Spirit of the Mang'anja.* B. Litt. Thesis, Oxford University, 1966.

Schoffeleers, J.M. *Symbolic and Social Aspects of Spirit Worship among the Mang'anja.* Ph.D. Thesis, Oxford University, 1968.

Schoffeleers, J.M. & Linden, I. "The Resistance of the Nyau Societies to the Roman Catholic Mission in Colonial Malawi." In T.O. Ranger & I. Kimambo, eds., *The Historical Study of African Religions.* London: Heinemann, 1972.

Scott, David Clement & Hetherwick, Alexander. *Dictionary of the Chichewa Language.* (1929). Blantyre: CLAIM, 1970.

Seligman, C.G. "Note on Dreams." *Man*, 120 (December 1923).

Shepperson, George. "The Military History of British Central Africa: A Review Article." *The Rhodes-Livingstone Journal*, 26 (December 1959).

Singano, E. & Roscoe, A.A., eds. *Tales of Old Malawi.* Limbe: Popular Publications, 1974.

Snow, Barbara. "Street Art in Malawi." *Focus on Malawi* (September 1984).

Soka, L.D. *Mbiri ya Alomwe.* (1953). Limbe: Malawi Publications and Literature Bureau, 1975.

Stannus, Hugh. "Native Paintings in Nyasaland." *Journal of the African Society*, IX, XXXIV (January 1910).

Stannus, Hugh. "The Wayao of Nyasaland." *Harvard African Studies*, III (1922).

Steere, Edward. *Collections for a Handbook of the Yao Language.* London: Society for Promoting Christian Knowledge, 1871.

Strumpf, Mitchell. "Ethnomusicology in African Studies." Staff Seminar Paper No. 28, February 1983, Chancellor College, Zomba.

Sundkler, B. *Christian Ministry in Africa.* London: SCM Press Ltd., 1962.

Taylor, Margaret. "Angoni Stories." *NADA*, 4 (December 1926).

Taylor, Margaret. "More Angoni Stories." *NADA*, 5 (December 1927).

This is Malawi. "Brian Hara Tells Story." (April 1981).

This is Malawi. "Mede Preserves Malawi's Culture Through Works of Art." (March 1976).

Thomson, T.D. "Place-Names in Nyasaland." *The Nyasaland Journal*, 6, 1 (January 1953).

Twynam, C.D. "Incidents in the Posts of Nyasaland." *The Nyasaland Journal*, 7, 1 (January 1954).

Twynam, C.D. "Nyasaland Mails and Stamps." *The Nyasaland Journal*, 1, 1 (January 1948).

Werner, Alice. "A 'Hare' Story in African Folk Lore." *Journal of the African Society*, IV, XIII (October 1904).

Werner, Alice. *Introductory Sketch of the Bantu Languages*. London: Kegan Paul, Trench, Trubner and Co. Ltd., 1919.

Werner, Alice. "'Ngoni' Stories." *NADA*, 5 (December 1927).

Werner, A. "A Native Painting from Nyasaland." *Journal of the African Society*, VIII, XXX (January 1909).

Werner, A. *The Natives of British Central Africa*. London: Archibald Constable and Co., 1906.

White Fathers. *Nkhani za Nyama*. Likuni: White Fathers' Press, n.d.

Whiteley, W.H. *A Study of Yao Sentences*. London: Oxford University Press, 1966.

Whiteley, W.H., ed. *A Selection of African Prose, Vol. 1*. London: Oxford University Press, 1964.

Winspear, Frank. "A Short History of the Universities Mission." *The Nyasaland Journal*, 9, 1 (January 1956).

Young, W.P. *The Rabbit and the Baboons and Other Tales from Northern Nyasaland*. London: The Sheldon Press, 1933.

Young, W.P. *The Rabbit and the Lion and Other Tales from Northern Nyasaland*. London: The Sheldon Press, 1933.

Young, W.P. *Why Rabbit and Hyena Quarrelled and Other Tales from Northern Nyasaland*. London: The Sheldon Press, 1933.

Zingani, Willie. *Njala Bwana*. Limbe: Popular Publications, 1984.

Zingani, Willie. *Madzi Akatayika*. Blantyre: Dzuka Publishing Co., 1984.

www.ingramcontent.com/pod-product-compliance
Lightning Source LLC
Chambersburg PA
CBHW032119020426
42334CB00016B/1003